The Rhine

Also by Ben Coates

Why the Dutch Are Different

The Rhine

Following Europe's Greatest River
from Amsterdam to the Alps

BEN COATES

NICHOLAS BREALEY
PUBLISHING

London · Boston

First published in Great Britain in 2018 by Nicholas Brealey Publishing
An imprint of John Murray Press
An Hachette UK Company

7

© Ben Coates 2018

The right of Ben Coates to be identified as the
Author of the Work has been asserted by him in accordance
with the Copyright, Designs and Patents Act 1988.

Maps drawn by Rosie Collins

A CIP catalogue record for this title is available from the British Library

ISBN 978-1-47366-217-9
Ebook ISBN UK 978-1-47366-218-6
Ebook ISBN US 978-1-47368-305-1

Typeset in Bembo by Palimpsest Book Production Ltd, Falkirk, Stirlingshire

Printed and bound by CPI Group (UK) Ltd, Croydon, CR0 4YY

Nicholas Brealey policy is to use papers that are natural, renewable
and recyclable products and made from wood grown in sustainable forests.
The logging and manufacturing processes are expected to conform to the
environmental regulations of the country of origin.

Nicholas Brealey Publishing
John Murray Press
Carmelite House
50 Victoria Embankment
London EC4Y 0DZ
Tel: 020 3122 6000

Nicholas Brealey Publishing
Hachette Book Group
Market Place Centre, 53 State Street
Boston, MA 02109, USA
Tel: (617) 263 1834

www.nicholasbrealey.com
www.ben-coates.com

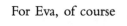

For Eva, of course

Contents

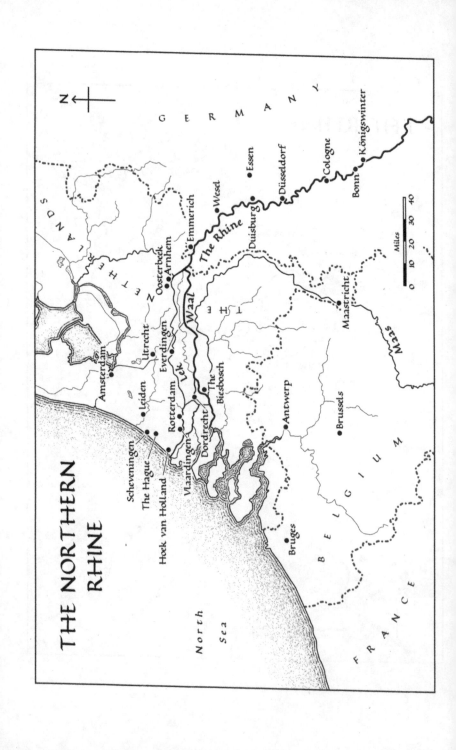

Introduction

Liquid City: Amsterdam and the Delta

A BOUT A YEAR after I arrived in the Netherlands, it began to snow. Not the drizzly slush which usually falls in western Europe these days, but proper snow of the kind which I hadn't seen since I was a child; big flakes which settled wherever they landed, carpeting the streets of Rotterdam like foam on the surface of a bath. Within a few hours, the streets around my home were coated with a thick layer of white powder and the canals had frozen solid. The trams stopped running and most of the shops were closed. The Dutch, it seemed, had returned to the Ice Age.

I'd moved to the Netherlands in 2010, through a strange combination of whim and good fortune. A flight which was carrying me from Peru to London had been diverted due to bad weather, and I ended up moving in with the young Dutch lady who'd offered me a place to stay for the night. Within a few months of my unexpected arrival, I'd become surprisingly well integrated: I had a Dutch job, house and girlfriend, and was beginning to speak the language pretty well. However, the change of weather thrust me abruptly back into the role of stranger in a strange land. The Netherlands which I'd been getting to know looked suddenly unfamiliar again, and I felt strangely unsure of how to behave. In England, I knew the protocol: any hint of snow and I'd call in sick to work, grab a toboggan or snowboard and head for the hills. But what did one do in a snowy place where downhill sports are out of the question, because the highest hills are barely tall enough for a dog to hide behind? The answer, according to my Dutch girlfriend, was obvious: 'Get some ice skates!'

At first, it seemed like a ridiculous idea. I hadn't skated in years, and in my native Britain ice skating was a minority pursuit anyway – something done only by teenagers on awkward first dates, or by couples in sequinned leotards competing for trophies. In the Netherlands, though, the opposite was true: ice skating was apparently almost as popular as drinking coffee and eating cheese. Almost every Dutch person I spoke to had a pair of ice skates stashed somewhere, even if they didn't get to use them very often, and skating champions were revered in the way star footballers or Olympic sprinters might be in other countries. During rare cold spells, the news would be dominated by endless speculation about the chances of holding an *Elfstedentocht* (Eleven Cities Tour) following the frozen canals for more than a hundred miles through the north of the Netherlands. In my first year in the Netherlands, I'd worked hard to understand and assimilate with the society I'd joined; drinking tiny little glasses of beer, talking unnecessarily loudly and eating sandwiches for breakfast. Now, taking up ice skating seemed like a logical next step towards integration.

And so I succumbed to peer pressure, and trekked across a white-jacketed city to a rundown little sports shop somewhere down by the river Maas. Inside, an old man with a Joe Stalin moustache quickly convinced me to spend a week's salary on some top-of-the-range skates; enormous boaty things which looked like plastic ski boots with stiletto blades welded underneath, ready to slice open anyone who dared to make fun of them. I carried my new toys home under my jacket, hid them under the bed and asked my girlfriend (now my wife) not to tell anyone I had them.

The next day, I walked to the end of my road, sat on the edge of a small river and nervously strapped myself in. The streets were quiet, muffled by the thick carpet of snow, and no one else was around. The ice on the river seemed very thick – about four inches, as far as I could tell – and I lowered myself gingerly onto it. After a few wobbly minutes, I was off, making thin black tracks through the white candy floss coating the top of the canal.

I'd never really paid much attention to the small river which passed close to my house – the Rotte, for which the city of Rotterdam is named – but now realised it actually stretched for miles, heading way out into the countryside and connecting with other channels big and small. Scooting low under a railway bridge, I headed north out of the city, past ancient windmills and boats straightjacketed by ice. After two hours of skating, I still hadn't run out of road. I stopped and bought a glass of strong, syrupy *glühwein* and drank it sitting on the ice for a while, before skating on towards the horizon.

Strange as it may sound, that day on the ice was the first time I'd ever thought of Dutch rivers as things which actually led somewhere. In other countries, I'd often used rivers as a way of getting from one place to another: in nearly a decade of indolent backpacking, I'd sailed along the Nile from Aswan to Cairo, rafted the Ganges, Trisuli and Pacuare, and ridden ferries along the Zambezi, Yangtze and Mekong. In the Netherlands, however, it was easy to think of rivers as mere background noise rather than significant features of the landscape. Centuries after the Dutch began their great project to reclaim land from the sea, the country was still covered with an extraordinary amount of water, with countless canals, streams, drainage ditches and artificial lakes criss-crossing the country. Walking and cycling along and over them every day, I'd grown used to ignoring them, never thinking about what they actually were: blue highways leading to other places.

Within a few days of my skating trip, all the ice had melted. But I was captivated by what I'd seen: an alternate map of my adopted home country in which rivers, rather than roads or railways, were the main arteries connecting communities. I wondered, if I kept following the rivers, how far could I go?

One day in the Rotterdam library, I looked at a few maps of the region, and found the answer: quite far. The Rotte river on which I'd skated was actually a minor tributary of the Maas, which itself formed much of the lower reaches of the river Rhine. This meant I could, in theory, skate, run, swim or cycle along the river not just as far as a *gluwhein* stop a few hours from home, but all the way across the Netherlands, into Germany and beyond – all the way, in fact, to the top of the Swiss Alps, half a continent away.

A few years previously, I'd lived for a while not far from the Nile in Uganda, and had become briefly fascinated with tales of Victorian explorers who set out to find the mythical source of the river, trekking for months through unexplored wildernesses. Obviously, exploring the Rhine wasn't quite in the same league, but following it all the way to its source had a pleasing purity of purpose. To live entwined with one of the world's most famous rivers yet never see its source seemed like living next to a great cathedral but never going inside; or dwelling at the foot of a mighty mountain but never seeing its summit.

I already fancied I knew the Rhine region well. Writing a previous book about the Netherlands, I'd explored one small stretch of the river in detail, travelling by boat and train from a ridiculous reconstruction of Noah's Ark in Dordrecht to the great flood defences near the North Sea. Further afield, I also knew much of the German Rhine well, having visited cities like Bonn, Düsseldorf and Cologne perhaps every other month for several years, for both work and pleasure. As a student and underpaid political aide, I'd spent a couple of happy summers exploring Alsace and the southern Rhineland, and later, as overpaid speechwriter and lobbyist, new to the Netherlands and missing the mountains, had flown numerous times for weekends in the Swiss Alps, Austria and Liechtenstein. However, there were still many stretches of the river which I'd never seen, and I knew less than I'd like to about the region's history and culture. A journey up and down the river seemed like an irresistible opportunity to explore further and learn more. I began studying maps and guidebooks, and planning to travel the whole way along the river by bike, boat, train and foot. I bought maps, found apartments to rent in various Rhine cities, and braced myself for long days on the road and long nights in the bar. When the summer came, I thought, I'd set out along the river, following it from the Netherlands all the way to its mountain source.

Rowing, like making your own pasta or pretending not to have a hangover, was harder than it looked. The first few strokes went well enough, but as my borrowed rowing boat picked up speed, I quickly found myself slaloming from side to side across the river like an out-of-control skier. No matter how hard I tried, it was impossible to get both oars to push neatly through the water at the same time without sending great tidal waves of spray towards nervous pedestrians on the riverbank.

I'd worked in Amsterdam on and off for years, and knew the city well, but thought taking to the water might offer new perspective. I was right: from water level on the river Amstel, things looked very different than they did from the street. The normally hectic city was quiet, and the small Dutch houses, which lined the water, loomed high overhead, like skinny mountains with red-tiled peaks. I rowed clumsily northwards, splashing and cursing my way towards the steeples of Amsterdam's old city centre. One oar clunked clumsily against a stone wall as another skimmed uselessly across the surface, and I looked enviously at a green-headed duck as he paddled effortlessly by. Luckily the weather was, by Dutch standards, spectacular, which is to say, neither windy nor rainy, and only a little grey.

There were few boats moving on the river, but I passed dozens of houseboats, each moored to the riverbank, with its own little bridge and pot plants on the roof. Some were beautiful old Dutch barges – thick bananas of black-painted steel sitting proudly above the waterline – but most were more ordinary: one-storey wooden cubes, like floating garden sheds. The architecture was mundane but the locations were spectacular, and this was reflected in the prices: a typical Amsterdam houseboat could cost far more than a similarly sized apartment. Slipping slowly under a bridge, I was swiftly overtaken by a Dutchman of about my age in a kayak, gliding effortlessly home from the supermarket with a cargo of grocery bags. I fumbled with my oars and waved a greeting, and he gave me a wry nod as if to say 'you clearly don't belong here'.

As always, I was amazed by how much life there was on the water. A dozen young people cruised by in a motor dinghy, happily flirting with one another and drinking little plastic cups of orange Aperol. Then came an old man in a motorboat with a black dog asleep in the bow, hollering at the youngsters as he passed: 'Watch out! There's a police speed check around the corner!'

Some fishermen on the bank were inflating a small boat, and I remembered the day, a few months previously, when I'd encountered a fellow youngish Englishman on a bridge near here, busily inflating the plastic children's dinghy which he'd just bought at a nearby supermarket. Once the boat was inflated, he loaded it with a dozen cans of Heineken and wriggled in, his legs hanging precariously over the sides like a giraffe in a bathtub. I asked tentatively what he was doing, and he shouted over his shoulder as he drifted away between the big barges, while cracking open a beer: 'Having a proper cruise, innit!'

★

In many ways, Amsterdam was an absurd place for me to begin my exploration of the Rhine. As several people had pointed out, the location generally considered the mouth of the Rhine lay not in Amsterdam but some fifty miles to the south-west, on the North Sea coast at Hoek van Holland. However, my choice of starting point wasn't entirely as ridiculous as it appeared.

While some rivers follow a direct course from A to B, the Rhine is a little more complex. From its source at Lake Toma, high in the Swiss Alps, this river flows down through a small piece of Switzerland into the micro-nation of Liechtenstein, before continuing briefly northwards through Austria and into the pearl-like Lake Constance.* Leaving Constance, the Rhine then heads west into Switzerland again, before abruptly turning north at Basle, serving as the Franco-German border for a while, and then heading lustily northwards through the left flank of Germany. That might already seem complicated enough, but after crossing the border into the freewheeling Netherlands, the Rhine becomes even more anarchic, fracturing into a vast cobweb of smaller channels, some man-made and some natural, with names which could make an English speaker swallow their tongue: the IJssel, Nederrijn, Benede Merwede and Dortse Kil. The only river actually called the Rijn in the Netherlands is a small stream which trundles through the centre of the country, while the Dutch river which carries most of the Rhine's cargoes to the sea is called the Maas, and the vast delta of the southern Netherlands is known as the Rhine–Maas–Scheldt delta.

For a novice hydrographer, it was all quite confusing, but it's sufficient to say that the Rhine delta covers much of the south-western Netherlands, and waters originating in the German Rhine are found all over the place. The Dutch map is littered with names inspired by the river and its tributaries – Rijnsaterwoude, Rijnsburg, Rijndijk, Alphen aan den Rijn, Nieuwerbrug aan den Rijn – and the country's most famous painter (born in the city of Leiden) is Rembrandt van Rijn. Amsterdam, Vlissingen and Deventer all lie in different corners of the Netherlands, but drop a rubber duck in Cologne and

---

* Technically, this account is an oversimplification, and there are several points in Switzerland at which the river could be said to begin. However, Lake Toma is generally accepted as the primary source of the Vorderrhein, or Anterior Rhine.

it could well end up bobbing through any of them. From above, the Dutch Rhine looks less like a road leading neatly from A to B, and more like a glass of beer spilled in an Amsterdam bar, messily spreading its way across the floorboards towards the doorway.

For me personally, the main result of this confusing geography was it made my route-planning difficult. Who could say where the Rhine really ended and where my journey should begin? After much studying of maps, I ended up choosing a route which seemed both geographically reasonable and fun: a quick pootle around Amsterdam, before heading briefly southwards along bits of the tiny Oude Rijn through North and South Holland to the wide river mouth at Hoek van Holland. From there, I could travel more slowly along the Nieuwe Maas, Lek and Nederrijn to the Dutch–German border, and then along the Rhine proper through Germany, France, Switzerland, Austria and Lichtenstein all the way to the source.*
Amsterdam wasn't known as a major Rhine city, but it was nourished indirectly by the waters of the Rhine, kept supplied with tourists by countless Rhine cruise ships, and linked to the river by a long canal. In that context, it seemed as good a place as any to start.

A second reason for starting in Amsterdam was that the city, perhaps more than anywhere else in the Netherlands, epitomised the way in which rivers like the Rhine shaped the lifestyles of the people living alongside them. Amsterdam is thought to have arisen as a small fishing village in the thirteenth century, based around a pair of dikes on either side of the river Amstel, which were eventually linked together by a bridging dam – the Amstel-dam. It was at first a pretty sleepy place, but that began to change rapidly in the mid 1600s, when a blockade of Antwerp lead to much trade being diverted to Amsterdam and sent Protestant refugees flooding

* Throughout this book, I take a few lexicographical liberties with the names of places to which I travel. Firstly, I occasionally describe stretches of water as being part of 'the Rhine' even if they're technically part of the numerous channels which make up the fractured Rhine delta, such as the Waal. Secondly, I generally rely on present-day place names and borders – referring, for example, to something which happened 'in Germany in 1800', even though the unified country of Germany didn't exist at that time. Thirdly, as an Englishman writing in English, I use anglicised place names – for example 'Cologne' rather than 'Köln', and 'Basle' rather than 'Basel'. These shortcuts may infuriate pedantic geographers, but should make things much easier to follow.

northwards in search of new freedoms and opportunities. In half a century the population of the city roughly tripled. By the late sixteenth century, Dutch explorers and traders were fanning out across the globe in search of new territory and riches. The Verenigde Oost-Indische Compagnie (Dutch East India Company, or VOC) was formally established in 1602, and quickly bloomed into a world-spanning colossus – a seventeenth-century version of Shell or General Motors. The Dutch became what the author Daniel Defoe described as 'the carryers of the world', running trading posts everywhere from present-day Indonesia to Taiwan, Japan, Brazil, South Africa and North America. The Dutch founded New York City, naming Brooklyn and Harlem after small towns in their homeland; bumped into Australia; and discovered New Zealand, naming the latter after the southern Dutch province of Zeeland. At home, they also embarked on a wildly ambitious project to physically rebuild their country; pumping lakes dry and reclaiming swathes of the boggy Rhine–Maas delta. For most of the seventeenth century, the Dutch were trapped in a blissful virtuous cycle. Foreign trade generated rich profits which could be invested in new boats and expeditions, and land reclamation unlocked new land which earned money to invest in more reclamation. The Dutch guilder was – like the dollar or bitcoin – accepted as currency all around the world.

In Amsterdam, the wealth of this 'Golden Age' transformed the city. It grew quickly from a relative backwater into one of the biggest metropolises in Europe, a bustling, cosmopolitan place where dozens of languages were spoken and riverside wharves were packed with exotic spices, fabrics and foods. Around the original Amstel-dam on Dam Square, concentric canals were dug and equipped with complex series of locks and sluices which meant they could regularly be flushed clean, with fresh water flowing from one side of the city to another. The most prominent water features were given grandiose, aspirational names: the Herengracht (Gentleman's Canal), Prinsengracht (Prince's Canal) and Keizersgracht (Emperor's Canal). Newly wealthy merchants built canalside houses which were modest in size but majestic in style, as narrow and deep as books on a shelf. Foreign visitors were astonished by what they saw in the Venice of the North: artists, innovators and poets; soaring churches; neat bridges and above all canals.

As in any country, it was almost impossible to untangle all the influences which had shaped the Netherlands' culture, but it was fair to say that almost everything which an outsider might think of as quintessentially 'Dutch' could be traced directly back to the influence of rivers like the Rhine. Windmills were made to pump boggy areas dry, and dikes built to hold the water back. The flat green fields reclaimed from the water provided food for dairy cows, who produced gallons of milk. Cheese was made from the milk, and tulips grown in the fields. Streets were paved with bricks so they wouldn't crack when the reclaimed ground subsided. The Dutch themselves used bicycles to ride along the flat sides of canals and the tops of dikes, wore clogs to protect against the silty mud, and grew tall from all the milk and cheese. Perhaps most importantly, the waterways which criss-crossed the country were the major source of its prosperity; the golden ticket which made a rain-soaked corner of Europe a cultural and economic superpower. Water, once the greatest enemy of the Dutch, ended up making them rich and Amsterdam one of most picturesque and profitable cities in the world.

Abandoning the unwieldy rowing boat, I continued northwards on foot, following the Amstel and then turning west along the Herengracht canal. The outer fringes of Amsterdam were a confusing sprawl, but as a pedestrian, the old centre was still delightfully easy to navigate, with the four major canals circling Dam Square like rings on a dartboard. I arrived in the area known as the Negen Straatjes (Nine Little Streets); a delightful warren of seventeenth-century townhouses, cafés and boutiques. I hadn't walked through this part of Amsterdam for more than a year, and thought I could detect a change. The city had long been famous as a place of refuge and recreation, but in recent years had risked getting a bit rough around the edges, with a few too many visitors coming to do fun things which were illegal back home. In response, the city authorities had begun closing brothels, increasing tourist taxes and tightening drug laws. Inevitably, the changes were hotly debated, and the authorities struggled to strike the right balance. Too much tolerance of excess and Amsterdam might become thuggish and seedy, but too little and it risked becoming an insipid Potemkin village where loved-up couples loved to wander but it was hard for Dutch people to actually live or work.

It may have been my imagination, but the result seemed a modest improvement: Amsterdam's streets were a little cleaner than they had been in the past, and the atmosphere a little calmer. There was still an amazing number of tourists, but the old city was wonderful: brick-lined canals, ancient townhouses, and thousands of bicycles weaving along the narrow streets like fish in a stream. In the usual Amsterdam way, many people were sitting outside their houses on their own front steps, sharing bottles of wine and eating little cubes of cheese as the world bustled by just a few feet away. At midday on a rather grey Tuesday, the whole city had the bohemian air of a park on a sunny Sunday, and the locals looked like 'after' pictures in an advert for a fitness regime. I stopped to take photo of a bridge just as a girl of about six announced loudly to her mother, in Dutch: 'Oh what a beautiful bridge! I think it's very, very, very old. Like from the 1960s!'

Near the Westerkerk (Western Church), I found a nice café and sat outside on the cobbles drinking herbal tea, which tasted like canal water. My spoken Dutch was decent but patchy, but when the waitress realised I was English she complimented me on it lavishly. Not for the first time, I was glad to have been born in a country where language skills were in short supply. For a Dutch person to be considered 'fluent' in English, they had to be able to recite Shakespearian sonnets by heart, but for Englishman to be 'fluent' in Dutch, they merely had to order a drink.

My tea finished, I kept walking east from the Westerkerk towards De Wallen, through deep canyons formed by black-painted ancient houses. Like all the best cities, Amsterdam felt more like a village than a great metropolis. In the space of thirty minutes, I'd walked halfway across it and seen three people I knew; acquaintances who were all bemused to learn where I planned to go next. 'Following the rivers to the Alps?' one of them said. 'Why do you want to do that? Can't you just take the train?'

My acquaintance's low opinion of the Rhine wasn't unusual. In years gone by, few would have doubted the importance of such a great river. When roads were bad, rivers offered an easy way to transport goods and people. When populations were growing, rivers offered food to keep them fed. When great factories were growing, rivers provided water for power and cooling. And when wars were common, rivers provided natural moats to keep invaders out and ways of moving soldiers to wherever their deadly skills were needed. Well into the twentieth century, many Europeans would have seen a river near their home as being like oxygen or Wi-Fi; something it was impossible to live without.

In the twenty-first century, though, rivers have rather fallen from favour. In an era when tulips can be flown from Kenya to Amsterdam overnight, peace treaties negotiated by tele-conference, wars fought by drone, and products printed using blueprints downloaded from China, the idea that the slow, steady flow of water and ships might help shape nations has come to seem rather quaint. In Europe, rivers have become mild curiosities rather than major national assets; nice places to walk a dog or relax with a coffee, but considerably less important than oxygen or Wi-Fi.

Of course, this isn't to say the world is completely disinterested in rivers. Politicians and diplomats still lose sleep over the control of the Tigris and Euphrates, and fret over proposals to control the Nile, divert the Mekong or dam the Congo. But the Rhine never quite gets the attention it deserves. Magisterial histories of Europe barely mention it, and Europeans shrug when it's discussed. Younger Dutch people, in particular, often seem oddly prejudiced against the Rhine region, dismissing its cities as boring even as they flock to nearby rivals such as Paris and Berlin. In the twenty-first century, the Rhine has become like Buddhism or the bond market: something which everyone has heard of, but few people really know much about.

In an age of hyperbole, the Rhine also suffers from comparison with behemoths like the Amazon or Congo. Viewed through another lens, however, it's easy to argue that it is one of the greatest of them all; one of the major axes around which world history turns. Winding its way some 800 miles through Europe, it's the second-longest river in central and western Europe, behind only the Danube. Altogether, around 50 million people live in its watershed, nearly as many as live in Italy. It has also inspired some of history's most famous writers, poets, artists, diplomats and statesmen, often serving as a fulcrum of European war and history. 'The Rhine,' as Victor Hugo wrote, 'is unique; it combines the qualities of every river . . . Mysterious, like the Nile; spangled with gold, like an American river; and, like a river of Asia, abounding with phantoms and fables.'

To a certain extent, all rivers serve a dual purpose: along their length they unite, but across their breadth they divide. The Rhine is no exception. Along its length, it forms a key artery of Europe's trade system; one of the major outlets through which Dutch, German, French and Swiss industries ship their products to the world. The port at Rotterdam is by far the busiest in Europe, handling well over a million tons of cargo a day; more than twice as much as its nearest rival. It's perhaps not a coincidence that several countries which the Rhine traverses – the Netherlands, Switzerland, Liechtenstein, Germany – are among the richest in the world. Together, Germany and the Netherlands, the last two countries through which the Rhine flows, export more than the United States and Mexico combined.

Yet viewed across its width, the same river has also been a source of division. Under the Romans, the Rhine served as the edge of empire; the point at which they effectively gave up their expansionist plans and reconciled themselves to glaring across the water at the savages beyond. Over subsequent centuries the river was fought over countless times, including during two world wars – conflicts sparked in part by a desire to control the Rhineland, and fuelled by coal and steel from the river's middle reaches. Today, the Rhine is at peace but still forms, in various places, the border between France and Germany, Germany and Switzerland, Switzerland and Liechtenstein, and Austria and Switzerland; a reminder that modern frontiers can still be tangible things rather than just faint lines on electronic maps.

Without the Rhine, Europe would be a very different place. Germany would be far poorer, the Netherlands would be a soggy backwater, Switzerland would be even more isolated, and the North Sea would be far emptier of trade. Without the river, there might have been no world wars, and no European Union. The French might be speaking German, or the Germans speaking French. The cars which plutocrats drive might be Japanese rather than German, and the paintings which visitors to Amsterdam marvel at might be Italian rather than Dutch. As Halford John Mackinder wrote in 1908: 'The Rhine is unique among the rivers of Europe in its influence upon history.'

★

With all that in mind, I sat by the water in Amsterdam and scrawled a list of several key aspects of the river which I wanted to explore. Firstly, and most simply, I wanted to learn more about how the Rhine had shaped – and continued to shape – the countries it flowed through, and the people who lived there. Secondly, I was keen to explore how the Rhine region was changing. In the years leading up to my journey, this area (like much of Europe) had been beset by crisis. Economies had stumbled. Germany was racked by a refugee crisis and France had been hit by brutal terrorist attacks. Austria had nearly elected a fascist as president, Switzerland had introduced legislation against Muslims, and the 'tolerant' Netherlands had seen anti-immigrant riots. Further afield, the British had decided that the best way to promote free trade was by leaving the world's largest free trade area. Authoritarian leaders in the east of Europe were threatening the unity of the Union. An American president was threatening to collapse NATO and block European imports, acting like the geopolitical equivalent of a dog who'd somehow managed to catch the car he was chasing.

The threat posed by these changes was often exaggerated, but to my mind, it added a new dimension to my questions about the relevance of the Rhine to the modern age. In a world where international trade was viewed as a betrayal, and many leaders were more inclined to build walls than bridges, what role could the Rhine play? Was the river still important when profits were made online as often as on the factory floor; when people travelled by plane rather than riverboat; and when cultural influences were spread by memes and viral videos rather than by artists moving downriver? And in an age when culture was increasingly globalised, was there such a thing as a unified 'Rhine culture', which was shared across borders, uniting people such as the Dutch, Swiss and Germans? I set off to find out, Amsterdam receding behind me and the Alps far ahead.

PART ONE
The Netherlands

I

Turning the Corner

Hoek van Holland to Rotterdam

I SLEPT IN the sand dunes, sheltered from the wind by a big sign which said 'No Camping'. At 6 a.m. I was woken by a big seagull insistently pinging its beak on the dirty saucepan in which I'd cooked a nourishing dinner of hotdogs the evening before. It was early summer, and the weather was – by Dutch standards at least – beautiful; warm and sunny, with fluffy popcorn clouds scattered high in a bubblegum-blue sky. Down by the shore, happy children chased dogs through the splashy surf, and a father gave his sons a serious lecture in how best to throw a ball. A short way offshore, a handful of surfers tried in vain to ride the undersized waves; soggy little black-suited ninjas dancing in the waist-deep water. Behind them, out to sea, I could see dozens of modern windmills protruding from the choppy sea like skinny white giants, waving their arms in glee at the unusually good weather.

The journey down from Amsterdam had been delightful; an erratic but picturesque sixty-mile bike ride which zigzagged across much of the north-western Netherlands, heading southwards to Alphen aan de Rijn and then turning along the Oude Rijn (Old Rhine), a scenic little stream which meandered through flat fields and quiet villages, carrying more ducks and swans than boats. From the grand cathedral city of Leiden I spun west to the coast at Scheveningen, and down through the sand dunes to my sleeping place near the best-named village in Europe: Monster.

I'd returned to the Netherlands from a longish spell working in Africa only about ten days' previously and was struck, as I always am on such occasions, by just how *tidy* everything was. Even in relatively drab suburbs of cities like Amsterdam, everything was in its place; functional, orderly and spotlessly clean. I passed the occasional patch of graffiti, but the trees were all neatly trimmed, the pavements swept clean enough to eat off, and the grass cropped as close as a soldier's haircut. Accustomed to living close together, and to carefully keeping the sea at bay, the Dutch applied the same orderly principles to their daily lives. Whole towns had the bland tidiness of a gated college campus or retirement community. It wasn't always exciting to look at, but there was undoubtedly something impressive about how neatly everything fitted together in a country where 500 people were squeezed into every square kilometre. For a nation renowned for its anarchic liberalism, it all seemed terrifically sensible.

After chasing the seagull away, I packed up my tiny tent, made a saucepan of muddy instant coffee and sat drinking it on the sand. The scenery was beautiful; an endless beach which stretched northwards for perhaps fifty miles almost uninterrupted. Not for the first time, I wondered how the Dutch had managed to keep their coastlines secret from all the thousands of sand-seekers who flew over them on their way to Italy, Greece or Turkey. This neglected spot was surely one of the best beaches in Europe.

I cycled a mile or two down the coast, along a quiet road tucked behind the sand dunes. As always in the Netherlands, cycling was a delight. There were no cars, no inconvenient road crossings, no sudden dead-ends, and no pedestrians ambling along clearly marked bike lanes. The only interruptions were welcome ones: cycle-specific traffic lights, clear signposting and even big cone-shaped rubbish bins into which passing cyclists could toss their litter without slowing down. I sped effortlessly along, with a steady sea breeze pushing at my back like a helping hand. In the space of barely a mile, I passed few pedestrians but scores of other cyclists – not British-style weekend warriors with expensive bikes and scuba-style clothing, but a cross-section of Dutch society: smartly suited businessmen, wobbly old ladies, mothers with young children perched precariously on their handlebars. I thought, pretentiously, of novelist Flann O'Brien's 'Atomic Theory' of cycling, set out in *The Third Policeman*, which argued that if someone spent too long on a bike, they risked swapping atoms with your machine. 'You would be surprised at the number of people in these parts,' said one of O'Brien's characters, 'who are nearly half people and half bicycles.'

After five miles or so, I reached the end of the beach, where an incredibly long concrete sea wall stretched out into the hazel-grey surf. This was, literally, the *Hoek van Holland*, or 'corner of Holland', where the most significant branch of the lower Rhine, the Nieuwe Waterweg, spilled into the North Sea. I left my bike locked to a railing and walked out along the sea wall, with the fresh water of the river mouth on my left and the salty sea to my right. The view back along the beach to the north was spectacular: a vast ark of sand stretching all the way to the hazy horizon, as pale and powdery as crushed ivory. In the other direction, however, things were rather less scenic. Across the wide mouth of the river lay the so-called Maas Plain (Maasvlaakte), a large area of industrial land which had been reclaimed from the North Sea as part of the ongoing Dutch project to artificially increase the size of their tiny country. Here, there were no beautiful beaches, just an ugly mass of cranes, docks, electricity pylons and stacks of shipping containers the size of buildings. Modern wind turbines rolled slowly in the breeze, and a cluster of thick chimneys smoked like cigars thrust upright on the riverbank. The Dutch Rhine, it seemed, was Janus-faced: serenely beautiful on one side; robustly industrial on the other.

Approaching the end of the wall, I half hoped to see some tangible evidence of the geographical significance of the river mouth and its role as an aquatic crossroads; a splash of deep blue river water spilling out into a bright green sea, perhaps, with seawater and Rhine water bleeding slowly together like ingredients in a cocktail. The reality, though, was rather more prosaic. The grey-green river widened slightly and then merged seamlessly with an identically grey-green sea, like a road leading into a car park. I tried hard to feel moved about the prospect of leaving the coast and beginning my journey inland, but in truth it was all very sensible and undramatic. I remembered the old joke about Toronto looking how New York City would look if it were run by the Swiss. Here, the Rhine looked how the Amazon or Nile would look if they were run by the Dutch.

I walked back across the sand to my bike. It was late morning by now, and the handful of bars along the beachfront were becoming busy with local families eating *uitsmijter* fried-egg platters and enjoying the scenery from behind the shelter of high glass screens, as if spectating in a high-security courtroom. In the era before the likes of Easyjet drew the crowds elsewhere, Dutch coastal towns like this one had been among the busiest seaside resorts in Europe; places where the wealthy would go to rest, bathe and take in the salty air. In the early 1800s, the Dutch royal family had even made a habit of racing up and down the sands north of Hoek van Holland on wheeled sand yachts. 'Credible greybeards . . . have asserted that they often saw Prince William V and his court sailing with incredible speed, almost as fast as our modern railways,' one observer recorded. Now the atmosphere was pleasant but slightly seedy; more Jersey Shore than royal retreat. A sign on the sand gave a phone number to call for '*Eerste Hulp Bij Zeehonden*', 'First Aid for Seals', and I thought how strange and terrible and wonderful the world was; that in some places people had nothing, and here they had so much to spare that even sick seals had their own ambulance service.

Historically, this part of the Rhine delta was a fairly desolate place. Long before the cocktail bars and surfers arrived, Hoek van Holland lay at the edge of a vast tidal basin, surrounded by salty bogs with the consistency of mashed potato. The fishermen and hunters who lived here ate well from the many streams and rivers, but were constantly menaced by the tides; forced to live atop muddy little hillocks (*terpen*), they had to run for higher ground whenever the tide turned. To the outside world, the Rhine delta was seen as a harsh, desolate place; it was dangerously close to the northern seas where sailors would encounter whirlpools, boiling seas and monsters which could swallow a ship whole. When the Roman commander Pliny visited the region, he reported seeing nothing but bleak, treeless salt marshes populated by people who 'seem to be shipwrecked'. He briefly considered conquering the local tribes in the name of Rome, but decided against it. Why bother, when all they had was bogs and fish?

Daily life on the lowlands might have been soggy and miserable, but with their position on the coast, barely a hundred miles from England and with easy access to the North Sea, Baltic Sea and the Atlantic, small settlements like Hoek van Holland later acquired an outsized strategic importance. In the sixteenth and seventeenth centuries, as the Dutch built up their navy and merchant fleet, the Rhine in particular emerged as a key outlet for the country's internationalist ambitions. The Dutch developed a navy which was, for a while at least, bigger than the English and French fleets combined. Rotterdam, a mid-sized town not far from the river mouth, grew to become a major trading centre, the departure point for great expeditions which explored, colonised and built trading links with far-flung places such as Indonesia, Brazil and Ghana. Wooden sailing ships ferried goods such as timber, wool, dried fish and grain up and down the river, and along the Dutch coast to Scandinavia, the Baltics, England, Belgium and beyond. Fishing fleets based near Rotterdam and The Hague also provided an important source of both food and income. The rivers and the sea, long thought of as an existential threat to the country, ended up making it rich.

Later, the river mouth became an entry point for thousands of intrepid travellers making 'Grand Tours' of Europe. In the eighteenth and nineteenth centuries, these tours were a rite of passage for upper-class young people (mostly men), who headed out across Europe on greatest-hits tours of classical antiquity and the Renaissance highlights, ticking off cathedrals, libraries and galleries in much the same way today's gap-year students tick off temples, islands and beach bars.

The Grand Tours had no fixed itinerary, but most tourists aimed for Rome, Venice or the Alps as their furthest destination, and travelled through some combination of the Netherlands, France, Germany and Switzerland on their way. As such, Hoek van Holland made an obvious entry point to Europe for travellers arriving from London. Most roads in those days were bone-jarringly uncomfortable, and the Rhine offered an obvious alternative; a relatively bump-free highway going from the North Sea all the way to Strasbourg, Basle and beyond. In the nineteenth century, regular ferries connected Hoek van Holland with the east of England, and a two-week tour from (say) Rotterdam to Cologne and back typically cost a little over three pounds. London bookshops were filled with guidebooks promoting the delights of Dutch and German travel, alongside adverts for enormous suitcases and (in case things went badly wrong) funeral supplies from 'Jay's London General Mourning Warehouse'. Travellers crossed the Channel in their thousands, many heading straight up the Rhine by boat and train. 'The era in which we live will be called the nomadic period,' *Putnam's Magazine* declared in 1868. 'With the advent of ocean navigation . . . began a travelling mania which has gradually increased until half of the earth's inhabitants . . . are on the move.'

Grand Tourists came from all over Europe and North America, but many were British – the stereotypical traveller was a wealthy young man who'd finished studying the classics at Oxford or Cambridge, and then set out on a foppish pilgrimage to see the wonders of western civilisation in person, while bedding women, drinking wine and commissioning portraits with little thought for the cost or consequences. Many snottily saw completing a Grand Tour as a qualification in its own right; proof that they were more cultured and knowledgeable than those who hadn't travelled. Dr Johnson said any Englishman who'd not travelled to Italy would always be 'conscious of an inferiority, from his not having seen what it is expected a man should see'. Naturally, many also returned loaded down with souvenirs – not snowglobes or keyrings, but crates packed with paintings and statues, wines and luxury foodstuffs, thick books and innovative scientific instruments. Even in the early days, the tours were astonishingly popular: as early as 1785, Edward Gibbon reported that 40,000 Brits were enjoying trips to the Continent every year. It wasn't just just rich young nobles who made the journey, though; in the 1770s, a three-ton Indian rhinocerous called Clara was dragged upstream on a barge pulled by teams of horses, as part of a money-making tour arranged by a Dutch sea captain, which took her to Mannheim, Basle, Rome and Vienna. Along the Rhine, spectators gathered on riverbanks as Clara passed, utterly astonished by her mighty size and ironlike flanks, so different from the cows and ponies they were used to.

In the early years, voyages across the North Sea and then up the Rhine were slow, and currents could be rough. One traveller who crossed from Harwich in 1789 reported that 'the wind was boisterous and changeable and the sea very high . . . I was bitter sorry, we were 30 hours at sea'. In time, though, new steamships made tours much faster. In 1816, people were astonished when a steamship made it from Rotterdam to Cologne in only four and a half days. Then came guidebooks. In 1836, John Murray published his first 'little red book' guiding confused Brits across the Continent. Scores of other guidebooks followed, including the influential *Up and Down the Rhine for £5*, which advised travellers that for a Rhine cruise, 'Nothing is really needed beyond a small carpet bag, containing . . . the ordinary dress you wear in London, and an umbrella . . . and a wide-awake hat, if you have them.' By 1856 a reported 120 different travel books had been written about the Rhine in English. They included the wildly popular guides published by Karl Baedeker, which had distinctive raspberry-red covers and were the *Lonely Planet* or *Rough Guides* of their day, recommending the best places for a confused visitor to sleep, eat or hire a donkey.* Inspired by the likes of Baedeker, a pioneering trickle of Grand Tourists turned into a flood: in 1827 the main steamship line between Cologne and Mainz was carrying 18,000 passengers each year, but by the 1860s it was taking more than a million.

Like backpackers complaining that Angkor Wat or Machu Picchu are getting overcrowded, Grand Tourists were often disappointed to find that the hidden treasures which they'd fantasised about visiting were actually getting quite busy. One bitter tourist of the early 1840s complained: 'Steamers are everywhere loaded to sinking; inns are full to suffocation, and landlords stand shaking their heads, gabbling German, French, English, Italian, and Russian.' 'Imagination cannot conceive of what motley cast and colour are the crowds which in these days rush up the Rhine,' wrote another, 'guide-book in hand, and ignorant of every language under heaven.'

A further challenge was the food. Visiting the Netherlands, the Brits mocked the locals' 'Popery and wooden shoes', but praised the butter and beef. 'Good Rhinish wine and salmon, and bad cooks' was Joseph Shaw's review. Further upriver, they were horrified by the French habit of eating frogs but generally impressed by the wide range of fruits available, shipped up from the Mediterranean. More xenophobic Brits often pointed out the contrast between British and continental cuisine, claiming that the superiority of British food reflected the superiority of British people. 'A true Englishman who loves roast beef and pudding cannot breathe freely out of his own island,' Lord Boyle wrote. More than a century later, looking around Hoek van Holland at the deep-fried monstrosities

---

* In 1942, when the Nazis ordered the bombing of England in retaliation for a raid on Lubeck, officers used Baedeker's star ratings to select their targets, declaring they would destroy everything in England which 'had three stars in Baedeker'.

on sale, and the Dutch people ordering fries for breakfast, I thought he may have had a point.

Leaving the beach, I aimed inland, cycling along the northern bank of the river – still the Nieuwe Waterweg at this point. Considering Hoek van Holland's importance as a geopolitical hinge point, there were few signs of dynamism or prosperity. For modern-day Grand Tourists who arrived here by ferry, their first sight of continental Europe would consist of little more than a few rows of semi-detached post-war houses, a couple of snack bars and a lot of shops selling cheap T-shirts, raincoats and baseball caps. I stopped briefly for a cup of tea with milk, and had to explain twice to the waitress that I planned to pour the milk into the tea rather than drink them separately – an action which she, as a non-Brit, clearly thought was utterly absurd. A sign on the bar said in English 'Tipping is Not a City in China'.

Continuing towards Rotterdam, the cycle lane continued right along the riverbank, tracking the water like a canal towpath. The river was tranquil, steely-coloured and immensely wide: perhaps two or three times as wide as the Thames in Westminster. A flat grey barge – a so-called 'bulk' carrier, bearing a loose cargo such as grain or gravel – charged up the middle of the channel, its wake washing high up the sloping concrete banks. A little blue passenger jet circled high overhead, waiting to land in Rotterdam, and I remembered reading recently that the King of the Netherlands had admitted to a secret double life, working part-time as airline pilot for KLM. I wondered if he might be on board, adjusting the thrust and trim while his crown bumped on the ceiling.

Across the river, the Port of Rotterdam continued to reveal itself as an endless show-reel of harbours, chimneys, refineries, cranes, turbines and pylons unspooling for dozens of miles along the southern bank. I'd seen similar views of the port many times before, while driving and cycling through the area, but never ceased to be amazed by the sheer size of it. At about 12,500 hectares, the badly branded 'Europoort' was, at the time of my journey, about the size of the city of Manchester, and still growing. It was by far the biggest port in Europe, handling more shipping containers each year than Zeebrugge, Barcelona, Southampton, Felixstowe and Le Havre put together. The river was a big part of its success: every day, nearly 300 vessels passed through the port on their way inland, continuing their journey away from the coast on rivers including the Rhine.

I'd visited the port itself a few days previously, on a boat tour looping its way through one of the busiest areas. As I should have expected, it wasn't a particularly scenic voyage: giant chemical refineries; massive blue cranes shaped like dining chairs with their backs to the water; walls of shipping containers stacked like cereal boxes in a supermarket. The scenery was more reminiscent of Port Talbot than of tranquil Amsterdam or Delft. However, the sheer scale of the port was spectacular, and it wasn't hard to see why people who worked in or lived near it saw it as a source of deep pride. From the water, everything looked so big that the sense of scale was distorted: containers looked like matchboxes, giant cranes like delicate surgical instruments and enormous ships like bath toys. The biggest lighthouse in the Netherlands was a tiny piece of striped candy, dwarfed by the cranes around it. Warehouses bore the names of world-beating companies most people have never heard of: Cabot, Emerald, Vitol, LyondellBassell, Vopak. My city-loving friends in Amsterdam and The Hague might have been only dimly aware that the port existed, but it was truly the hidden engine room of the Netherlands: the only way the tourist-friendly, bicycle-filled, socially liberal cities were affordable was because of the tough, rough indus-triousness of places like these, tucked away in the watery underbelly where no one would see them. We cruised on past a small artificial island on which thirty or so sealions were basking in the sun like fat tourists in wetsuits. One splashed into the water and bobbed perilously close to a passing container ship; I hoped the first aiders were still standing by. Across the water, I could see the giant refineries of Pernis – a place where I'd occasionally worked, and often deliberately misspelled in emails to my boss.

The riverside area around Rotterdam had a long history as a trading centre, but its emergence as true global hub dated to a stroke of luck in the 1640s, when under the terms of the Treaties of Westphalia the river Scheldt, in present-day Belgium, was closed to international shipping. Traders around Rotterdam were (like those in Amsterdam) quick to exploit their rivals' demise, and an astonishing explosion of international trade ensued, transforming sleepy riverside towns into colourful emporia. From the 1600s onwards, as global trade increased, the Netherlands was ideally located to benefit, lying as it did on the western flank of Europe, between Germany and the markets of the United States and Britain. The waters around the river mouth were free of ice all year round, while the British Isles formed a convenient buffer sheltering the Dutch coast from the worst Atlantic storms. Crucially, the Rhine itself also seemed designed for shipping; a deep channel which carved its way right through one of the most populous and productive regions of Europe, it was filled with a mixture of winter rainwater and summer snow melt which meant that (occasional flooding aside) the water level barely changed from season to season. Visitors arriving from London were astonished by the number and variety of ships buzzing around the river mouth, and the haste with which Dutch merchants rushed back and forth between vessels and the quaysides. The Netherlands, one nineteenth-century poet famously wrote, was 'a land that rides at anchor, and is moored /. in which they do not live, but go aboard'. The quaysides along the river (like those in Amsterdam) teemed with unprecedented, exotic sights: parrots, rhinoceroses, amber, ivory, sugar, opium, indigo and saffron.

By the mid 1800s, the Port of Rotterdam was thriving – so much so, in fact, that the stretch of river which lead from the city to the sea was increasingly crowded and unable to accommodate the larger cargoes which now arrived almost continuously. In response, the Dutch authorities did exactly what they usually did when confronted with such a problem; they proposed an ambitious, hugely expensive plan to completely reshape the natural environment. By the 1860s, major canals were very much in vogue: Egypt's Suez Canal was scheduled to open in 1869. Near Rotterdam, teams of men spent nearly a decade digging in the mud to consolidate the river's fractured, cobwebbed sea mouth into a single lock-free channel. Over the years that followed, the waterway was progressively widened and deepened, and by the time I visited it was up to 675 metres across, wider than the combined wingspan of ten Boeing 747s. Just as its architects had hoped, the new waterway provided an economic boost to the whole region. Cargo shipments grew from a mere 1.2 million tons of throughput just before the new canal opened, to a staggering 42 million tons at the dawn of the Second World War. Further upstream, the Germans also radically reshaped the Rhine in the nineteenth century, with the great engineer Johann Gottfried Tulla leading a massive project to dredge the riverbed, speed the flow of traffic and reduce the risk of flooding. The length of the river between Basle and Worms was reduced by nearly a quarter, and more than 2,000 islands were removed. Rotterdam, situated some twenty-five miles from the sea, had effectively become a coastal city.

During the war, the port of Rotterdam was utterly ravaged, first by Nazi bombing raids and then by Allied raids during the Occupation. After the war, though, the port recovered dramatically, thanks in part to massive Marshall Plan investment in shipping facilities around the mouth of the river. At first, this investment was effectively a gamble – the Dutch began building big new harbours long before it became clear Europe could generate enough trade to pay for them. Luckily, the bet paid off quite spectacularly, and by the early 1960s, Rotterdam was the largest port in the world.

Thanks in significant part to Rhine-based trade, the Dutch economy accelerated past those of its rivals. In 1960, for example, the Gross Domestic Products (GDPs) of Belgium and the Netherlands were roughly the same, around $12 billion per year. By 2008, Belgium's had increased to an impressive $500 billion or so, but the Netherlands' was nearly double that, close to a trillion dollars a year. In 2016, the Netherlands exported more merchandise than the UK, despite having only one-quarter of the population.

Boosted by these strong exports, the Dutch economy enjoyed an unparalleled run of economic growth: for more than twenty-five years leading up to 2008, the Dutch never had two consecutive financial quarters in which their economy didn't grow. This wasn't all due to the Rhine or the ports, of course, but the delta's role as a hub for international trade played a big part in the story. As the port's boosters never tired of pointing out, today anyone in northern Europe who drives a car, travels in an aeroplane, uses something plastic, has paint on the walls, eats processed food or wears modern clothes is almost certainly consuming chemical products which have bobbed along the Rhine through Rotterdam. In 2015, one canny Dutch entrepreneur even managed to sell 300 containers full of sand to a Sheikh in Qatar, which were promptly shipped from Rotterdam to Doha – the equivalent, surely, of selling rain to the English, or snow to Eskimos.

However, travelling around the port and chatting to people who worked there, I did detect some reasons to worry that its future might not be quite as glorious as its past. In particular, whenever I visited I was amazed by how few people there were. In my mind's eye, a port was a place of sweat and steam, filled with puffing steamships sounding their horns, wooden crates being carted up gangplanks and burly stevedores hauling on thick ropes. The reality was inevitably rather different: in the container yards which lined the river, there were no massed workers clocking on and off, but rather a continuous steady whirr of automated vehicles shunting containers around, following magnetic tracks laid in the floor and driving themselves to power points for automatic recharging. Rather than being a place of sweat and steam, the port was a place where skilled labour seemed surplus to requirements, all cars were driverless and the algorithm reigned supreme. In many ways, I found it all very impressive, but it was also bad news for the people who'd once depended on the port for their livelihoods. According to local news reports, the hardest hit looked set to be the crane drivers; once known locally as 'Kings of the Terminal', they were now increasingly being replaced by robotic systems. In 2016, many of Rotterdam's crane drivers had gone on strike for the first time in well over a decade, bringing operations to a grinding halt with a protest over plans to give even more jobs to robots. Trade unions claimed around 800 out of 3,500 crane-driving jobs at the port were under threat, to which one port manager tactfully responded by telling a reporter 'Robots don't . . . strike'. When I stopped to take a photo of one unmanned yard filled with busy automated trucks, a passer-by joined me and shook his head in amazed horror. 'How did they let this happen?' he despaired. 'The guys who worked here, why did they give up their jobs?' I resisted the temptation to ask him in which country his jeans and trainers had been made, and how many Rotterdammers had been employed in the making of them.

More generally, there were also reasons to question how long the Netherlands' run of economic good luck could continue. At the time of my tour, the Dutch economy had recovered from a bumpy few years, and despite some worries (house prices, job insecurity) was still in the rudest of health. In 2017, the Netherlands' GDP exceeded that of Norway and Ireland combined. However, even if the threat posed by robot army could somehow be headed off, there were plenty of other things for port workers to worry about. Shipping companies had lost business to railways linking Europe with Asia, and to massive underground pipelines which carried chemicals from Rotterdam's refineries to Belgium and Germany. More generally, while the port had brought huge wealth to the delta, it also brought a strange kind of vulnerability. Like a bird living on a buffalo's back, the southern Netherlands produces relatively little itself and is heavily dependent on servicing the trade of other countries. Rotterdam's size and influence is such that it has become, as *The Economist* put it, 'a barometer of the world economy'. When the global economy took off, the Dutch economy rode on its coat-tails. But if and when the global economy cools and trade slows, it may be the Netherlands which catches the worst cold. A small change in the global oil price, for example, or in the Chinese demand for steel or the Irish demand for paint, could wreak havoc on the local economy. If a bombastic American president decided to slap high tariffs on German car imports, or the Brits cut themselves off from Europe, the consequences for the Dutch could be disastrous. Openness to trade had long been the Netherlands' greatest strength, but reliance on it could also be a weakness. Only a fool would bet against the Dutch, but on the Rhine, the shipping news wasn't entirely good.

Continuing my journey inland, the south side of the river remained fascinatingly un-picturesque, an unending panorama of monstrous industrial architecture whose function I could only guess at. The north side, however, where I was cycling, offered brief flashes of the old Netherlands of picture postcards: flat, emerald fields; dopey Friesian cows; thatched farm cottages; and herons stiffly standing sentry over murky canals. A string of little towns and villages with unpronounceable names flicked past, and I remembered reading how, during the war, the Dutch resistance had used local place names to test people suspected of being foreign invaders. If someone couldn't pronounce a word like 'Scheveningen', they were probably a foreign spy. I liked to think I spoke decent Dutch, but as I passed a sign pointing to 'Rijskade-Knooppunt Kethelplein', I was relieved no one was around to test me.

Skirting around the edge of Schiedam, I spun on towards Rotterdam city centre. This west side of Rotterdam had a large immigrant population, including many Moroccans, Turks and Surinamese, and the streets I cycled through were busy with all the usual facets of urban immigrant life: shops selling headscarves and international phone cards; kebab joints and Middle Eastern restaurants; and a beautiful bone-coloured mosque. In a strange way, Rotterdam's ethnic diversity was another of the Rhine's great legacies. In the 1960s and 1970s, as trade through the city's ports increased, thousands of Turkish and Moroccan immigrants had come to work in local factories, warehouses and harbours. A couple of generations later, most were well integrated but there had also been predictable tensions between some locals and more conservative Muslims, exacerbated by the loss of blue-collar jobs in the robot-run port. The far-right politician Pim Fortuyn built his political base in Rotterdam, and the right-wing rabble-rouser Geert Wilders made near annual visits to the river suburb of Spijkenisse, calling it his home town and conducting walkabouts which usually were attended by more journalists than voters. In 2017, Wilders launched his election campaign with a speech in Spijkenisse in which he denounced 'Moroccan scum' for 'making the streets unsafe', a stunt which appalled most observers but was wildly popular with an odd coalition of cultural conservatives, grumpy nationalists and people whose livelihoods were threatened by the shifting Rhine economy. When the votes were counted, several of the places where far-right support was strongest were close to the river. Ironically, a region which had thrived economically thanks to free trade was now a power base for hucksterish politicians who thought 'globalisation' was a dirty word.

A short while later, I arrived in the centre of Rotterdam. I'd lived in the city on and off for about seven years, and always had something of a love–hate relationship with it. At its best, it was a vibrant, diverse and sometimes thrilling place, with a spiky, post-industrial aesthetic reminiscent of Brooklyn or Berlin which made other Dutch cities look twee and old-fashioned in comparison. As an outsider trying in vain to assimilate, I also loved how authentically Dutch Rotterdam felt, uncontaminated as it was by mass tourism and completely free of stag parties and tour groups. As early as the mid 1950s, the *New Yorker* had called it 'the one city in Europe that has turned the disasters of war and occupation into a triumph'. That may have been an exaggeration, but for me it had come to feel more or less like home.

On bad days, however, I despaired of the city's endless concrete and grime; its surfeit of ugly post-war buildings and lack of pretty canals, churches and cobbles. Rotterdam was often compared to an American city, with its wide, straight thoroughfares, tall office buildings and shopping malls. This Atlanticist attitude was sometimes a good thing, giving the city a certain dynamism, modernism and optimism. But it could also be unpleasant. At its worst, Rotterdam was brash, consumerist, individualistic, uncultured and car-obsessed. It was, one non-Rotterdammer complained to me, the kind of place where many people would be more impressed by the size of your flat-screen television than by any kind of culture, literature or history.

However, despite these grumbles I considered myself an honorary Rotterdammer, for better or worse, and today I was glad to be back. Shouldering my bike, I ascended the steps of the Erasmusbrug; the great white harp-shaped bridge connecting the northern and southern banks of the channel. The river below was amazingly busy – in the space of a minute, I counted six big cargo ships passing underneath, as well as three bee-coloured water taxis. High-rise towers stretched away from the water like a bar graph. To a time-traveller arriving by boat from a previous century, Rotterdam would be unrecognisable. *Cook's Guide* of 1874 said 'a more picturesque town we never beheld', and that while 'Venice is all poetry, Rotterdam is the poetical and practical combined'. The Nazi bombing raids of the 1940s put paid to all that, though, as did the hasty reconstruction which followed, when rubble was piled in the city's canals. By Dubaian standards the city's small cluster of skyscrapers would be unremarkable, but in the Netherlands – where soggy ground meant buildings were rarely more than a dozen storeys high – Rotterdam's collection of gleaming modern tower blocks made an astonishing, futuristic sight. Gazing over the water at these daring buildings, I half expected to see the Jetsons whizz by on a monorail.

Looking south across the water, I had a clear view of one of the most impressive buildings on the lower Rhine: Hotel New York, a turreted brown-stone building which loomed like a fortress on a promontory jutting into the main channel of the river. The building was constructed in 1901 as the head office of the Holland America shipping line, and had played an important role in the history of the Rhine, the Netherlands and Germany; its two turquoise clock towers once forming a gateway through which thousands passed on their way to new lives in the New World.

The history of German and Dutch emigration to the Americas is often overshadowed by the experience of other groups, such as the Irish, but its scale was astonishing. Between the mid 1840s and mid 1850s alone, around 750,000 Germans migrated to the United States. Later, in 1882, the total hit 250,000 in a single year. The emigrants included famous families such as the Astors and Rockefellers, and were so numerous that at various times there were serious plans to make Texas, Wisconsin and Missouri into 100 per cent German states. By no means all the emigrants passed along the Rhine, but many did, travelling to the coast by train or by steamship from river cities like Cologne and Koblenz. Rhine boatmen often were paid commissions by transatlantic shipping companies for delivering passengers, and Rotterdam once teemed with middle-men selling tickets to places including Ellis Island. Like the later Moroccans and Turks in Rotterdam, the Germans and Dutch sometimes faced a rough reception in their new homes – in the nineteenth century, groups including the 'Know Nothing' party claimed Germans were bringing crime and stealing American jobs. Benjamin Franklin asked bitterly: 'Why should the Palatine Boors be suffered to swarm into our Settlements, and by herding together establish their Language and Manners to the Exclusion of ours? Why should Pennsylvania, founded by the English, become a Colony of Aliens, who will shortly be so numerous as to Germanise us instead of our Anglifying them, and will never adopt our Language or Customs, any more than they can acquire our Complexion?' Alt-right sentiment was clearly nothing new.

Overall, though, the Europeans in America were a great success story. Germans imported traditions such as Christmas trees, hamburgers and kindergartens; they founded companies including Pfizer, Boeing and Heinz. Not to be outdone, the Dutch added words including coleslaw and cookies to the American vocabulary, and the Dutch accent was sometimes said to be the source of the famous Brooklyn drawl. Rhine cities left their mark in place names across the United States, including Cologne, Minnesota; Manheim, Pennsylvania; and Rotterdam, New York. By 2016, an astonishing 45 million Americans officially reported themselves as being of German descent, along with more than 4 million claiming Dutch ancestry, 8 million French and about a million Swiss. 'America,' wrote a wistful traveller called Isiah Thomas as he watched ships leaving Rotterdam in the late 1700s, 'stands comparatively like the sun in the heavens – the centre of light, and the wonder of the admiring world, who feel the influence of its rays. The persecuted will find ease and rest, and tortured virtue and exiled worth will take refuge [there] from every quarter of this old world.' I wasn't sure he'd be able to say the same today.

I freewheeled down the slope of the Erasmusbrug to the south bank, entering a giants' playground of office buildings with precarious sloping facades and misshapen profiles. The south side of the river in Rotterdam had for years been relatively deprived and undeveloped. Now, though, after a rough few years, the local property market was once again soaring. Wealthy professionals were buying up homes in the riverside areas they once would have scorned, converting graffitied former warehouses into boho suburbs where kids could play in the streets and youthful dads could practise their skateboarding. For someone who'd known the city for a while, it was amazing to see how quickly things had gentrified, both around the river and elsewhere. Grotty bars had been converted into chic bistros, boutiques had opened under railway arches, and areas where it had once been impossible to buy a croissant were now seething with kale and quinoa. All the men had beards, and there were more tattoos than in a Russian prison.

It was getting late by now, and I decided to seek some sustenance before the light faded completely. I rounded the front of Hotel New York and pedalled over a small bridge to my final destination, a long, low-slung warehouse hulking on the riverbank. Inside, a draughty space had been converted into a kind of open-plan food market dedicated to selling craft beers, ethnic cuisines, arty books and expensive platters of Dutch cheese and ham. As in so many places in modern Europe, heavy industry had given way to decay, and decay had now been replaced by people with MacBooks cooing over recycled industrial architecture, faded fourth-hand furniture and expensive organic food. The whole place was a terrible hipster cliché, and I loved it. I bought a beer, and then another, and wandered around the food stalls, helping myself to free samples and eating enough cheese to give a cardiologist a heart attack.

As night fell, I could easily have gone home, recrossing the river and then following the Rotte a mile or two northwards. However, my house didn't have a roof terrace or pay-per-view movies, or a cleaner, or a mini-bar, and I opted instead to stay somewhere which did. The SS *Rotterdam* lay a few hundred metres south of the bar in another riverside harbour. The giant Titanic-style ocean liner had once done a roaring trade ferrying emigrants and wealthy tourists along the river from Hotel New York all the way to New York itself. Now it was stuck on the river in Rotterdam, operating as a floating hotel. Inside, the ship had a pleasing air of faded glamour, like an old cinema or theatre. A maze of narrow corridors led to various bars, dining rooms and dance floors, all heavily decorated with mirrors and chandeliers. Up on the top deck, I found a panoramic view of the glinting city in one direction and, in the other, the endless sprawl of floodlit cranes and humanoid pylons and flaring gas chimneys of the port. Far below me, the river flowed steadily towards the sea, carrying a convoy of low-slung barges towards the port. I looked at the glittering lights of Hotel New York, imagined the generations who'd passed this way in search of a better future, and thought: why did they ever leave?

2

Water Wars

Vlaardingen and the Dutch Delta

I AWOKE TO find my bed tilting like a ski ramp: the ship was sinking. Fumbling for the light switch in the darkened cabin, I stumbled up in a panic: when I booked a cheap room on the SS *Rotterdam*, I hadn't realised it was due to make a voyage. I dashed out into the corridor and to a porthole, lurching from wall to wall as I went, bracing myself for a terrifying plunge into the icy sea. But no: the porthole offered only a circular view of the stationary riverbank in Rotterdam, to which the ship was still firmly moored. It was only my head which was plummeting up and down, riding rough seas of confusion after an evening of strong brown beers.

Confusion abated, I quickly showered and changed, pausing only to run straight back into the shower when I realised the little tube of hotel body lotion which I'd been rubbing on my face was actually toothpaste. My alarm had gone off at the ungodly hour of 8 a.m., and I bumbled through checkout like a man who'd just finished an ultra-marathon. The breakfast, as so often in Europe, was a horrifying selection of cold slabs of processed meat and cheese, laid out like ingredients on a cookery show. I asked a waitress if there was any cooked bacon, and she laughed as if I'd made a terrific joke. 'The cold ham is over there!'

With the river's vast hinterland beckoning, I didn't want to linger too long around Rotterdam, but was keen to explore a little more of the coastal delta by water taxi before heading inland. The little speedboat set off along the river to the west, backtracking slightly towards Hoek van Holland. The weather was chilly, and the fare for a ten-minute ride more than I'd usually spend on a night out, but there was surely no better way to see the river at this point: wide and choppy; alive with cargo bulkers, ferries and other taxis speedily criss-crossing the channel like stones skimmed across a pond. Tucked in off the main channel to the north, I caught a glimpse of the small harbour at Delfshaven, another place I'd often visited in the past. It was here, in 1620, that a group of religious radicals had allegedly spent the night before setting sail for England and then Virginia, where they moored their ships (including the *Mayflower*) and founded a colony at Plymouth Rock which was one of the first permanent European settlements in North America. The Netherlands, one of them wrote before leaving, was 'a strange and hard land'.

After about ten minutes I disembarked from the taxi and walked a mile or so along the river to my first destination, the small town of Vlaardingen. I'd never been there before, and had idly assumed it would be nothing but apartment buildings; another post-war commuter town drained of life by its proximity to Rotterdam. I was pleasantly surprised, therefore, to find a pretty riverside town, centred around a long, thin canal which lead off the side of the main channel. Down near the big river, things were still relatively industrial, but further inland the town became increasingly picturesque, with brick-paved streets overlooked by lovely seventeenth-century houses. Across the canal, rows of modern motor launches and yachts sat waiting for the weekend.

I walked north along the canal. A bell trilled loudly and a bridge opened like the cover of a book to allow a small motorboat to pass. It hurtled through at speed, its only passengers a pair of boys of about ten years old. '*Hallo meneer!*' they cried, 'Hello sir!', waving excitedly as they passed. Nearby, a fisherman sat untangling a ball of line, preparing for a long day sitting and staring at the water. We chatted for a minute and he introduced himself as Sjoerd – one of those names which sound normal to Dutch ears, but to an English speaker sounded like the consequence of an upended table halfway through a game of Scrabble. I gestured at his empty net and asked how the fishing was going. 'Wonderful!' he said.

In many ways, the Rhine delta had always been a great place to be a fisherman. Riverside towns such as Vlaardingen were sheltered from the worst of the coastal weather, but had easy access to some of the world's prime fishing grounds. Fishermen from here could harvest rich stocks of herring and cod in the North Sea, Baltic or

Atlantic or – if they preferred – head inland to catch other fish and eels in the delta itself. For centuries, a bishop in Bonn, a merchant in Mainz or a cook in Koblenz could all enjoy fish caught by fishermen in such a town and ferried along the Rhine.

For much of modern history, fish provided the economic backbone of countless small towns in the delta. By the 1500s, thousands were employed as fishermen and boat-builders and fish merchants. Five centuries later, fishing was no longer a principal occupation, but Dutch seafood was still a rare bright spot in a national cuisine otherwise dominated by mashed potato and gluey *frikandel* meat sticks. Around the Rhine delta, one fish in particular dominated: the herring, a small, silvery beast which was served disgustingly cold or soaked in vinegar, from trucks which looked like British ice cream vans. For the Dutch, herring was a widely loved delicacy, and the landing of the first catch of the year – the *Nieuwe Haring* or 'New Herring' – was a major event, announced in newspapers and on chalkboards outside restaurants, and sometimes celebrated with mini-carnivals on the quayside.

Like having cheese sandwiches for breakfast, eating herring was something of a minority pursuit outside the Netherlands. In the past, though, herring were almost unbelievably abundant across northern Europe, and as common a sight on dinner tables as beef or chicken might be today. According to the ancient Dutch scholar Saxo Grammaticus, in the twelfth century one sound off the coast of Denmark contained so many herring that passing boats would become stuck in the water, and fishermen could reach in and scoop out fish with their bare hands.

The Dutch love of herring could largely be blamed on a disgusting discovery made in the 1390s by Willem Beukelszoon, a fisherman from Zeeland. He somehow figured out that if a certain part of a fish's digestive system was left intact while the rest of the guts were removed, the whole fish would taste stronger and stay fresher for longer. To me this sounded a bit like discovering cats' toenails tasted delicious – potentially true, but really not something anyone should ever be in a position to find out. At the time, though, Beukelszoon's discovery was a true breakthrough. By gutting and salting herring at sea, and packing them in wooden barrels, fishermen could avoid rushing back to port, and instead spend days or weeks travelling to far-flung fishing grounds. At a stroke, the simple wooden fishing boat became a kind of floating fish factory, and the humble herring went from local delicacy to tradeable commodity.

Thanks to Beukelszoon's* breakthrough, the Dutch fishing industry boomed, and there were soon thousands of fishermen heading out to sea in so-called herring *buizen*, or busses – banana-shaped sailing boats which were sturdy enough to brave stormy seas but shallow-drafted enough to navigate small river harbours like the one at Vlaardingen. Thousands of Dutch fishermen roamed far and wide: in 1745, a resident of an island near Oslo reported seeing 200 Dutch fishing vessels in a single day. Large workforces were employed to clean and pack fish for export. It was back-breaking work, with many hazards: some North Sea herring companies employed one woman whose job description included licking the eyeballs of any colleagues who were unfortunate enough to get fish scales lodged there.

Dutch fishermen grew famous for their skill in finding fish, sometimes following seagulls who chased shoals of herring far out to sea. Ports far apart were connected by the herring trade, and Dutch fishermen became regular visitors to scores of towns across northern Europe. One writer visiting the Shetland Islands in the 1770s was surprised to find of the Scots that 'almost all of them speak as much Dutch . . . as serves the purpose of buying and selling, [and] some of them speak . . . the low Dutch fluently'. Centuries later, Dutch fishermen were still a regular sight along the coast of Scotland. According to the writer Donald Murray, when a German ship was captured by British forces near the Scottish town of Lerwick during the Second World War, one prisoner of war was greeted on shore by cries of 'Hello Ralf!' from the locals, who recognised him from fishing trips before the war. Fishermen were usually too busy working to have much fun, but some found time to befriend local ladies. 'That place,' a retired Dutch fisherman once recalled of sleepy Lerwick, 'is Sodom and Gomorrah.'

Still in Vlaardingen, I doubled back along the quayside to the

---

* There are several different ways of spelling Beukelszoon's name; this is the one used by the Dutch Rijksmuseum, which includes in its collection a picture of him looking hungry, fish in one hand and gutting knife in the other.

former home of Abraham van der Linden, one of the town's most prosperous fish merchants in the 1700s. This was a beautiful three-storey brown-brick building perched next to the water, with a high gabled roof and a candy-striped flagpole over the front door. Inside, the main feature was a grand dining room with a massive marble fireplace and a table laid with fine china. The painted ceiling looked as if it belonged in the Vatican; all trumpeting angels and cherubs reclining on clouds. Shuffling around in my hoody, I could easily imagine the grand gentlemen sitting here to enjoy a lavish fish supper, looking out through the big windows at the fishing fleet which had made them rich. Clearly, the herring business had once paid well.

It would be an exaggeration to claim delta fishing triggered the famous Dutch 'Golden Age' economic boom of the seventeenth century, but it was undoubtedly one of the building blocks. It was partly through fishing that the Dutch developed their considerable skills in sailing, mapmaking, navigation and shipbuilding which helped them build a global empire. As one nineteenth-century English visitor rather enviously put it: 'whatever greatness Holland has achieved in commerce has undoubtedly grown from the appren-ticeship served by its sons on the waters . . . out of its fisheries'. Herring fishing was, he said, 'the chief branch of their industry, their grand source of wealth [and] the golden mine of the republic'. In turn, the needs of herring towns like Vlaardingen also encour-aged the Dutch to expand their empire further. When war with Spain disturbed the supply of salt from Spain and Portugal, for example, the Dutch were forced to roam further afield, collecting salt from Cape Verde and the Caribbean. As the great Dutch trading company – the VOC – grew larger, herring also served as an important fuel: in 1636, the Admiralty in Amsterdam ordered that in order to feed one hundred sailors for a month, Dutch ships had to carry no fewer than 450 pounds of cheese and four tons of herring. Dutch fishermen helped make their country rich, and fostered skills which helped make it even richer. Amsterdam, as one local saying went, was built on a foundation of herring bones.

However, the glory days didn't last. From about 1650s onwards, Dutch fisherman faced increasingly tough competition from their English, Scottish and Scandinavian rivals. Fish became harder to find, and herring fleets shrank to a fraction of their former size. By 1838, when a British journalist visited Vlaardingen, it was already noteworthy for being 'the only town [in the Netherlands] whose inhabitants now continue the fishery with spirit'. A few years later, another foreign observer wrote: 'Towns in Holland which were at one time famous and wealthy fishing ports are now fading away into ruins.' It was even said that over-reliance on herring had encouraged the Dutch to think slowly; fed a dull diet of herring and potatoes, they became unimaginative and unadventurous, lacking the sparky innovation of their more gastronomically promiscuous neighbours.

By the mid twentieth century, fish populations had become so depleted that they were unable to replenish themselves – a textbook example of what economists call a 'tragedy of the commons', in which something which is owned by no one ends up being over-used by everyone. In the 1960s, the global catch of Atlantic herring hit 4 million tons per year; by the 1980s it had plummeted to 0.9 million tons. Vlaardingen's golden goose had stopped laying eggs.

In the 1970s, the EU introduced the Common Fisheries Policy, which set strict rules for how many Dutch boats could set sail and how many fish they could catch. From an environmental perspective, the result of all this meddling was positive, and fish stocks recovered somewhat. However, for individual fishermen, the combination of low fish stocks and strict rules was disastrous. In Vlaardingen, the last major fish processing factory had moved elsewhere in 2012. Some fishermen tried to pool resources and ease competition, but it rarely worked. 'Fishermen are like frogs in a wheelbarrow: they usually jump in all directions,' one fisherman told a researcher.

As jobs dried up, the EU inevitably netted much of the blame. Eurosceptics claimed the fisheries policy was an exemplar of EU policy in general: well intentioned and perhaps marginally effective, but hideously inefficient, undemocratic and costly. Anglo-Dutch conflict over fish also continued. Not long before I visited Vlaardingen, the ever-infuriated *Daily Mail* had reported just one Dutch fishing vessel had 'caught in English coastal waters . . . nearly 23 per cent of the entire English quota' thanks to 'bureaucrats in Brussels' who set the quota rules. During the Brexit campaign,

Boris Johnson appeared on television clutching a live lobster and saying it was time for Britain to leave the EU because Europeans were 'stealing our fish'.

Vlaardingen was charming, but as I wandered around the town, it was hard to escape the conclusion that the collapse of the fishing industry had hollowed out a once prosperous place. Vlaardingen was a genuinely lovely place, but it also had many of the tell-tale signs of a town in gentle decline: empty buildings, overflowing bins and a surfeit of cheap takeaway places. There was little going on, and none of the boats were moving. In the last few years, even the once popular fish festival had apparently been renamed so it didn't directly include the word 'herring' in the title. Vlaardingen, sadly, struck me as a place with a great future behind it.

I decided it would be rude to visit without doing my bit to reverse the town's decline. After a bit of hunting around, I found what I was looking for: a proper Dutch herring seller, housed in a canal-side cabin about the size of a shipping container, adorned with patriotic bunting and big chalkboards advertising snacks which were '*Gezond en Lekker*', 'Healthy and Tasty'. The jolly grey-haired Dutchman behind the counter seemed delighted to have a customer. I asked him how business was, and he replied with a gesture towards the empty chairs on the terrace behind me and a single word: 'Quiet!' Traditionally, the Dutch eat herring by dropping them whole down the throat, like a fire-eater's sword. I took the coward's option: a couple of cigar-sized fish entombed in a finger roll. The fish was salty and slippery, like a slug which had been fermented in a bucket of green seawater. I remembered once being tear-gassed in Swaziland, and thought the effect had been much the same.

Unwilling to bankrupt myself by calling another costly water taxi, I mounted my bike and cycled back towards the centre of Rotterdam. To my right, the river harbours were crammed with fantastical pieces of nautical construction equipment: drillers and dredgers and pile-drivers, as immense and multicoloured as fairground rides.

Down in the shadow of the giant Erasmusbrug, I boarded a ferry heading east, joining a large crowd of commuters and shoppers who gleefully ignored the 'no cycling' signs and hurtled down the slippery gangplanks onto the boat. By the time we departed it was packed with bikes, lined up along the deck like cavalry waiting to go into battle. A few belonged to tourists, but most were the well-worn steeds of older Dutch people on their way home from the shops, their bikes heavily laden with jars of coffee, loaves of bread and big wedges of wax-covered cheese. Where else in the world, I wondered, would a seventy-year-old housewife who struggled to walk do her shopping by boat and bicycle?

I'd made the same journey by boat from Rotterdam many times before, but always found it delightful. The weather had (in a typic-ally Dutch way) changed completely in the space of an hour, and it was now warm and sunny, with bright splinters of sunlight reflecting off the choppy water. The river itself was the colour of an old metal saucepan and what an expert hydrologist might call pretty damn big. The ferry moved surprisingly quickly, and within fifteen minutes or so we reached the point where the Maas forked into another of the southern Netherlands' great rivers, the IJssel.★ I disembarked near the point of the fork, at Krimpen aan den IJssel. Walking a few minutes up the IJssel, I arrived at the thing I'd come to see: four enormous concrete towers, the size and shape of elevator shafts, flanking a big road bridge across the river. Suspended between each pair of towers was a giant slab of steel, each bigger than a double-decker bus, hanging high over the water like the blades of a guillotine. As a sign up on the bridge explained, if the water level in the river rose more than about two metres above normal, the two slabs would slide down into the river, cutting it off from the sea and ensuring people living upstream didn't take unplanned swimming lessons.

Of course, flooding in the Netherlands wasn't a recent phenom-enon. For much of its history, the Netherlands flooded almost as much as it didn't. Heavy rain in Holland, Germany or elsewhere could massively swell the rivers, while big spring tides could push salt water up from the coast. Many fields in the delta were only useable for a few months a year, and people were used to living on the top of hills and dikes. The rivers themselves fluctuated constantly, regularly spilling over their banks and carving new routes

---

★ That's not a typo – in the Dutch language, the letters IJ are a digraph – a pair of letters effectively treated as one, always capitalised and pronounced 'eye'.

with carefree abandon. In the German town of Pfotz, locals in the seventeenth century told of church bells which could still be heard ringing deep beneath the water, a ghostly echo of churches that had been drowned years earlier. Swampy water was a breeding ground for dysentery, typhus and even malaria, and biblical flooding was common. In 1342, for example, one Dutch resident recorded that 'the floodgates of heaven were open, and rain pelted down onto Earth like in the 600th year of Noah's life . . . [until] water was all over the land'. Up the river in Mainz, he wrote, the water around the cathedral 'stood as high as to a man's belt'. 'The people in Holland,' one visitor wrote, were 'like the dwellers on the slopes of Vesuvius . . . always within an ace of destruction'.

From the early 1600s onwards, the Dutch made a concerted effort to banish the water from their land for good. Hundreds of windmills were built across the country – some of them for grinding corn and sawing wood, but most for pumping water. By paying for new windmills to be built, investors could unlock huge tracts of land for housing or agricultural use, earning a handsome return on their investments. When Karl Marx visited the Netherlands in the 1830s, he reported there were a total of some 12,000 windmills nationwide, based on (according to Marx) technology copied from Germany. 'The air makes bondage . . . in Germany,' he wrote, but 'at the same time . . . the wind was making Holland free'. Later, steam pumps were used to drain vast 'polders' as well as a certain muddy lake – the 'schip-hol' or 'ship-hole' – which was dried out and used as the site for a major airport. Many of the most famous features of the Dutch landscape – windmills, grassy dikes, flat green fields – began life not as picturesque features, but as functional pieces of engineering designed to keep people alive.

Despite these heroic efforts, however, fear of flooding was never completely mopped up, and the Dutch still often got their feet wet. In 1809, for example, perhaps 100,000 people were displaced by floods in the Rhine delta, with several hundred people killed, along with thousands of pigs, cows and horses. 'Sometimes,' one nineteenth-century visitor recorded, 'the waves of the German Ocean, rushing with irresistible power up the Maas, dash themselves furiously on the dikes. Then sounds the alarm bell in every fishing village in every coast-hamlet, and . . . on [the helpers] come, one after the other, as fast as they can hurry, bringing with them hurdles, sails or whatever may be ready to hand for the purpose of strengthening the threatened dikes.'

Decades later, floods were less common but one could still detect a hint of neuroticism under the laidback veneer of Dutch culture. Everyone was obsessed with buying insurance, and my mobile phone buzzed regularly with automated messages from the Dutch government's emergency warning system, practising for the day when (if) the dikes collapsed. As I'd seen in Amsterdam, the fight against flooding had also done a huge amount to shape the way the Dutch viewed the world around them. For many people, nature was not something wonderful and encompassing, but a menace to be carefully managed and approached with caution; a place (as Koos van Zomeren once wrote) 'that you can go and visit if you have a car'.

The worst Dutch flood of recent times occurred in 1953, when an unprecedented combination of high spring tides, strong winds and a major storm sent huge waves rushing from the North Sea inland across the Rhine delta. Flood defences in the region had been neglected and damaged during the recent war and were quickly overwhelmed, with many homes completely submerged. Along the river, many dikes failed. People were left clinging to chimney pots, trees were turned into battering rams, and thousands of dead cows grotesquely littered the mud-covered landscape. Altogether, nearly 2,000 people were killed and perhaps 70,000 left homeless, with some 200,000 hectares of land left under water. Coming just a few years after the end of the war, it was a devastating blow.

However, the Dutch would not be defeated for long. After the flood waters receded, a Delta Committee spent years compiling a gargantuan six-volume report, which argued that the vast cost of building new defences paled in comparison to the cost of future floods. The authorities eventually cooked up a plan – the Delta Works – which would effectively close off the Rhine delta from the sea, reducing the length of the Dutch coastline by roughly half. Many environmentalists were aghast, but by 1958 the first component of the Delta Works had been completed: the same giant steel floodgates which I now saw suspended over the river in Krimpen. As hundreds of miles of dikes were built or raised, the delta was converted from a wild, stormy place where fishermen had to keep their wits about them to a relatively placid, heavily managed region where people were more likely to get sunburn than experience a flash flood.

Nevertheless, the authorities still had to be constantly vigilant. The inflow from the Rhine across the German border was carefully monitored, with floodgates opened or shut depending on a delicate calculation of many factors. When I began researching the delta, I quickly found myself flooded with North Sea Spatial Agendas and National Coastal Visions. To a non-specialist, they were mostly either boring or baffling, but did offer a fascinating insight into how the Dutch authorities saw the river delta: essentially, it was something which should be controlled in the same way one might coerce an unruly toddler or an untrained dog. 'Average winter water levels in the IJsselmeer will not be allowed to rise to sea level until at least 2050,' read one hefty tome. 'The probability of dying as a result of a flood for any individual should be no greater than 0.001 per cent per year,' said another.

Yet even all this might not be enough. In theory, the Delta Project meant the end of Rhine flooding woes. In practice, though, the Dutch still found themselves stuck in the role of the proverbial boy with his finger in the dike – terrified to let their guard down lest the water suddenly flow over. Climate change was increasing flood risks, and more homes and businesses were being built close to rivers. Upriver, floods were still common. In 1995, for example, heavy rains raised water levels in parts of the Rhine basin by up to five metres in twenty-four hours, forcing the evacuation of 250,000 people, along with 200,000 cows and pigs. More recently, in 2011, the Rhine overflowed in Bonn, Cologne and Koblenz, causing shipping to be suspended and killing a kayaker. In 2013, surging water levels again caused shipping to be halted on the German Rhine, and thousands of soldiers were deployed to strengthen the flood defences, causing an estimated €8 billion of damage in Germany alone. 'That was a bad one!' an old man who lived by the river in northern Germany once said when he caught me inspecting the tidemarks on his house. 'My bed almost floated away!'

I continued my journey southwards, spinning easily along a dike which tracked the river like a towpath. The scenery was by Dutch standards mundane, but still enchanting: windmills on the horizon, fat cows in the fields, and greenish lily-filled canals in between. Approaching the city of Dordrecht, I took another ferry across another stretch of water (the Beneden Merwede), and then skirted around the edge of the town. With the wind at my tail, I moved briskly until I ran into a traffic jam – a swarm of ten-year-old schoolchildren cycling down the street on a class outing; all helmet-free and carefree. Rounding a sharp corner, one boy managed to crash into a parked bulldozer and tumbled across the road. His teacher, a young man on a slick racing bike, barely batted an eyelid, carefully checking the bulldozer for damage before telling the boy to catch up with his classmates. 'Ride faster, or you'll get left behind!' he said. A little further on, I was surprised to come across a giant industrial works on the riverbank; a seething mass of tangled pipes, chimneys and ball-shaped chemical containers which would have looked more at home at the Europoort. A sign by the gate announced it was the Chemours chemical factory, owned by the artist formerly known as DuPont. I thought I recognised the name, and when I checked my notebook I realised why – the plant had been at the centre of a minor scandal when it was revealed that thousands of tons of a chemical used to make Teflon were being discharged into the river every year, and that tests reportedly had shown higher than pleasant levels of carcinogenic chemicals in local residents' blood. Chemours argued strongly that no harm had been done, but the details of the story remained rather murky, and the local authorities said they were 'not 100 per cent sure' whether the chemicals being pumped into the river were safe. On balance, I decided not to go for a swim.

Like flooding, pollution in the Rhine was hardly a new problem. In the nineteenth century, the population of cities along the river exploded. German factories and mines began to send huge volumes of goods downriver, and the river quickly became polluted with fuel, fertilisers, sewage and waste. In the 1860s, countries along the river began to restrict factory discharges and chemical shipments, but as shipping and industry increased, the problems continued to worsen. In 1979, the quantity of pollutants floating in the current was estimated to be 30 million metric tons – equivalent to about one-quarter of all the cargoes carried on the Rhine that year.

Invasive species such as zebra mussels also arrived, carried into the Rhine in ships' ballast tanks. Nuclear power plants were another problem: reactors in France and Germany pumped huge amounts of heated water into the river, encouraging the breeding of bacteria, which consumed oxygen. Fish stocks went into catastrophic decline, and salmon – which servants on the upper river had once allegedly complained about eating three days a week – disappeared. In 1970, *Die Welt* claimed the Rhine was 'Germany's largest sewer'.

The undoubted nadir for the Rhine's ecosystem came in 1986, just after midnight on a grey November evening. A Swiss traffic police patrol was driving along a road just outside the Rhine city of Basle when officers spotted flames shooting from the roof of an unlit building close to the riverbank. They alerted the fire brigade, who arrived within minutes to find a serious fire had broken out at Warehouse 956 of the Sandoz chemical works. There was no sprinkler system, and the blaze was soon raging out of control. As hundreds of firefighters arrived, the police drove through the darkened city using loudspeakers to warn sleeping citizens to stay inside and close their windows.

By 5 a.m., the fire had been extinguished. The warehouse was a smoking ruin, but firefighters felt a justified sense of relief at a job well done. However, it soon became apparent that the real disaster was only just beginning. While fighting the fire, the firefighters had pumped enormous amounts of water out of the Rhine and sprayed it over the burning warehouse. Perhaps 15,000 cubic metres of water flowed back into the Rhine through the sewer system, carrying with it chemicals from inside the factory. As curious residents of Basle ventured out into the smoky morning, they were greeted by a remarkable, horrible sight: the Rhine had turned red.

Over the following days, a stripe of red liquid dozens of miles long slid down the river at a little less than walking speed. A spokesman for Sandoz claimed it was a 'harmless dye stuff', but it soon became clear it was anything but. Thousands of dead fish, waterfowl and eels washed up on the banks. Live fish reportedly were found with their eyes popping out and their skin covered with sores. Within a week, Dutch officials reported mercury levels at the German border were three times the normal level. In France, sheep which drank from the river died, and drinking water supplies were shut off. In Germany, more than 20,000 people had to drink water from fire trucks. The chief inspector of the Rhine River police in Basle told a reporter: 'the Rhine is now dead. The whole ecosystem is destroyed.'

Just a few months after the Chernobyl nuclear accident, tensions were running high. As the scale of the disaster became known, noisy street protests erupted in Basle. Swiss authorities were accused of being negligent in enforcing safety regulations, and criticised for waiting more than twenty-four hours before warning the Dutch, Germans or French about the toxic spill heading their way. At a public meeting, one Sandoz director was spat on by protesters and pelted with dead eels. Protesters in Basle said the city should be renamed 'ChernoBasel'.

In time, the crisis passed, as crises do. with However, public attitudes towards the river would never be the same again. Support for the Green Party in West Germany soared, and political parties in Switzerland and the Netherlands were forced to adopt bolder green policies. The disaster also highlighted the fact that the river itself didn't respect national boundaries, and its protection hence depended on delicate negotiations between neighbouring countries. A Dutch plan to protect salmon, for example, sparked a long dispute with the French, who refused to invest in 'fish ladders' to bypass hydro-electric dams and preferred to load salmon on trucks and drive them around the dams before releasing them.

Eventually, though, a bold clean-up programme was agreed by the governments of West Germany, France, Switzerland and the Netherlands. Dutch dredgers scooped tons of contaminated silt from the riverbed. Millions of euros were channelled into fish-breeding programmes, water treatment plants and filters. Strict new rules governed industrial activity along the river, and by the mid 2000s, levels of pollutants such as cadmium, lead and phosphorus had been sharply reduced.

The situation was still far from perfect. The sheer volume of river traffic made accidents and spills somewhat inevitable, and as the Chemours dispute in Dordrecht showed, drinking water was a particular problem – depending on which figures one chose to believe, perhaps 30 million people depended on the Rhine for their tap water. The Dutch government claimed pollution had 'a negligible effect on public health', but in 2013, scientists found Dutch tap water was contaminated with prescription drugs including anti-depressives, which had been passed into sewer water through urine, and warned many people appeared to have been exposed to the anti-anxiety drug oxazepam. In Amsterdam, another survey found that the level of cocaine and ecstasy in Amsterdam's waste water was higher than in any other city in Europe – another explanation, perhaps, for the persistent cheerfulness of most Dutch people. Overall, though, efforts to clean up the Rhine had been a wonderful success story. In 2002, nearly three decades after the Sandoz tragedy, the UN reported more than sixty different species of fish were living in the Rhine, including rainbow trout, flounder and catfish, as well as stone moroko, spined loach, bighead carp and tubenose goby. The river which environmental experts had declared was 'dead' had made a remarkable recovery, rare proof of how international cooperation could not just limit but actually reverse catastrophic environmental damage.

Scooting further around the edge of Dordrecht, I crossed the river again – or one of its branches, at least; a clean, green, relatively wild-looking channel. On the far side of the river lay the Biesbosch, another place which I'd never visited before but which had acquired near mythical status in my imagination. In the course of several years of living in the Netherlands, I'd regularly bored my Dutch friends and relatives by grumbling about the lack of real wilderness around. Dutch postcards and picture books often dwelt on nostalgic rural imagery – docile dairy cows, emerald fields, tranquil waterways and idling windmills – but as far as I could see, the truth was that outside the historic centres of cities like Amsterdam, much of the modern Netherlands was an Americanised sprawl of busy roads, superstores, billboards and flyovers. Dutch people often talked reverently about the '*Groene Hart*' or 'Green Heart', of supposedly unspoilt rural land lying between major cities of the south, but on numerous visits I rarely found myself more than a few hundred metres from the nearest petrol station, motorway, housing development or overhead power line.

In that context, the Biesbosch ('Reed Forest') promised to be a real treat – a vast area of wetland and forest which the authorities described as 'one of the largest and most valuable natural areas in the Netherlands'. 'You'll love it there!' one friend in Amsterdam had said. 'It's like going back in time, to before people existed.' Cycling up the sloping ramp from the ferry, my hopes were high. The weather was still unusually warm, and the area east of the river was immediately beautiful. Acres of smooth, glassy water spread below doughy white clouds, while fat Friesian cows clomped along the horizon atop their own reflections. In the distance was a drowned forest of blackened, bollard-like tree stumps which could almost have been in swampy southern Virginia or the paddy fields of South East Asia. The world looked like a mirror.

The Biesbosch was created in another of the Rhine's great floods, way back in 1421. In November that year, on the feast day of Saint Elizabeth, a storm surge sent great waves sweeping across much of the delta. The low-lying area between Rotterdam and Dordrecht was devastated, with many villages submerged and thousands of people drowned. Maps from before and after the flood showed the geography of the delta transformed, with big river channels dissolving into masses of smaller creeks and inlets, and a large area of farmland converted overnight into an inland sea.

More happily, the flood also created a new natural attraction – the Biesbosch – a vast area of tidal wetlands, islands, mudflats and willow forests, all thickly veined with rivers and creeks fed by the Rhine. Many acres of farmland had been lost, but for centuries after its creation the Biesbosch remained a place of work, home to thousands of farmers, fishermen and huntsmen. The brackish waters were rich with salmon and eels, and also reeds, which were gathered in great witches' broom bundles and used to make chairs and thatch roofs. Later, during the Second World War, the inhospitable backwaters served as a hiding place for Dutch Jews, resistance fighters and downed British pilots. '*De duitsers durven de Biesbosch niet in,*' one local museum noted proudly; 'the Germans didn't dare go into the Biesbosch'!

From the 1950s onwards the region was transformed again when the epic Delta Works blocked the rivers' connections with the sea and reduced tidal flows. The waters turned brackish, and the turbulent became tranquil. Today, the Biesbosch was an important habitat for fish and birds, as well as a transit lounge for geese making the long journey from Europe towards Africa in the winter.

Predictably, it also wasn't quite as wild as I'd been lead to believe. The open expanses of water were beautiful, but – in the usual Dutch way – Mother Nature was kept firmly in her place. Small patches of forest were criss-crossed with cycle lanes, tarmac footpaths and concrete footbridges, and at the heart of the 'wilderness' was a slick visitor's centre and museum, complete with dozens of older Dutch couples drinking coffee on a terrace. In the distance, I could see the big puffing chimneys of the surrounding industrial zones, and power lines slung were along the horizon like hammocks. The marshes themselves were attractive, but it would be hard to describe them as wild or unspoilt. The overall effect was of a poorly maintained golf course rather than an epic wilderness. Having been reliably assured that the Biesbosch was one of the Netherlands' last true wild places, it would have been easy to feel disappointed about how developed it all seemed. However, the scenery also offered a helpful reminder that the balance between the competing roles which the river played was often a delicate one. In the modern world, the natural and the wild are not always kept separate from the artificial and the domesticated. Some places are still pure and 'unspoiled', but in many others, forests are encroached on by cities, deserts are ringed with skyscrapers and rivers are places where tubenose gobys jostle for space with cargo ships and containers. The Rhine, like an overworked parent juggling family and careers, was often forced to play numerous roles all at the same time: as a major shipping channel; as an agricultural and industrial water supply; as a source of drinking water; as a cherished habitat for birds, fish and wildlife. To be annoyed that it wasn't unspoiled would be to miss the point – given how much pressure it was under, it was impressive that the Rhine managed to support any wildlife at all. The balance between the competing interests of traders, tourists and environmentalists would always be a delicate one, but after a bleak few decades, the river seemed to be doing well.

With the day nearly over, I returned to the ferry and doubled back towards Dordrecht, along a dike-top cycle lane which ran around the edge of the Biesbosch. The scenery again looked half Dutch and half Louisianan, with swampy little creeks and dead forests protruding through the evening mist like distant skyscrapers.

Following signs along the waterfront, I tried to find a beaver. As part of the broader Rhine clean-up programme, a handful of beaver couples had been introduced to the Biesbosch from the River Elbe in the 1980s; by the time of my visit, their numbers were reported to have swelled to as many as 200. At first, I was desperate to see one, but then remembered an article which friends of mine had thoughtfully sent me a few days previously, about a man in Russia who'd been bitten by a beaver while out walking and bled to death in the forest. Edging nervously down the path, I nearly bumped into a Dutch woman with dyed blonde hair bellowing deafeningly at her husband: '*Ik heb nog steeds geen bevertje gezien!*', 'I still haven't seen a beaver!'

As the sun set behind the trees, I sat on a riverside deck behind the hostel where I was to spend the night, watching electric-blue kingfishers flitting through the reeds and keeping a nervous eye out for carnivorous beavers. When I thought I saw one – a dark, doglike creature nosing slowly through the crystal-clear water – I turned and ran quickly inside.

3

The Final Frontier

Utrecht and the Roman Rhine

FOR A SMALL place, Utrecht had a big chip on its shoulder. The city was only twenty-five miles or so south of Amsterdam, and equally beautiful, but had never quite got over the sense it was an inferior smaller sibling; a Stephen Baldwin to Amsterdam's Alec. 'Don't compare us with Amsterdam!' pleaded the first page of the free tourist guide I collected at the train station. 'Please stop doing it! We have been regarded as the little sister of Amsterdam for far too long!'

I'd arrived in Utrecht on a blustery blue lunchtime after a long bike ride along the rivers from Dordrecht. Utrecht lay roughly two-fifths of the way from the North Sea to the German border, and I'd never really thought of it as a riverine or nautical city. However, it was by any definition one of the major cities of the Dutch Rhine, lying on the Kromme Rijn (Crooked Rhine); a small, bending branch of the delta.

Like a snake wriggling free from a zookeeper's grasp, the river had gradually changed course and slithered further away from the city centre. Today, Utrecht was far less famous internationally than its rivals Amsterdam, Rotterdam and The Hague, and like a proud mother defiantly claiming her dropout son was actually very clever, was left tirelessly promoting its modest modern attractions: it was home to the headquarters of Dutch Railways, the location of one of the Netherland's largest conference centres, and birthplace of the only Dutch pope! However, it had a rich history as a staging post for trade and conquest along the river. It was also lovely. I visited often, and always thought it was easily one of the nicest cities in the Netherlands, packed with twisting little streets, wonky old townhouses and pretty hump-backed bridges which could grace the cover of any book of Dutch clichés.

Leaving my bike locked near the station, I walked through the city, following the left bank of the imaginatively named Oudegracht (Old Canal), which was notable for the fact that it lay several metres below street level, sunk down like an open-topped subway tunnel. The canal would once have been part of the Rhine itself, busy with traders and fishermen and soldiers, but was now little more than a placid moat bifurcating the old city, lined with tunnel-like bars and restaurants. I walked on past a florists' market, and paused to buy a plate-sized syrupy *stroopwafel*. A few corners later came Utrecht's version of Hollywood's Walk of Fame; gold casts of the handprints of Dutch celebrities of whom I'd never heard. Spotting one plaque, a passing woman clutched at her friend's arm and let out a squeal of excitement: 'The best actor: Cees Geel!'

After twenty minutes or so of idle wandering, I reached the city's proudest landmark, a fourteenth-century bell tower. The mammoth brick structure had once been the highlight of a grand cathedral, but when that collapsed in a storm in the 1670s, it was left standing isolated from the rest of the reconstructed church, floating free like an errant exclamation mark at the end of a sentence.

In the cobbled square behind the tower, I stopped in a puddle of green light to study a map I'd scrawled on the back of a receipt, and realised I was standing right on top of what I'd been looking for: a long crack, about as wide as a thumb, scored through the pavement and lined with stainless steel. From deep within the crack, a bright sheet of green light shone upwards into the sky, like a force field in a sci-fi movie. At the edge of the square, the crack disappeared into a wall, only to reappear around the corner, the green curtain of light crossing a narrow street in front of a Surinamese takeaway. Amid the bustling shoppers and speeding cyclists, the light was easy to miss, yet it marked what once would once have been one of the most important frontiers in Europe: the Roman boundary of the civilised world, beyond which lay barbarism.

The Romans arrived in the lower Rhine region around the summer of 57 BC. They had by then racked up an impressive record of military victories as they extended their power beyond Rome, romping through their regional heats as they saw off rivals such as the Etruscans and Carthaginians. The Roman Empire stretched roughly from rainy northern England to sunny Syria, from Portugal to the Black Sea. Tens of millions of people lived under Roman rule, and the whole Mediterranean was effectively a Roman lake.

Most of the Netherlands and northern Germany, though, remained quite literally off the map. In 57 BC, the lower Rhine region was a bewildering patchwork of tribes now largely forgotten to history, with names which sounded more like varieties of pasta than fearsome warrior races: the Aduatuci, Eburones, Menapii, Moroni, Treveri, Batavi, Cugerni, Canninefates, Toxandri, Marsaci and Tungri. These tribes lived a relatively uncivilised existence, roaming constantly in search of food and pasture, and were at the mercy of tides which frequently swept across the swampy plains. Human sacrifices were not unheard of, and some tribesmen did their hunting with boomerangs.

To the Romans, the tribal areas of the present-day Netherlands were effectively *terra nullius* – a blank space on the map which could easily be claimed by anyone who could be bothered to do so. The simpletons who lived there were 'people at the end of the world', and their territory was the very definition of 'uncivilised'; a place where 'neither vines, olives or fruit trees grew'. The few Romans who dared venture as far as the Rhine delta reported that even the tides were against them. According to Tacitus, one of the most diligent chroniclers of the Rhine frontier, 'One moment the water came up to [men's] armpits, and the next it was up to their mouths'.

The people who inhabited the north were naturally assumed to be just as savage as the seas. Referred to under a single catch-all name, 'the Gauls' were mocked for their hilarious hairstyles and the fact they wore trousers rather than tunics – a habit the Romans thought utterly appalling. Like many imperialists, the Romans also thought the people they conquered were lazy. 'A [tribesman],' Tacitus claimed, 'thinks it tame and spiritless to accumulate slowly by the sweat of his brow what can be got quickly by the loss of a little blood.' According to Tacitus, the average tribesman's typical day was not unlike that of a modern student, involving a hangover, a lie-in, a warm bath, a big meal and another round of beers. 'Drinking bouts lasting all day and all night are not considered in any way disgraceful,' he grumbled.

Of course, the Romans' view of the tribes was often exaggerated.

In practice, the peoples of the Rhine were not a single tribe but a jumble of different peoples and ethnicities, many of whom were not quite as uncivilised as the Romans liked to pretend. The Celts, for example, traded widely and produced intricate metalwork, even panning in the Rhine for flecks of gold which had been washed downstream from Switzerland. Some tribes had rich languages and cultures; the word *Rhine* is often said to come from the Gaulish word *Renos*, meaning 'that which flows'. The epitaph on the grave of one Batavian tribesman gave some indication of the esteem in which his tribe held themselves: 'Here I lie now, immortalised in stone. Is there anyone who might be able to rival my achievements? I do not think so, but should they succeed, remember: I set the precedent. I was first.'

It was true, though, that the tribes were little match for the Romans' awesome military machine. The tribes' access to iron was limited so their weapons were mostly rock-based, and the heavily armed Romans cut a swathe through the region, killing thousands. The invaders typically showed the locals little mercy: Caesar wrote of one skirmish in which his soldiers chased a tribe until they were 'fatigued and exhausted after running', cornered them on a riverbank and then 'drew their swords, and slaughtered many of them'. However, not all battles were so one-sided. On another occasion, Caesar also wrote that the tribes 'showed such determination in their bravery that when those in the front rank had fallen, the men behind them stood upon the slain and continued the fight from on top of the corpses'. As the piles of bodies grew higher, he wrote, 'survivors used the heap as a vantage point for throwing missiles at our men, or catching spears and throwing them back'. Yet despite such heroics, even the bravest tribesmen struggled to hold back the well-trained Roman army. The leader of one lowland tribe, the Nervii, reported that after a brief encounter with the Romans, only 500 of his initial army of 60,000 men remained able to fight. Across Gaul, Caesar's troops were said to have killed a million tribespeople and enslaved perhaps a million more.

Not everyone was killed, of course. Like gangsters building a vice empire, the Romans also co-opted their defeated and intimidated rivals, allowing (for example) the Batavians, who held an island in the middle of the Rhine, to pay their taxes to Rome in the form of military service. However, those who refused to cooperate were shown no mercy. The Romans thought nothing of breaking truces, attacking refugees and deliberately provoking tribes to react so they'd have an excuse to crush them. They also believed people they'd conquered should be grateful for having been 'liberated' from poverty and darkness. One Roman soldier wrote scathingly: 'They pick up mud with their hands . . . and they use this earth as fuel to heat their food and themselves, half frozen as they are by the northern cold. They have only rainwater to drink . . . And these people say that being conquered by Rome is tantamount to slavery!'

As the Romans continued their drive northwards, however, they found it increasingly hard going. From about 47 BC onwards there was a growing acceptance the lands north of the river would never come under Roman control. The strength of the tribal resistance was a major factor, but there were also other reasons for stopping at the river. For one, the other side of the Rhine looked to many Romans distinctly unappealing, filled as it was with either thick forests or swampy marshland, skinny cattle and ramshackle encampments. Stopping at the water's edge also made it easier to keep Roman troops supplied, as grain and fodder could be brought in by boat from the south. Above all, the river (or, in the Netherlands, rivers) made a convenient barrier between the Romans and their enemies on the opposite side; a border wall keeping godless heathens out of the Roman heartland. Eventually, Claudius decreed the Rhine would serve as what became known as the Limes Germanicus, the 'Germanic frontier' or the outer limit of the Roman Empire. The banks of the river were fortified with a string of walls, ditches and watchtowers which wouldn't look unfamiliar to a fan of modern prison-break movies. Utrecht – site of a *trajectum* or river-crossing on the Kromme Rijn – became a key frontier outpost; a Helmand or Basra of the first century. As Florus wrote: 'the Empire which had not stopped on the shores of the ocean was checked on the banks of the Rhine'.

I left the glowing green Limes and walked into the cathedral square, where I'd booked an underground tour of Utrecht's Roman ruins. It began several metres below street level, inside a crumbly cavern which looked like a wine cellar. A friendly female guide with curly hair and basketball boots began by explaining the history of Roman colonisation in the area, laying cloth maps on the stone floor and explaining how the fortress in Utrecht had been built to standard flat-pack design (four watchtowers with four walls between). Later, the English missionary Willibrod had used the city as a base from which to spread Christianity in Europe, and the Dom was built on top of the ruined Roman fort. 'You probably noticed when you arrived here that you were walking steeply uphill,' the guide said, referring to the barely perceptible slope in the pavement leading from the canal to the square. 'That's because of all the different castles and churches which were built on top of one another, until the whole thing was a big hill.' Leading a small group of visitors around a corner, she pointed out a crumbly old section of a Roman wall which looked (for want of a better metaphor) like a crumbly old section of a Roman wall.

Emerging briefly into the daylight, we walked a short distance across the Dom square and descended another flight of stairs into a dungeon-like underground space. I was issued with a big flashlight and set free to roam around the ruins, following a metal walkway which circled broken sections of wall in the darkness. Various points along the wall were carefully strewn with a jumble of Roman relics and bits of broken cathedral – smashed pottery, rusty iron weapons and tools, beheaded statues and crumbling archways. At the rear of the cavern, a smashed piece of terracotta bore a clear paw print, the legacy of some cat which had run across a wet tile centuries earlier. 'This is fantastic!' a Dutchman standing near me exclaimed. 'Two thousand years of history in just a few minutes!'

Tour over, I left the group and emerged blinking into the sunlight. My phone rang: my wife, a proud Rotterdammer who'd been raised just north of the river. I told her I'd been learning how the peoples of the northern banks of the Maas and Rhine had been some of the only ones in Europe to successfully resist Roman conquest. 'I told you!' she crowed. 'People from North Rotterdam are *tough*!'

The Roman fortress in Utrecht was just one of a string of military forts and trading centres built along the Rhine. Other bases along the river also evolved into major settlements: Moguntiacum (Mainz), Bonna (Bonn) and Colonia Agrippinensis (Cologne). However, the Rhine wasn't an impermeable border. The Romans traded extensively with the tribes across the water, and wherever possible co-opted them. One of the greatest strengths of the Roman Empire was its ability to ensure rivals were not only subjugated but assimilated. Tribesmen queued up to become auxiliary soldiers, posted for decades to some far-flung corner of the empire, on the simple promise that they could obtain citizenship once they retired. The empire thrived in part because many people would rather become a Roman than fight a Roman.

At first, the areas the Romans conquered along the river were run basically as military jurisdictions, with little thought given to what would now be called 'nation-building'. In time, though, the Romans also began to focus on development. New towns were laid out in straight lines and grids, and ramshackle huts replaced with temples, theatres, libraries, bathhouses, shops, graveyards and handsome villas. Porridge was replaced by bread, and beer by wine. Local leaders whose fathers would have prided themselves on their fierce resistance to Rome now delighted in wearing Roman clothes, living in Roman houses, and trying to teach their children Latin. Germanic tribesmen, known for their toughness, were prized recruits for the Roman army. During the invasion of Britannia, German soldiers swam the Thames in full suits of armour on their way to winning the Medway.

The Rhine soon became not just a frontier but a major artery. Although the Romans were famous for their roads, in truth travel by road was still hard going. Wherever possible, then, goods were shipped by boat along the rivers. One historian later calculated that if it cost one coin to transport an item on inland waterways, it would cost between six and twelve coins to transport the same thing by road. As trade flourished, an area where people had recently subsisted on little more than grain and game now grew fat on Andalusian olive oil, Italian wine and Egyptian dried fruits. Boats brought in food, clothing and ceramics, as well as barrels of fish sauce (a sun-heated brew of fish guts, blood and anchovies was about as popular in Roman times as ketchup is today). Like modern-day customs officers, Roman tollhouses charged duties on passing boats. Plutarch wrote of his annoyance at a trip delayed by inspectors who 'go through bags not their own, searching for hidden items'. Proper river crossings were built, along with places where travelling traders could rest their horses and perhaps visit the baths, which served as a kind of public swimming pool, friendly local bar and conference centre all rolled into one. Hadrian reported seeing someone who couldn't afford a towel drying themselves on a wall. In time, the river became a kind of magnet attracting anyone who sought to get rich off the mighty Roman military machine – ferrymen, bridge builders, importers of amber and fish-paste. Thanks largely to trade and river defence, the stretch of land between Cologne and the North Sea was one of most prosperous in northern Europe. For a while at least, the Roman Rhine was a pretty pleasant place to be.

It was getting late, but I decided to wander a little further before heading to my hotel. As darkness fell, Utrecht looked truly spectacular; the ancient shopfronts reflected in the wine-dark water, the bridges glowing from beneath as if trolls were warming themselves by riverside fires. Reaching the canyon-like Oudegracht, I descended a steep, slippery staircase to the canalside. The reflection of the moon sat perfectly in the centre of the coal-coloured water, like an ivory lily pad crumpled by ripples. At the waterside, a young couple who'd just finished dinner were preparing to head home in a two-seater kayak, squabbling tipsily about who'd get to sit in the front seat and who'd have to ride behind. 'No, Jan!' the woman scolded. 'I'll steer.'

The next morning, I cycled out of Utrecht towards the suburb of Leidsche Rijn. The journey itself wasn't exactly inspiring, passing through dull modern suburbs of elevated train tracks, warehouse-like supermarkets and housing estates which looked like office parks. Hidden away amid all this, though, was something rather special: a full-sized replica of a Roman Limes fort (the Castellum Hoge Woerd). As tall as a two-storey house and made out of cappuccino-coloured wood, it immediately gave a clear sense of what it would have been like to be at a Roman fort on the Rhine. I climbed up onto the high walls and walked along them for a while, gazing out across the modern housing estates and imagining forests filled with riotous tribesmen.

Inside, the fortress was more like an Apple store than a museum. The walls, ceilings and floors were all sparkling white, and the floor looked clean enough to serve a cheese platter on. Shining glass display cases housed a selection of Roman relics recovered from the mud beneath Utrecht: silver coins, palm-sized statuettes and broken pots. The main feature, though, was stunning: a Roman Rhine boat which had been found buried in mud nearby. As long as a tennis court and very shallow, it would once have been used to transport wood and other goods along the river to Utrecht. Now, it lay incongruously amid the shiny white space, looking like a giant brown tobacco leaf crumbling under the spotlights. Ever keen to gather some local colour, I sidled over to another visitor – an attractive woman of about my age, wearing a bright blue shawl – and politely asked what she thought of it. When she rudely failed to reply, I belatedly realised she was, in fact, a wax dummy: an astonishingly lifelike mannequin placed there to show Dutch children what a real Roman looked like, and to humiliate awkward Englishmen.

For all their grand building projects and military might, the Romans' hold on the Rhine region was always rather tenuous. Like modern-day soldiers fighting Afghan or Syrian insurgents, the Romans found that whenever they thought they'd defeated one tribe, another would quickly rise in their place. Attacks and counter-attacks ravaged the region. In 12 BC, for example, the Sugambri tried to launch an attack across the river but were intercepted by Roman forces who (according to Cassius Dio) sailed 'down the Rhine as far as the Ocean', 'leaving a trail of devastation along the way'. Battles between the Romans and the northern tribes were nearly always won by the former, but the cost could be appalling.

The turning point arguably came in AD 9, when the empire was rocked by the annihilation of three Roman legions at Teutoberg Forest, in present-day north-western Germany. A leader of the Cherusci tribe called Arminius tricked the Roman governor Varus into marching a large army right into tribal territory, where they were ambushed by an enormous force. The Romans were heavily outnumbered. After a bloody four-day battle, Varus realised there was no chance of escape, and flung himself on his sword. The victorious tribesmen celebrated by cutting out the eyes and tongues of the conquered Romans, reserving particular vitriol for the 'legal pleaders' – lawyers who they felt had long persecuted them with meddlesome rules. One tribesman was said to have been seen holding the severed tongue of a Roman lawyer high in the air and crying triumphantly: 'At last, viper, cease to hiss!' In total, the Romans lost perhaps 35,000 men, women and children. 'Hemmed in by forests', a Roman scholar later wrote, the Roman army had been 'exterminated almost to a man by the very enemy whom it had always slaughtered like cattle'.

Over the years that followed, the Romans tried to reassert their authority, but never came close to pacifying the lower Rhine. They became less rigorous about punishing incursions, and suffered regular insurgent attacks. One notable revolt by the Batavi in AD 69–70 destroyed many riverside camps and left the fort in Utrecht badly damaged – archaeologists would later find a thick layer of burnt wood and blackened stone plus a trove of fifty coins hidden by a Roman solider fearing he was about to be slaughtered. Elsewhere, the empire found itself harassed by rebels at the fringes, in Persia, Libya, Morocco and Scotland. The centre couldn't hold, and things began to fall apart. By trying to extend their powers too far beyond their natural heartlands, the Romans, Augustus said, had acted like 'those who fish with a golden hook, the loss of which, if the line should happen to break, could never be compensated by all the fish they might take'.

By the third century AD, tribal incursions across the Rhine had become a regular occurrence. Cities began to shrink. The empire was ruled by a series of incompetent playboy emperors, and as they failed to maintain stability and peace, people living in places like Utrecht treated orders from Rome as optional or even irrelevant. Like a downed villain in a Hollywood film, the Romans staged a few late fight-backs, but the damage was done – the tribes had confirmed the 'impenetrable' Germanic Limes were actually a soft underbelly which could easily be attacked. Even Mother Nature seemed to turn against the Romans, as the sea rushed in to destroy their beloved coastal temples and pushed sandbanks across their shipping lanes. In AD 406 came a knockout blow: an invasion by a coalition of Germanic tribes led by the fearsome Vandals, who poured across the Rhine near Mainz. The raid happened in the depths of winter, and it seems likely the river was frozen, enabling the invaders to simply walk across. The Romans barely put up any resistance, and they sacked cities including Mainz, Worms and

Strasbourg. It was a devastating psychological blow. To Prosper of Aquitaine, it seemed 'the frame of the fragile world' had collapsed. A few years later, a large force of Goths entered Rome itself, raping, pillaging and destroying temples. The Romans began to pull back from the Limes. All along the river, Roman forces – as one contemporary witness put it – 'vanished like shadows'. The Rhine had proved to be a Rubicon, and the Roman occupation of the Low Countries was over.

The next morning, I set out to explore the river south and east of Utrecht. Studying a map in my hotel, I'd planned what I thought would be a nice run, from the tiny town of Everdingen to the slightly less tiny town of Wijk bij Duurstede. The route I'd planned was fairly long – twenty miles or so – but I was usually a keen runner, and hoped it would be challenging but survivable.

Shivering in shorts and a thin hoody, I grabbed an artery-clogging train station breakfast of *gevuldekoek* marzipan cookies, and took a local train to Culemborg, an unremarkable town fifteen miles south of Utrecht. From there, I jogged north-west on a quiet lane for a couple of miles to Everdingen, a hamlet from where I'd chosen to start following the river Lek, another of the Rhine's many Dutch branches. It was hard going at first, but the weather was a runner's dream: bright and sunny and blue, with crisp clean air which made my breath hang in the air like smoke from a cigarette.

There was little more to Everdingen than a few houses and a kink in the dike-top road, but after a few wrong turns, I found what had inspired me to start running here: an impressive star-shaped fort, a couple of hundred metres across, squatting low between the riverbank and a dike, surrounded by a wide moat thick with swans, ducks and lily pads. The last time I'd been here, the fort had looked like a wreck, and I was surprised to find it had since been converted into premises for a craft beer company – proof, if it were needed, that the hipsterfication of the western world truly knows no bounds.

The river here was very different from the other stretches I'd seen so far – not sturdy and industrial but wide and swampy, its edges demarcated by soggy fields and paddocks with great bites taken out of them as if a hungry whale had recently passed by.

Continuing eastwards, I ran happily against the current, the water slopping gently a few metres to my left. Cows and horses idled on the riverbanks, but the channel itself was quiet, with no traffic at all apart from a solitary blue bulker which bobbed slowly past. Despite the flat terrain, it felt strikingly like England: a green and soggy landscape of tangled hedgerows and muddy dog-walkers and church spires peeking over the treetops. I half expected to round a corner and bump into the local cricket team on their way home from the Dog and Duck, rolled copies of the *Daily Telegraph* under their arms and bellies full of bitter.

North of Culemborg, I took a small ferry across the river to the opposite bank, accompanied by a group of half a dozen priests. I was a little surprised when they started cursing loudly about Feyenoord's recent performance, and when I looked closer I realised they were actually house-painters wearing black paint-proof smocks rather than cassocks, and carrying bottles of Pepsi rather than communal wine.

There were no scenic footpaths on the uncivilised northern side of the river, so I ran on the cycle lane, a narrow strip of red tarmac threading its way along the top of another high dike, running parallel to the riverbank. I'd been running for perhaps an hour by now, and as the tarmac rolled by underfoot I felt myself finally settling into the familiar runner's rhythm, my feet falling under me in infinite circles with minimum effort. In the Netherlands, I remembered, running always felt different than in other places, the unrelenting flatness making it possible to hit a steady rhythm which was hard to attain elsewhere. Mile after mile ticked past in a kind of yogic trance, interrupted only by occasional stops to check my map and rest my blistering feet.

This part of the delta hadn't always been so tranquil. After the departure of the Romans, the Germanic tribes rushed to fill the gap which remained, seizing abandoned settlements and resurrecting neglected trade routes. One tribe in particular enjoyed remarkable success. Compared with the likes of the Romans or Vikings, history has not treated the Frisians well. Today, their once mighty culture is all but forgotten; there are no gladiatorial movies or television dramas to popularise their achievements, and they merit barely a passing mention in even the most magisterial histories of Europe. Yet their story is truly remarkable. From a small base on the rivers Lek and Kromme Rijn, they built a trading network which stretched from present-day Germany to France, Britain and Denmark. They helped popularise goods such as honey in northern Europe, and according to some historians, effectively invented the concept of money. It's not much of a stretch to say they were one of most powerful and influential peoples in the history of northern Europe, perhaps even the world.

In prehistoric times, the Frisians lived mostly in the north of the present-day Netherlands, in a band of boggy territory stretching roughly from The Hague to Groningen. The Roman general Drusus met them after he crossed the Rhine in 12 BC, and they went on to play a strange mixed role in Roman history: they were mocked by Roman scholars for their ramshackle houses and primitive life-styles, but valued for their skills in navigating the rivers. Frisians served in the Roman army in many places, including Britain, and Frisian traders built a network stretching up the Rhine at least as far as Cologne. However, they retained a fiery independent spirit, and regularly participated in tribal revolts against Roman rule. Fusion between Frisian and Roman culture was limited, and when the Romans retreated from the river zone, the Frisians quickly seized the opportunity to fill the power vacuum left behind.

Within a few decades of the Romans leaving, the old Roman roads were in bad shape, being so rutted and potholed that it was difficult to move anything heavy or fragile. Rivers such as the Rhine offered an obvious alternative, and the Frisians, with their boating skills, were ideally placed to exploit the opportunity. Frisian traders soon spread outwards from their small patch of coastline to domin-ate trade along much of the North Sea coast, as well as far along the Maas and Rhine. A charming, if slightly misogynistic, ninth-century poem gave a flavour of what awaited Frisian men whenever they returned home: 'He's so very welcome . . . when his boat is back. He's the one who provides for her, and she welcomes him, washes his clothes dirtied by the sea and gives him clean ones.'

Despite their worldliness, the Frisians remained a pretty rough, tough crew. One visitor called them 'the hard men from the sea, ill-omened and terrible'. But the sheer breadth of their network also enabled a certain cosmopolitanism. At a time when much of the rest of Europe was living on simple breads and beers, the Frisians enjoyed veritable feasts of game, seafood and dairy products, supplemented by luxuries such as honey and wine, which they imported along the river. Like many people of the delta, the Frisians were also canny salesmen; encountering early Christians on their journeys along the Rhine, they quickly began forging little bronze 'keys to paradise' and selling them to believers, an ancient version of the atheist selling religious trinkets in the cathedral gift shop. And as their network grew, their name became a byword for good business sense. By the seventh century, the North Sea was known to the English as the 'Frisian Sea', and anyone who sold goods was not a 'merchant' or a 'trader' but a 'Frisian'.

After an hour and a half of running, just as my legs were starting to stiffen, a small sign at the roadside announced I was nearing my destination: Wijk bij Duurstede (pronounced 'Wike by Dure-stay-da'). The river, which had been quiet for hours, was suddenly busy again with big barges of the kind which I'd not seen since Rotterdam. Roads filled with traffic, and the scenery became less rural English and more suburban-industrial Dutch. Running over a final bridge towards town, I belatedly realised why: Wijk bij Duurstede lay at the riverine equivalent of a major motorway junction, where the Amsterdam–Rhine canal met the Lek, where the Lek met the Kromme Rijn, and where all three merged into the single channel of the Rhine. From here on, I wouldn't be following a confusing web of rivers but a single channel – the Rhine proper – all the way to the Alps.

Wijk bij Duurstede was a pretty little place adorned with a turreted castle, a small harbour full of leisure boats, and what purported to be Europe's only drive-through windmill, a tall brick tower with an archway cut through its base like a mousehole in a skirting board. Leaving the river, I headed a short distance inland. On a chilly weekday, I appeared to be the only pedestrian in town, and many of the shops looked shut. Once, though, Wijk bij Duurstede was one of the most important cities in Europe. Known as Dorestad, it sat at the centre of a vast Frisian trading empire. The Frisians arrived here in about the seventh century, taking over an abandoned Roman fortress and building a large harbour and settlement. Jetties extended far along the riverbank, and boats from the north of Germany and Scandinavia brought all sorts of exotic products: bearskins, walrus tusks and caramel-coloured amber. Hunting dogs were brought to help chase down game, and slaves to provide the muscle needed to move boats against the river currents. Local iron ore was melted in furnaces to produce tools and weapons, while the imported antlers of red deer and moose were carved into combs, needles, dice, whistles and even ice skates. One of the biggest trades was in barrels of wine from the middle Rhine, which were too heavy to easily transport by road. As a sign in one of the local museums put it, Dorestad was, in economic importance, 'not unlike our present-day Europoort terminal in Rotterdam'.

The Frisians' other great claim to fame was their currency. The Romans had used coins, of course, but after the collapse of their empire most trade was based on barter, namely swapping one good for another. The Frisians, though, thoroughly resurrected the concept of money, casting thick silver coins which were decorated with monsters and gods, recognised throughout their trading zone. Frisian money was currency in its truest sense; a convenient way to transport value, accepted over a wide area, and durable enough to survive thousands of transactions without falling apart. Quite suddenly, comparing the value of a boatload of German wine with that of a load of Essex corn was straightforward. As the historian Michael Pye put it, the Frisians transformed 'the idea of the value of things . . . A new way of thinking became possible'.

However, Frisian supremacy couldn't last forever. As their trading empire grew, they increasingly found themselves bumping up against their greatest regional rivals, the Franks. This Germanic tribe had something of a reputation for being hard to get on with. 'It is,' Sidonius Apollinaris wrote, 'a sport for them to throw their fast axes through the air from a great distance.' The Franks were, he said, 'monsters' with red hair who 'wear tight clothes that are stretched tight across their big male parts'.

Despite such low opinions, the Franks sometimes allied with the Romans, working as mercenaries and becoming quite familiar with Roman culture. Like the Frisians, they also gradually adopted the

Roman spirit of restless expansionism. From about 450 they headed south, gradually extending their control over a wide swathe of present-day Netherlands, Belgium, Germany and France. The Franks, as the Frisians had, steadily filled the power vacuum left by the retreating Romans, like river water rushing to fill a suddenly empty harbour.

For a while, the Frisians and the Franks managed to mostly steer clear of one another. In time, though, the Franks began butting up against Frisian territory along the Rhine. The two peoples fought repeatedly, and control over Dorestad passed back and forth before between them. In AD 734 the Frankish ruler Charles Martel finally defeated the Frisians and drove them north, away from the Rhine delta. The Frisians became subjects of the Frankish Emperor Charlemagne and abandoned their pagan beliefs – in Michael Pye's memorable phrase, they 'stopped smashing skulls and accepted Christianity'. The Frisians had enjoyed a good run as the traders and rulers of the lower Rhine, but now their time was over.*

However, the end of Frisian dominance did not mean the end of Dorestad. In fact, the great emporium enjoyed a new heyday under Charlemagne, who skilfully united swathes of the Germanic and Gallic regions, forming a vast empire stretching from Rome to Aachen and beyond, with the Rhine an essential link between these twin poles. Under Charlemagne's rule, Dorestad continued to thrive, spreading to the opposite bank of the Kromme Rijn and serving as an internal transfer point within Charlemagne's empire, where boats arriving on one river could hand over goods to those departing on another. By the early to mid 800s, however, it had begun to fall out of fashion, having been superseded by nearby rivals. The city's economy was also undermined by environmental changes. As the curve in the Rhine increased, and the Kromme Rijn gradually silted up, Dorestad lost its once perfect riverside location.

The subsequent history of the region is complex, but the final nail in Dorestad's coffin was arguably hammered in by the Vikings,

---

* The Frisians' physical legacy is limited, but their name lives on in the north-west Netherlands, in the province known as Friesland and in the Frisian Islands, where many people speak Frisian or *Frysk*. Germany also has districts called Ostfriesland and Nordfriesland, or 'East Friesland' and 'North Friesland'.

who came to the region in the ninth century, burning villages, killing livestock, terrorising large settlements like Utrecht and stealing treasures from cathedrals. In one famous raid in AD 837, Walcheren, a large island in the Rhine delta, was utterly ravaged, the Vikings burning and looting old Frisian trading posts before carting off women and children. Dorestad itself was attacked no fewer than four times between AD 834 and 837. After about the 860s, the once great emporium was barely mentioned in historical records. The Frisian capital of Europe became little more than a tranquil backwater; another Rhine town where the distant past would forever be more glorious than the future. The Frisians themselves, meanwhile, were condemned to be forever overlooked and under-appreciated – the Ringo Starrs of European history.

With cold hands and aching legs, I hobbled through the cobbled town and caught a train back to Utrecht, arriving just in time to see golden lights flickering to life on the Dom. The long run had left me utterly exhausted, and I stumbled sleepily through the labyrinthine streets. In an effort to save some money, I'd booked a bed for the night in a cheap youth hostel: a bleak, prison-like place with plasticky bunk beds, plasticky carpets and plasticky bed sheets. It had more in common with a Soviet prison than the glories of a Roman or Frankish villa. Nevertheless, I collapsed straight into bed without even opening the bag of crisps I'd bought for dinner.

Unfortunately, I turned out to be sharing my room with a young man who spent almost the entire night sitting up in bed, talking loudly on the phone with his girlfriend, breathlessly cooing the clichés of a fool in love: 'I love you more. No, I love you more! No, you hang up!' Whenever I got out of bed, he would quickly shove his phone under his pillow, lie down and pretend to be asleep, making loud snoring noises while I implored him to make his calls elsewhere, before picking up the phone again as soon as I got back in bed. Needless to say, I slept badly, cursing and kicking at the bed slats above me as the fool in the top bunk chattered on. When I crept out early in the morning, he was finally fast asleep. I filled his shoes with crisps on my way out of the door.

4

A Bridge Too Far

Arnhem and the Dutch–German Border

EVERY SEPTEMBER, THE skies west of Arnhem are filled with parachutes. First come the planes, big-bellied propeller-driven antiques, slowly droning into sight under the low grey clouds. Then the doors open and they appear one by one: dozens and dozens of jumpers, dangling precariously beneath dome-shaped military parachutes, descending slowly towards the fields like black toadstools falling from the sky. The crowds cheer, the brass bands play and the brave veterans are thanked, and then the visitors leave and everyone gets on with their lives for another year. But in the history books Arnhem remains, like Normandy or Nagasaki, forever famous for the unpleasant things which happened there a lifetime ago.

Within the Netherlands, the region around Arnhem is known for something far simpler: for being (in Dutch terms) a long way from everything else. Arnhem lies far closer to Germany than it does to Utrecht, surrounded by miles of farmland, and has a reputation (at least among residents of more westerly Dutch cities) as a slightly backwards place filled with whatever one calls 'hillbillies' in a country which doesn't have hills. 'The people are very different there,' friends in Amsterdam and Rotterdam had warned me darkly, as if discussing some remote corner of Sudan or Siberia rather than somewhere only an hour's drive away. 'The far east!' one exclaimed. 'My god, it's boring there!'

With those prejudices in mind, I was pleasantly surprised to find Arnhem was a glossy, well-heeled place, with few farmers to be seen and no cows clomping through the city streets. Wandering along the riverbank, there was less of the provincial Dutch tweeness I'd expected, and more of the gentle cosmopolitanism of a British or German cathedral city.

Historically, the Rhine in this region was a famous faultline between the two religions which once cleaved the Netherlands; those 'under the river' being largely Catholic, and those to the north of it mostly Protestant. Today, though, Arnhem residents seemed to have united around a new common religion: shopping. The streets were narrow and winding, but filled with countless expensive chain stores and fashionable boutiques. Despite its turbulent history, it felt like somewhere people lived well.

Arnhem is situated directly on the north bank of the Nederrijn or Dutch Rhine, and the river provided the city with an impressive backdrop: wide and steely, with well-built stone banks and a breezy riverside promenade lined with open-air restaurants and bars. The weather was perfect – bright blue skies, blazing sunshine, the river wide and sparkling in the sunlight. I stopped to photograph a colourful Turkish restaurant called RijnMozaïk (Rhine Mosaic) and was nearly run over by three young men just arriving in town by bicycle, towing little trailers piled high with fishing equipment. 'Arnhem!' one of them exclaimed. '*Vet, joh!*', 'Cool, huh!'

I stopped for lunch at one of the many terrace cafés. The daylight was golden and I enjoyed sitting in it for a while, watching joggers and cyclists breeze past. I'd been trying to be vegetarian, but my willpower crumbled and I ordered a cheeseburger. As the great Sarah Palin once said, if God didn't intend for us to eat animals, how come he made them out of meat? A pair of couples about my age arrived, and seeing that the café was busy, unhesitatingly crowded onto the table around me, elbowing and shoving as if they were crowding into the last lifeboat on the Titanic. The Dutch, I remembered, treated personal space not as a sacred zone which should never be violated, but as a public sphere in which all were welcome. To my horror, one of the women put her phone on the table and began to play loud dance music through the speakers. I felt like shoving her in the river, but being English, I obviously couldn't complain.

After lunch, I cycled out of Arnhem to the west, following the river current to Oosterbeek, a leafy village on the north bank. Today, it was a sleepily pleasant place where retirees tended their villas and groups of children cycled to school. Once, though, it wouldn't have been too much of an exaggeration to say it was a place where the fate of Europe hung in the balance.

★

For most of modern history, conflict was about as rare in the Netherlands as mountains. In the centuries after the Dutch won their independence from Spain, their governments largely clung to a policy of remaining neutral in the wars which ravaged Europe. Violence of any kind was almost unheard of, and the Dutch escaped the First World War almost completely unscathed, even as neighbouring Belgium was pulverised.

That sense of being a safe haven changed abruptly, however, with the outbreak of the Second World War. For the Nazis, spreading westwards from Germany towards Britain, Belgium and France, the Netherlands made an irresistible target; a short-cut and a staging post, it possessed valuable international ports and a long coastline which could be used to launch attacks on Britain. Ignoring pleas from the Dutch that they didn't want any trouble, Hitler abruptly attacked the Netherlands in May 1940. German paratroopers were sent to try and seize control of the government precinct in The Hague, and other troops were sent overland into the northern provinces. The Dutch army fought fiercely but were ill-equipped, and thousands were killed. Queen Wilhelmina fled with the Cabinet to England by boat. On 14 May came the decisive blow, when Rotterdam was hit by a massive bombing raid which triggered apocalyptic fires, destroying the port and reducing the city centre to rubble. Faced with such epic destruction, and warned by the Nazis that more bombers were on their way to cities including Utrecht, the Dutch promptly surrendered. The French and Belgians soon followed.

In some parts of the Netherlands, daily life continued almost uninterrupted under Nazi rule, thanks partly to Hitler's view that the Dutch were natural brothers-in-arms for the Germans, being fellow members of the Aryan master race. In many other places, though, people suffered terrible hardships. As the Nazis consolidated their control and fortified the coastline around the river mouth, thousands of Dutch went hungry or were treated brutally by both the Nazi occupiers and Dutch collaborators. In The Hague, thousands of homes were demolished to make way for beachfront bunkers. In Utrecht, men were grabbed off the streets and taken to Germany to work in factories. In Rotterdam, people starved amid the ruins. In Amsterdam, a young girl with a diary moved into a secret annex in her father's office. Tens of thousands of people, many of them Jews, were taken on one-way journeys to concentration camps.

For four long years the hardships never ceased, but by the summer of 1944, the end was finally in sight. Hitler had invaded the Soviet Union in 1941 hoping to strike a knockout blow which would win the war, but had instead ignited a grinding war of attrition which saw his army being crushed between two fronts. The Allies were regularly launching 1,000-bomber raids on German cities such as Cologne; the exhausted German army was increasingly mutinous; and Hitler, increasingly removed from reality, was struggling to control an enormous occupied territory. The Allies, meanwhile, were in no mood to forgive and forget. Winston Churchill promised to 'make the German people taste and gulp each month a sharper dose of the miseries they have showered on mankind'.

In 1944, the Allies crossed the Channel from England to Normandy. The dominoes began to topple: Paris fell on 25 August, followed by Brussels and Antwerp in early September. As Nazis surrendered en masse, the Allies swept across France and Belgium, greeted in town after town by crowds singing and dancing and cheering. There were still many fierce battles, and the Allies faced huge problems keeping their racing armies supplied with enough food, fuel and ammunition, but to many soldiers liberating Europe had begun to seem as easy – as one British commander put it – as a 'combine harvester going through a field of corn'.

However, there remained at least one great obstacle blocking the Allies' path across Europe: the river Rhine. As the Nazi retreat began, the river emerged as an obvious natural bulwark – what the historian Lloyd Clark memorably called 'a liquid security blanket, behind which their shattered nation could cower'. 'If necessary,' Hitler said, 'We'll fight on the Rhine.'

In Allied military headquarters, British and American leaders argued intensely over how best to breach the river. It was clear the Rhine would have to be crossed if they were ever to reach Berlin, but with some 2 million Allied soldiers stretched across the Continent, from the North Sea to Switzerland, the British and Americans disagreed about how to use them. Should they focus on a single 'narrow front' to puncture through the Nazi front lines like a knife? Or should they fight on a 'broad front', sweeping the

Germans back across the Rhine like a broom? After much debate, they eventually agreed to launch a 'single full-bodied thrust' to establish a bridgehead across the great river near Arnhem. Thirty thousand soldiers would be dropped by parachute and glider deep behind enemy lines, where they would capture the bridges. Simultaneously, tanks and infantry would strike out northwards from the Allied lines near Eindhoven, forging a route across the recaptured bridges and then on towards Berlin. The codename for the first, airborne element would be Operation Market, and for the second, land-based component, Operation Garden. Together, they were Operation Market Garden. The name sounded as twee and genteel as an English summer party, but the stakes were high. Just as in Roman times, the Rhine had become a final frontier, a last line of defence against the enemies of civilisation. 'When you think about the defence of England, you no longer think of the chalk cliffs of Dover,' British Prime Minister Stanley Baldwin once said. 'You think of the Rhine. That is where our frontier lies today.'

In Oosterbeek, I cycled a quick loop through the village, circling northwards away from the river. It wasn't exactly packed with attractions, but there was one I was curious to see: the Bilderberg hotel. In certain dark corners of the internet, Oosterbeek was notorious as the birthplace of the Bilderberg conference series, an annual event attended by about a hundred of the world's most important politicians and financiers. The conferences were initiated in Oosterbeek in 1954 and quickly became the subject of countless conspiracy theories, with the 'Bilderbergers' blamed (among many other things) for secretly planning the 9/11 attacks, covering up Barack Obama's communist plot to take over America, and tricking Americans into liking the Beatles. More than sixty years after their founding, the conferences had long since outgrown the original venue, but for some, this faded Dutch hotel remained a by-word for a rapacious international elite. It all sounded like a load of rubbish to me, but I couldn't resist stopping for a quick cup of coffee and a caramel *stroopwafel*. I spent a few minutes idly browsing conspiracy websites on my phone, noting they often, for some reason, focused on the role allegedly played in the Bilderberg group by the state of Israel. The coffee was weak and the Wi-Fi wasn't working. An elderly couple at the next table were talking about how unusually clever their grandchildren were. On balance, it seemed unlikely that this village by the Rhine was really the place from where the world was run.

Beyond the hotel, Oosterbeek's wide streets lined with bike shops, bakeries and expensive-looking homes. Cycling east, I soon reached the Airborne War Cemetery, a square green field enclosed by tall trees, with the serene feel of a forest glade. A big white marble cross stood at one end, flanked by long rows of toothlike headstones, shining brightly in the sunshine. I locked my bike to a tree and walked up and down for a while, scribbling names and dates in my notebook. In total, nearly 1,700 people were buried or commemorated here – Brits, New Zealanders, Canadians, Australians, Dutch and Poles. Compared to the likes of Arlington or Ypres, the scale of the cemetery was modest, but like many such places it was quietly haunting, and I found it hard not to be moved by the dozens of tombstones, with a few elderly people shuffling between them clutching bunches of flowers. At one end of the cemetery, an old man stood resting a hand on an altar-like plinth which was engraved with the words 'Their name liveth for evermore'. I said hello, and when he looked up, I saw he had tears in his eyes.

On 17 September 1944, the Allied forces launched their assault on Arnhem. Hundreds of aircraft set out across the Channel: bombers, fighters, transport aircraft and dozens of gliders – flimsy plywood things which carried paratroopers inside, like flying horses of Troy. As they flew across the east of England, the aircraft made an astonishing sight: a never-ending stream of aircraft flying low and loud enough to rattle the teacups in the farmhouses below. Amazingly, one air crew apparently were told they'd be completing a short training flight around their home airfield in England, only to unexpectedly find themselves part of the largest airborne assault in history. They were understandably terrified, but their leaders were confident of victory. One British commander, John Frost, even took his golf clubs.

After about three hours in the air, the planes approached the target zone. The gliders disconnected from their tow planes and dived towards the flat fields around Arnhem, landing hard in the grass on long metal skids. Allied planes strafed German positions on the ground as the sky above Oosterbeek and Arnhem filled with parachutes; thousands of white domes descending like lanterns. The men of 10 Para jumped accompanied by their mascot, a live chicken, which was tucked into the front of a paratrooper's jacket.

The element of surprise was quickly lost, and the Nazis opened fire, their guns spitting skywards. Planes and gliders hurled sickeningly to earth. 'When we came back, the aircraft looked like a lace curtain,' one confused airman recalled. But overall, the landings were a remarkable success, and by early afternoon a total of nearly 20,000 Allied troops had been inserted behind enemy lines. In many places, the Nazis were taken completely by surprise. A serviceman called James Sims later wrote of finding a group of Nazi soldiers 'dressed in their Sunday uniforms . . . caught in the fields where we had landed, snogging their Dutch girlfriends'. 'Their faces,' he said, 'went redder and redder by the minute.'

From the landing zone at Oosterbeek, soldiers set out on foot for Arnhem, advancing along the same residential streets which I now cycled. Today, the area was the epitome of bland domesticity, but in 1944 it was anything but. One they'd got over their initial surprise, the Nazis quickly realised the major flaw in the Allies' plan: by blocking a few key roads, the Germans could isolate the paratroopers away from the river. The operation quickly descended into chaos. British paratroopers found their radios didn't work properly, and some soldiers were reduced to sending carrier pigeons back to England with messages. When the Nazis cut off the water supply to Oosterbeek, others were forced to drink from bird baths. Some Brits managed to fight their way into Arnhem and seize the northern end of one bridge over the Rhine. However, isolated and crippled by poor communications and a lack of supplies, they were unable to capture the whole bridge, and could do little more than sit and wait as enemy tanks rumbled into the city. The Nazis, an Allied soldier later wrote, were 'like fire ants – once stirred up they are deadly'.

After two days of fighting, the Allied soldiers remained pinned down in ruined houses as the Germans methodically pummelled them with artillery. The hospital in Arnhem was overflowing with injured Allied soldiers. One English soldier who survived a tank attack emerged to find 'Oosterbeek was unrecognisable; it was as if a giant had swept every building away'. Many were seriously wounded, but some less so. When one soldier collapsed with epilepsy-like convulsions, his colleagues feared he'd taken a piece of shrapnel to the brain, but a nurse offered a simpler explanation: he'd been poisoned by a lump of plastic explosive falling in his tea. He stopped drinking, and quickly made a full recovery. Many others were captured as prisoners of war. One group of British soldiers, detained by a Nazi sergeant major, expected to be interrogated about the invasion plan but found their captor, a keen student of the English language, had just one question: 'What is a bollock?'

Local Dutch people, meanwhile, did their best to support the liberators. Having suffered the miseries of a brutal Nazi occupation, some Dutch were confused by the good manners of the British, who asked politely if it would possibly be all right if they fired their guns from their bedroom windows. Other locals focused on keeping things nice and tidy. One soldier reported that after a car full of Nazi officers was machine-gunned by British soldiers, several Dutch women appeared and began sweeping the broken glass from the street. Elsewhere, an army chaplain prayed quietly with a group of soldiers, asking them: 'How many of you have read Mark chapter 17?' They replied that they had indeed studied it carefully, to which the father replied with a smile: 'Mark has only fifteen chapters.'

Despite such humour, the situation was dire. Days after they'd expected the battle to be over, the troops realised that while Operation Market Garden had not yet failed completely, it was likely to. One officer, General Brian Horrocks, called it 'the blackest moment of my life'. Thousands of soldiers had been killed and wounded, and the price paid by the local population was also severe. A British paratrooper, Leonard Moss, later told poignantly of what he'd seen when visiting one Dutch home:

> The inside of the farmhouse has been wrecked . . . Glass crunches underfoot, furniture is broken, deliberately smashed. There's not a whole plate or bowl anywhere. Sat in the corner, on a wooden stool, is a Dutchman. He's middle-aged, balding, dirty and small. He looks up, face stained with tears, eyes red. He makes a gesture with one hand as if to ask 'Why?' and then puts his head into his hands in desperation. His whole life, all he's worked for, has been destroyed.

I left the cemetery and headed back into Arnhem proper, cycling east along the bank of the river. The water was largely obscured from the road by a thick hedgerow, but the cycling was typically lovely, and the path so flat it would fit into an envelope. Nearer the city, the riverbank became car-free and prettily cobbled, with big tour boats parked along the quayside. I passed a small war memorial, and saw someone had graffitied on it a picture of a modern Predator drone. Whether this was a witty comment on the evolution of warfare or a disgraceful piece of vandalism, I couldn't quite decide. As often in such places, it was hard to reconcile the bitter history of the place with its present tranquillity. Had hundreds of soldiers really been machine-gunned to death here, during my own father's lifetime, down where that little girl was feeding the swans? Watching a flotilla of rowers glide past in the sunshine, I thought that the greatest tribute to the fallen was perhaps this: that Arnhem, once so filled with hatred and bloodshed, now seemed utterly mundane. 'Wasn't there some kind of war here once?' I heard a passer-by say.

In 1944, more than a week after the operation began, the liberators of Arnhem finally admitted defeat, and the Allied evacuation began. Hundreds of exhausted, wounded soldiers gathered on the muddy riverbanks, waiting hours for their turn to board one of the boats shuttling back and forth across the river. Even in defeat, there were moments of black humour. One soldier waiting to cross whispered to the sergeant in charge of loading the boats: 'Hey mate, where do we change for Liverpool Street Station?' The reply came back with a laugh through the darkness: 'Get out of the boat and catch the 303 bus heading west!'

Yet for the most part, the mood among the defeated Allies was understandably grim. One soldier later wrote a poignant eyewitness account of the final retreat across the river:

> I sit at the back of the boat, shivering like a small child. From my position, I can see the lines of troops waiting to be rescued, the lost, lonely, cold faces, some terrified, some resigned. Machine-gun fire continues to rake the water. A dead body bumps against the boat and is grabbed by the water and quickly disappears; he's one of the many I see carried on the current.

At 2.30 a.m., the last few airborne soldiers in Oosterbeek left their positions and slipped down to the water. And with that, Operation Market Garden was over.

Some would argue the operation hadn't been a complete failure. The Nazis' hold on the Rhine had been weakened, and the foundations arguably laid for the future liberation of the Netherlands. But few would dispute the Allies had paid a terrible price. Hundreds of Brits, Americans, Polish and other nationals had also been killed, and Arnhem and Oosterbeek ruined. Later, military leaders would be bitterly criticised for failing to understand how fiercely the Germans would fight to retain control of the bridges, given the way they served as barricades blocking the road to Berlin. One soldier's summary was succinct: 'it wasn't supposed to be like this'. The Rhine had not been taken, and the Allies had not secured their springboard to Berlin. The bridge at Arnhem was – as the saying went – a bridge too far.

Leaving Arnhem, I cycled east, crossing a big bridge high over a river. I checked my map and realised this was the IJssel, flowing into the Rhine from the north. Compared to the big, busy Rhine, the IJssel looked serene, with fat Friesian cows idling in apple-green fields which had been left deliberately exposed to the river in order to ease flooding elsewhere. I wondered what would happen to the livestock in the case of any catastrophic deluge, and hoped cows could swim. A mile or two further was the junction itself, where the two rivers merged seamlessly like the two halves of a zip. A small speedboat raced down the main channel leaving a fat foamy wake, and a dozen cows huddled on a small crescent of sand. Fishermen sat huddled outside their green dome tents like Eskimos outside their igloos. I overheard two of them angrily discussing the terrible quality and cost of Dutch healthcare, and remembered my last visit to a Dutch hospital, in a gleaming wait-free building which looked like a Google campus, and wondered if perhaps they didn't quite realise how lucky they were.

Backtracking slightly, I found a small war memorial: a round concrete plinth about the size of a large dining table, flanked by a couple of flagpoles, commemorating a British army division which had fought fiercely here to cross the IJssel. A small information board explained ungrammatically but poetically: 'Military and civilians participated in war roulette, involving survival or death, happiness or sadness'. I paused to take a photo and was interrupted by a couple in a camper van – middle-aged, jolly and German – asking for directions to Oosterbeek. I gladly began telling them the way, but after a few words was interrupted by a young Dutchman who rushed over to correct me: no, no, I hadn't explained it clearly enough; they had to go *first* around the corner and *then* over the roundabout. I thought again how strange and wonderful the world was; that in a place where the British and Dutch had once fought the Germans in their deathly game of roulette, the biggest concern now was whether the former had remembered to tell the latter to turn left at the traffic lights. 'I hope you all have a very good visit in Holland!' the Dutchman said.

Eventually the Rhine fell, of course – not in Arnhem, but further to the south-east, where several teams of Allied soldiers were racing for the honour of forging a literal bridgehead into the Nazi homeland, including around the German town of Remagen. In the Arnhem area, the key breakthrough came near the German river towns of Rees and Wesel. After the failure of Operation Market Garden, the Allies had to accept that the war which they'd hoped was nearly over would drag on for many months to come, forcing them to push the Nazis back (as one Canadian solider put it) 'yard by yard, dike by dike'. As winter approached, rivers froze and food supplies ran out. In cities such as Rotterdam and Amsterdam, park benches were chopped up for firewood, tulip bulbs served as food, and dead bodies were stacked like kindling outside churches. Hitler, meanwhile, launched a bold counter-offensive into the Ardennes hills of southern Belgium, and reassured German radio listeners that Allied commanders were incapable of ever invading the German homeland. Winston Churchill, the Führer said, was a 'drunkard', and President Roosevelt a 'fire-side chatterer with a poor knowledge of geography'.

Early in 1945, with Hitler's authority crumbling and the Soviets closing on Berlin, the Allies launched a new offensive across the rivers Roer, Maas, Lippe and Rhine. Keen to retain the element of surprise, they carried out elaborate tricks to fool the Nazi spies, installing inflatable rubber dummies of tanks and artillery pieces.

Ammunition and other supplies were stacked high along the sides of the roads leading north, in hopes that enemy reconnaissance aircraft would mistake them for mere dikes or hedgerows. One observer calculated that the ammunition alone made up a wall five feet high and thirty miles long. The Nazis, meanwhile, did their best to slow the advance, blowing up dikes so the Allies' path was blocked with floods of freezing water. Over the following weeks casualties were often heavy, but Churchill provided a rare moment of light relief when, in early March 1945, he embarked on a tour of the toothed fortifications which the Nazis had built to hold the Allies back. Warning the assembled journalists that 'this is one of those operations connected with this great war which must not be reproduced graphically', the Prime Minister unbuttoned his fly and urinated over the wall into Nazi territory.

In late March came the final assault across the Rhine at Rees and Wesel: the dubiously named Operation Plunder. A soldier called Denis Whitaker remembered: '5,000 guns erupted in a single, solid roar. Shells bursting over the eastern bank screamed like so many freight trains rushing through the night, the fire seemed to blanket the entire shore; it was hard to imagine how anything could stay alive on the other side of the river.' The riverbank in Wesel exploded in a wall of flame, reflected brightly in the water. Allied amphibious vehicles skidded down muddy riverbanks, and hundreds of RAF bombers appeared overhead, raining bombs on the Nazi positions. At one point, an American soldier paused to scrawl '300,000' on an artillery shell – the three hundred thousandth fired by the Americans in one hour. The effects were devastating: 'the whole town [of Wesel] looked as if it had been picked up and dropped down again', one soldier said.

By 1 a.m. Wesel had been taken, one of a series of beachheads established on the eastern bank of the Rhine. That morning, Churchill again visited the front line, gazing across the Rhine from an army observation post as artillery fire echoed across the water. Chomping on a trademark cigar, the prime minister was delighted to be in the thick of the action. 'The Rhine and all its fortresses,' he later wrote, 'have proved that physical barriers are vain without the means and spirit to hold them. A beaten army, not long ago the master of Europe, retreats before its pursuers.'

Churchill was perhaps exaggerating a little, but the crossing of the Rhine was certainly a decisive moment. After crossing the river, Allied armies fanned out in a six-week race across Germany. One after another, the cities of the north were liberated: Hamburg, Amsterdam, Groningen. In Arnhem, a combined British and Canadian force fought fiercely for several days to liberate the city. Barely a month after the crossing of the Rhine, Hitler committed suicide in his bunker in Berlin. The following week, Germany formally surrendered and Allied troops swept across the Netherlands, throwing chocolate, cigarettes and soap to cheering crowds waving tulips and orange streamers. Up and down the river, the mood was triumphant. The Dutch, Churchill later told MPs in London, had suffered terribly in the 'enemy's clutch', but had been 'strengthened by the compression they have endured.' Others, though, took a different view. One young German woman, Wilma Kuhler, wrote to a Welsh solider to thank him for burying her husband on the battlefield. 'Wars settle nothing,' she said.

I continued eastwards along the river, cycling along a tarmac bike path which threaded along the dikes like a seam. The weather was still glorious and the paths were packed with cyclists – so many, in fact, that I often had to get off my bike and walk – not a problem I'd ever had on cycle paths in the English countryside.

On my left, I passed dozens of pretty little trapezoid bungalows, followed by a boggy field ringed with signs offering *Bouwkavels* (plots of building land) for sale. A man with a notepad stood sketching what looked like a rough plan for a cottage to build there. I stopped briefly and peered nosily over his shoulder. 'It's going to be fantastic!' he said. Further on, grassy fields were studded with huge chunks of Ozymandian stone and concrete – more relics of war. The river itself was mostly quiet, but I saw one largish container ship surging down the silent channel, as incongruous as a monster truck on a country lane. To the south, across the water, the scenery was prettily featureless in the usual Dutch way, with empty green fields spreading out flat as flat as blankets at a picnic. I had the feeling that if I jumped high enough, I'd be able to see Denmark.

Just past the village of Pannerden, I stopped for a rest at a pontoon from where a small ferry packed with Dutch cyclists was heading across the Rhine. A gang of competitive forty-year-old Dutchmen pulled up behind me, junkie-thin and mahogany-tanned. They quickly inspected my bike and frowned at my baggy non-Lycra clothes, before bullishly discussing whether to 'Do the 120 today' or stop after 'just the 100'. Across the sparkling water were several small beaches where young women swam while their boyfriends lounged on the sand. Looking at my map, I realised they were in another country: at this point, the north bank of the river was Dutch, but the south was German. 'Shall we go to Germany for lunch?' I heard one male cyclist ask his wife, trying to decide whether to take the ferry. 'Yes, I suppose so,' she replied. 'Why not?'

I stayed in the Netherlands, but as I cycled further, there was a clear sense that change was afoot. German cars began to outnumber Dutch ones, and place names on signposts were followed by either (D) or (NL) depending which side of the border they lay. Just past the village of Spijk, I suddenly realised the road signs I was following were in a different font than they had been previously, and the path I was cycling on was the Runde Straße, which didn't sound very Dutch. Doubling back a little, I managed to pinpoint the exact point where the labelling changed, at a sharp bend in the road running along the riverbank. I checked my map again and confirmed this was it; the Dutch–German border, completely unmarked everywhere except on the paper in my hand. Even crossing between Dutch provinces or London boroughs there was usually a sign demarcating the change in authority, but here there was nothing; no flag, no lines on the road, no signs wishing me '*Welkom*' or '*Willkommen*'. Here, the nation state seemed like a thing of the past.

The Dutch–German border wasn't always so invisible. Thomas Jefferson crossed it somewhere near here in 1788 and was amazed by the differences between two countries which he (like many Americans) had assumed were largely identical. Jefferson wrote in his diary: 'The transition from ease and opulence to extreme poverty is remarkable on crossing the line between the Dutch and Prussian territory. [In Prussia] there are no chateaux, nor houses that bespeak the existence even of a middle class. Universal and equal poverty overspreads the whole.' 'The villages,' he noted in Germany, 'seem to be falling down.'

Today, it was hard to detect many differences between the two countries. By far the biggest was the cycle lanes. In the Netherlands, these had all been impressively smooth and well signposted, but in Germany they were cracked and bumpy, sprouting with weeds. Signposts were almost non-existent, and I had to swerve repeatedly to avoid sheep wandering across the path. Not far past the border, I encountered an elderly Dutchman who was turning his bicycle around in exasperation, giving up on German infrastructure and heading back to the sanctuary of the Netherlands. 'Terrible! Just terrible!' he cried.

As an Englishman, born on an island, I was endlessly tickled by the idea that I could jump on my bike and cycle to a whole other country. Most Dutch and Germans, however, naturally took it for granted. In border regions like this, people thought nothing of filling their car or doing their weekly shop internationally. Thousands of Dutch residents worked in Germany, and vice versa. Dutch elites took evident pride in their familiarity with German language and culture, and throughout both countries it was common to meet nationals of one country who were married to citizens of the other. The Dutch national hero William of Orange was born in present-day Germany, and even the Dutch national anthem included a direct acknowledgement of the countries' shared culture and heritage: a foreign visitor to King's Day in Amsterdam might be surprised to hear patriotic Dutchmen bellowing '*Ben ik van Duitsen bloed*', 'I am of German blood.'*

Travelling regularly between the two countries, I'd long thought that the people on either side of the border were strikingly similar in their attitudes. The Germans, like the Dutch, believed firmly in good order, and lived lives based on tidiness, planning and careful scheduling. Both were allergic to English over-politeness and prevarication, but both also suffered from a tendency to discuss problems at such length that it left no time to actually solve them. Both were also relatively conservative with respect to money – in both countries, the same word ('*schuld*') famously meant both

---

* There is some disagreement about the etymology of the phrase – but at the very least, the wording has strong German connotations, and it's somewhat surprising it has remained in the song.

'debt' and 'guilt'. However, some differences were obvious. The Germans, for example, were generally more formal: people could work together for years without ever using the informal *du* form of address, while the Dutch would be hugging the CEO within minutes of their first meeting. In the Netherlands, someone once told me, everything was permitted unless it was forbidden, but in Germany the opposite was true: everything was assumed forbidden unless it had been permitted.

Economically, the two countries were so integrated as to be utterly co-dependent. Thanks in large part to the Rhine, Rotterdam was sometimes referred to as 'Germany's largest port' and the Netherlands sent around a quarter of all its exports to Germany. The Germans also shipped masses of stuff to the Dutch – in 2017, 17 million Dutch people bought as much from Germany as did more than a billion Chinese. Politically, too, the countries were close allies, pooling their sovereignty formally through the EU and informally through constant efforts to defend their sensible north European values against foolhardy southern ones. For Angela Merkel, Dutch Prime Minister Mark Rutte made a regular sidekick at summits; a supportive Robin to her all-powerful Batman.

However, this didn't mean relations between the countries were completely untroubled. Despite their tolerant reputation, the Dutch had a long history of mild hostility towards their neighbours. This was perhaps understandable, given that some German thinkers argued the Netherlands shouldn't exist at all. Ernst Moritz Arndt, for example, in 1803 wrote a book arguing the Netherlands was 'a crying mutilation of the natural boundaries of Germany'. Others thought trade links made the distinction between the countries meaningless. Otto van Bismarck, the Iron Chancellor who forged modern Germany out of a ragtag collection of states, was once supposed to have said '*Holland annektiert sich selbst schon*' – 'Holland already annexes itself' – by relying so heavily on German trade.

After the Second World War, the Dutch naturally thought of the Germans the way a fieldmouse might think of an eagle from whose talons it had miraculously escaped; as an object of absolute terror and hatred. As Dutch Prime Minister Willem Schermerhorn said in June 1945, with typical Dutch directness: 'the Dutch people have a score to settle in almost every sector'. The Dutch quickly occupied a swathe of German territory near Arnhem, and argued they deserved generous reparations from Germany. Many Germans living in the Netherlands were designated enemies of the state and held in internment camps near the border before being deported, in an operation known as Black Tulip. Well after the war ended, people travelling from the Netherlands to Germany were greeted by signs warning 'You are Entering Enemy Territory: Be on your Guard!'

In time, though, Dutch views of their neighbours shifted. As the Iron Curtain descended across Europe, the Dutch came to recognise that Germany (or at least, *West* Germany) couldn't remain a ruined pariah state forever. Like a bitterly divorced couple getting back together for the sake of the mortgage, the Dutch and Germans pledged to forget the past and prosper together.

More recently, the authorities had made a concerted effort to fix what the *New York Times* once called 'one of Western Europe's most enduring prejudices'. Starting in the mid 1990s, the Dutch government organised special seminars aimed at softening anti-German prejudices in towns near the border, including special training for police officers in Arnhem on 'Getting Along with Germans.' There were numerous cultural exchanges and study-abroad schemes, and millions were spent on promoting trade along the Rhine corridor. In 2016, the two governments even signed a deal whereby 800 German sailors effectively were seconded to serve in the Dutch navy.

At the individual level, however, animosity lingered for decades. When, in 1966, the Dutch Princess Beatrix married a German prince in Amsterdam, the wedding was received with a distinct lack of enthusiasm on the part of some Dutch, who rioted in the streets. Decades later, Allied ex-servicemen were always given a warm welcome when they visited Oosterbeek and Arnhem, but curious German visitors less so. Martin Middlebrook wrote that 'efforts by German ex-soldiers' associations to join in the [remembrance] ceremonies are firmly rejected by local opinion; a wreath placed by Germans in the war cemetery on one occasion was swiftly removed'. In the early 1990s, a notorious survey by the Dutch Institute on International Relations found that 56 per cent of Dutch fifteen- and sixteen-year-olds had a negative view of Germans, while only 15 per cent felt positive. Majorities described Germans as 'racist', 'arrogant' and 'power-hungry'. In a revealing interview, the Dutch ambassador to Germany at the time, Peter van Walsum, said: 'Every society has a primitive need to set itself apart from a particular nation, race or religion. We Dutch have been . . . given a picture of Germany that has not changed since April 1945. As a result, tolerant Dutch citizens who would never discriminate against other foreigners see no deadly sin in behaving that way toward Germans.'

More recently, such sentiments had faded somewhat, and the Dutch and Germans were united against common enemies such as ISIS and Theresa May. Many Dutch even concluded that the Germans were setting a good example. 'Germany is like the country the Netherlands used to be, kind and tolerant,' one Dutch friend said wistfully to me. However, it still wasn't hard to detect some underlying unease among the Dutch about the speed with which Germany had bounced back to dominate the Netherlands again. Travelling around the Netherlands, it still wasn't unusual to meet older people who still eschewed all things German: cars, beers, washing machines, vacuum cleaners. 'It's always only French cars for me!' a Dutchman my father's age told me.

Outright hostility was rare, but for many Dutch, it was still acceptable to be unpleasant to Germans. As an outsider moving to Rotterdam, I'd learned that one of the surest ways to a certain type of Dutch person's heart was to express mild anti-German sentiment, preferably in the form of a joke referencing the theft of Dutch bicycles by German soldiers. When I wrote in a previous book about the war in Rotterdam, I was surprised to receive several emails from older Dutch readers objecting that I'd used the word *Nazi* to refer to soldiers in wartime, but *Germans* to refer to their countrymen today. 'They're *all* Nazis!' one irate correspondent said. At a personal level, many Dutch still viewed Germany as dominating and domineering, a little too fond of telling other countries what to do. 'I ate at a German restaurant the other day,' a guy on the train from Delft to The Hague once joked to me. 'The food was very good, but an hour later I was really hungry for power.'

From a German perspective, meanwhile, the relationship between the two countries naturally looked rather different. At the government level, the Germans viewed the Dutch as natural allies, forever striking a sensible middle ground between the capitalist, war-mongering excesses of America and the socialist, malingering excesses of the Mediterranean. The Dutch authorities occasionally got annoyed by German companies' use of the Netherlands as a tax haven, and the way in which Amsterdam acted as a magnet for drug smuggling and human trafficking. In general, though, they were pleased to have a competent partner to address common challenges. 'The Dutch are very sensible people,' a conservative German MP once told me over coffee in Berlin. 'Smart, successful. They're good neighbours for us.'

Now, after decades of low-level tension, the Dutch seemed finally to be viewing the Germans as something like a much bigger brother. They were irritated by how their sibling sometimes overshadowed them, and despaired at the foolish things he'd done in his teenage years, but were also respectful of his greater abilities, secretly affectionate and perhaps even a little jealous. The Germans, conversely, viewed the Dutch as a typical younger sibling – sweet and likeable, but also a little irresponsible. On a good day, their relationship could be summarised by something the German Chancellor Helmut Kohl once told a Dutch interviewer: 'We must not forget history, but we must also not be trapped by it.' But on a bad day, it was perhaps better summed up by the joke which was told to me by no fewer than three different people when I mentioned I was writing about Germany. 'Angela Merkel,' they said, 'arrives from Germany at Schiphol airport in Amsterdam. The immigration officer looks though her passport for a minute and then asks if he can confirm a few details. "Nationality?" he asks. "German," she replies. "Place of residence?" "Berlin." And then the final question: "Occupation?" "No," the Chancellor says. "Not this time."'

East of the border, I continued following the river towards Emmerich, the first of Germany's many Rhine towns. The cycle paths were still mostly deserted, but the weather was still beautiful. To me, the scenery generally looked more English than Dutch; not quite as tidy and a little more charmingly unkempt. If countries were people, I thought, the Netherlands would probably be a laid-back young architect in immaculate smart-casual office clothes. Germany, like England, would be a brilliantly productive but slightly eccentric professor, with wild hair and a skew-whiff tie.

Half an hour or so after crossing the border, I arrived in Emmerich. This was a fairly ordinary little German town made less ordinary by its terrific soaring suspension bridge, a 500-metre-long red-painted structure which looked like the Brooklyn Bridge. I locked my bike to a bench and walked along the riverbank for a while. Compared to the bustle of Arnhem, Emmerich was deathly quiet, with only a handful of people ambling along the waterfront. It was pretty, though. The riverbank had a charming little cobbled promenade, with a sculpture of a fisherman rowing a small boat and a stone obelisk pointing 179.1 kilometres westwards to Hoek van Holland and 681.9 southwards to Basle. Another sign pointed a few miles upriver to Kleve, a former German ducal city and the home town of Anne of Cleves, the fourth wife of England's King Henry VIII. A third sign pointed further along the river towards the town of Xanten, which I liked because it sounded like the name of a character in a superhero franchise or *Star Wars* film. ('Xanten, son of Xog, has returned to reclaim the throne of Zon from the rebel alliance!')

In the town centre, I stopped at a bakery and bought a disgustingly unhealthy lunch, sampling the very best of German cuisine: a litre of *schokomilch* milkshake, a sticky pastry and two Berliner doughnuts. My phone belatedly pinged with an automated message: '*Welkom in Duitsland.*' I was pleased to be back in Germany, and to be leaving behind some of the worst excesses of the Netherlands: atrocious table manners, grown adults reading comic books, and men wearing blue suits with brown shoes. I sat by the river for a while flicking through a German phrase book which I'd bought in the hope of brushing up my language skills. The book was printed in 1970 and seemed a little out of date; it began with how to order a porter to transport duty-free cigarettes through the customs posts on the border. It didn't include louche modern words like *girlfriend*, but did explain how to buy bath salts, how best to challenge a stranger to a game of chess, and how to buy tickets for an operetta. I practised asking a passing duck: '*Wird heute abend einen Operette gespielt?*' German, I decided, was rather like Dutch; it was so guttural and coughy that receiving a gentle 'good afternoon' was like being shouted at by someone with a chest cold. Perhaps the two countries weren't so different after all.

PART TWO

Germany

5

The Engine Room

Duisburg and Düsseldorf

A T NIGHT, THE old metalworks was a spookily beautiful place. The giant gas tanks were lit a bright Christmassy green, and the towering chimneys wore bright collars of scarlet neon. One house-sized pair of silos was floodlit in blood red, transformed from drab grey containers into a giant's glowing heart. Everywhere I looked, there were massive pipes, pylons, towers and turbines lit in bright primary colours. Dramatically oversized and dramatically lit, the whole place had the hollow grandeur of a film set. Climbing a steel staircase up through a web of pipes and cables above a big chemical tank, I half expected to see Batman hurling the Joker into a pool of toxic green slime.

Although now deserted, this – the Landschaftpark (Landscape Park) at Duisburg, just east of the Rhine in northern Germany – had once been one of the largest industrial centres in Europe, and one of the primary engines driving the German economy. It had also done much to shape the way the world saw the Germans, and perhaps even how the Germans saw themselves: productive, efficient, iron-willed and steelily unsentimental. Today, the boilers and smelters were silent, and the whole area had been converted into a giant urban park, filled with crumbling industrial architecture. Old rail-ways had been converted to child-friendly footpaths, high concrete walls were now vertical playgrounds for rock climbers, rusted storage bunkers were planted with wild flower gardens, and a former gas tank made a practice pool for scuba·divers. After some inevitable grumbles about white elephants, the whole project had turned into a staggering success, one of the highlights of the European Route of Industrial Heritage – a driving tour which was (one assumes) invented to make teenage daughters on holiday hate their fathers.

I wandered for hours amid the glowing ruins, seeing no one other

than a few late-night joggers who circled the park like planes waiting
to land. As midnight approached, I sat high over a giant spherical
tank of inky water to eat another spectacularly unhealthy travellers'
picnic. Like the Netherlands, Germany is not exactly world famous
for its fine cuisine – there is, perhaps, a limit to how enthusiastic
non-Germans can get about endless variations on pork with potatoes,
However, German food isn't without its charms, and whenever I
visited the Rhineland I enjoyed sampling local cuisines, which were
more varied than many outsiders appreciated. Unlike some countries,
Germany had no single national dish around which people could
unite, but rather a bewildering array of local specialities befitting a
nation which was (as the food historian Ursula Heinzelmann put it),
'in the middle of the European continent, between the Slavs and the
Romans, cold and heat, sea and mountains'. In the north of the
Rhine region, around Duisburg and Emmerich, the food didn't seem
wildly different from Dutch cuisine; pleasant but a little stodgy, with
chefs focused on keeping prices down rather than standards high.
Around Cologne, the food was also straightforward and hearty, with
an emphasis on novelty dishes which even other Germans might
struggle to identify in a line-up: *Hämmche* salted pork knuckles, *Halve
Hahn* cheese-on-rye sandwiches, and *Himmel und Ääd* mash-and-meat
with apple sauce. Further south, French and Italian influences began
to spill across the Rhine and the Alps, and German food acquired a
slightly lighter, Latin flavour; with meats cured rather than heavily
processed, vegetables roasted rather than pulped to oblivion, and wine
poured instead of beer. In Duisburg, though, all those delights were
still to come. Sitting in the darkness amid the towering pylons, I
unwrapped an old friend whom I'd picked up on my way to the
park: a mushroomy *jägerschnitzel* sandwich which was almost as big
as my head. It tasted delicious, and was probably filled with as much
energy as the generators and furnaces around me.

For someone keen to learn more about the cultural and historical
glories of Germany, Duisburg was not the best place to start: a
sprawling grey city of harsh streetlights, smoking chimneys, litter
and graffiti. Walking the streets around the Landscape Park, I found
myself in a land of kickboxing clubs, angry dogs on chains and
young men in tracksuits driving suspiciously expensive cars. The

horizon was lined with chimneys and the air tasted of burnt metal.

Duisburg was another city which had once grown wealthy thanks largely to its riverside location, close to the junction between the Rhine and the Ruhr. It was the site of a Roman Limes settlement known as Castrum Deutonis, and later became a member of the Hanseatic League trading club, attracting merchants from England, the Baltics and beyond. This trade brought a certain cosmopolitanism, but for much of the early nineteenth century Duisburg remained focused on trade in traditional goods: timber, fish, wax, pottery and furs.

In many ways, this made it typical of the German Rhineland at the time. By the late 1700s, Britain was already deep in the throes of the Industrial Revolution, her economy and society being transformed by innovations including the steam engine. New materials (iron and steel), new energy sources (coal and steam) and new machines (the spinning jenny and the factory line) enabled mass production. Britannia strained for new outlets for her energies, new materials and new markets. For the most part, however, this frenzied growth was confined to Britain. Keen to preserve their fearsome head start, the British did their best to ensure innovation wasn't contagious, banning the export of machinery and the emigration of skilled workers to neighbouring countries. As a result, the rest of the Continent lagged behind. The Netherlands, for example, had long been a place of refuge for innovators and scientists who had – during the famous Golden Age – made it one of the most economically and technologically advanced nations in the world. Yet as the Industrial Revolution began, instead of surging forward, the Dutch economy stalled. In the early nineteenth century the Netherlands remained a place where windmills were more common than steam engines, and horse-carts more common than railways.

Germany, meanwhile, was another late starter. Modern technologies were not completely unknown, of course, but despite its vast resources the country had singularly failed to keep pace with the modernising British economy. Foreigners often thought of Germany as decidedly behind the times. In 1798, for example, Marietta Stark wrote that for a Brit, visiting Germany was like travelling back a hundred years in time, given that 'the dresses, customs and manners of the people precisely resemble our ancestors'. When the English Queen Victoria announced her plans to marry the German Prince

Albert, her prime minister warned her that a German husband would only irritate her with his refusal to wash.

Of course, all this is not to say that nineteenth-century Germany was a poor or undeveloped place. However, well into the 1800s it remained a patchwork of kingdoms and fiefdoms, each with their own laws, regulations and tax rates. This lack of unity naturally hampered development: for a roaming merchant, even a short paddle up- or downstream could be like travelling to another country. Plenty of trade went up and down the Rhine, but large parts of the river remained relatively impoverished. A nineteenth-century traveller called Samuel Laing wrote of his surprise at 'how little industry or traffic [there is] upon its waters!' 'This ancient river Rhine flows stately and silently through vast populations . . . caring little for industry, commerce and civilisation,' he said.

In time, though, things began to change. The fragmented states of the north-west began slowly to unite, reducing barriers to trade. Tolls on river traffic were cut, dangerous rocks dynamited and some tributaries canalised, making it easier for ships to pass. In 1834 a _Zollverein_ (customs union) abolished tariffs between dozens of German states, giving a massive boost to trade. By the 1850s, a British visitor was amazed to hear that 3,000 dollars had been paid for a small patch of ground at Duisburg, on which a zinc factory was being built. 'The price paid for small lots of land would frighten an English farmer,' he gasped. Others hoped growing wealth and trade would make regional wars a thing of the past. 'The Rhine is crowded with steamboats,' an English journalist reported in 1854. 'Such communications will make war a game much more difficult to play, and . . . it will never be played again.'

Sadly, things didn't quite turn out that way. However, steam and steel-making technologies spread quickly across the Continent. As demand for steel to make bridges and boats and trains soared, German industrialists searched for places where they could find all the key ingredients for a profitable steel-based business: a readily accessible supply of iron ore, lots of cheap coal to provide energy, and big channels of water to help cool equipment and ship out heavy finished products. Water, shipping, iron and coal; the region where the Rhine met the Ruhr offered them all.

★

After a sleepless night in a hostel filled with shouty young German men, I took a local train a few miles south from the Landschaftpark to the centre of Duisburg. While waiting for the train to arrive, I mulled pretentiously over the little fence which lay between the tracks, preventing people from dangerously crossing over. In the Netherlands, I thought, there would be no fence, and people would run freely back and forth at will. In Britain, there would be no fence, and people would run freely back and forth until someone got hurt, and then there'd be an uproar in the newspapers and in parliament, and the station would have to be closed. And in Germany, there was a fence, and everyone stood patiently in their proper places on either side of it.

Compared with the glass-smooth high-speed trains I often took across Germany, the local train turned out to be an unpleasant surprise, graffiti-tagged and faded; more *CSI NY* than *Orient Express*. It moved quickly, though, and I soon reached Duisburg's Innenhafen or inner harbour, a long, canal-like strip of water branching off the Rhine, lined with old brick warehouses and factories on one side and ugly modern office buildings on the other. At the waterside, a handful of old harbour cranes were a rare relic of the industrial past, their long metal arms pointing over information boards which announced proudly that 'This was where the night sky once glowed red'. I wandered along an old train track to a 'Beach Bar' where a few young couples were drinking Fritz Cola on a patch of imported sand.

To many Germans, Duisburg was most famous as the stomping ground of Horst Schimanski, a fictional policeman who appeared in the *Tatort* TV series. I'd watched a few episodes in the past, and thought the detective was a good representative of Duisburg itself: good-hearted but a bit downtrodden, with the air of someone who'd had too many whiskies for breakfast. Others though, clearly disagreed. On previous visits to Duisburg, I'd noticed the locals took a certain spiky pride in their city's rough reputation. 'It's not perfect,' a young woman with a Duisburg tattoo on her arm once told me, 'But it's ours. And we love it!' Stopping to photograph a particularly ugly bridge, I met a friendly Japanese couple in their fifties who were excitedly doing the exact same thing. They lived in Kyoto but spoke good English and near perfect German. 'We come here every year, to eat the food and tour the region, visit some museums,' the woman explained. 'Our friends say it is mad, but we think it is wonderful!'

Such positive reviews of Duisburg would once have been common. As the German industrial revolution accelerated, the area around the confluence of the Rhine and Ruhr (known as the *Ruhrgebeit*) quickly emerged as one of the most thriving corners of Germany. In 1844 the first metalworks opened in Duisburg itself, right on the banks of the Rhine. A few years later came the coal-mines. By 1864, nearly 700 mines had been opened around the confluence of the rivers, employing about 100,000 people. By 1871, Germany was the second-biggest coal producer in the world, behind Britain but far ahead of the US, France or Belgium. Some coal from the Ruhrgebeit was exported down the Rhine to the Netherlands, where it was used to power the steam pumps which drained the Dutch polders, but much of it was used on-site to power the blazing furnaces used to manufacture steel. Duisburg's steel foundry quickly grew into the biggest on the Continent. German scientists and engineers also made great leaps forward. Ernst Siemens invented the dynamo, Karl Benz built the first practical motor car, and Rudolf Diesel patented a new type of engine. The Krupp steelworks, founded early in the nineteenth century by Frederich Krupp in Essen, grew into one of the world's most powerful companies. For those working there, the conditions could be unbearable – one old local story told of a factory worker arriving amid the flames of hell and crying '*Verdammt!* I forgot my winter coat!' However, rising incomes also meant new opportunities. By the early 1900s, once sleepy Duisburg was changing so fast that when soldiers came home on leave, they had trouble finding their homes. Like a puny teenager blossoming into an all-conquering muscleman, Germany, until recently an industrial laggard, had emerged as the dominant power in Europe.

Bored of wandering up and down the quiet Innenhafen, I took to the water. Arranging a boat tour on the phone from Arnhem, I'd been under the impression that I was signing up for what was effectively a private tour – me and perhaps one or two other curious visitors squeezed into a little dinghy, being shown around the harbours by a charming old local who knew the waterways like the back of his hand. I was therefore astonished on arriving at the designated jetty at the designated hour to find an enormous tour boat waiting for me, with about eighty jolly German pensioners offloading from coaches onto the open top deck. 'I hope they can fit us all on!' the woman queuing next to me chortled.

They did, and I found a seat at the stern, squeezed between a group of cheerful men my father's age, who were all wearing sand-coloured multipocketed waistcoats of the kind which a war photographer might wear for a day out in Mogadishu. None of them spoke more than five words of English, and I found their thick Bavarian accents very hard to understand, but we all sat happily nodding and grinning at one another and exchanging pleasantries. 'You're writing a report about the harbour?' an ash-haired man of about sixty asked me. 'Something like that, yes,' I replied. 'Leave him alone, Harald!' his friend interrupted, giving me a reassuring pat on the arm. 'Let him just write his reports.'

Luckily I'd come prepared for such interruptions, armed with a copy of the 1944 *Instructions for British Servicemen in Germany*, which my mother had given me on my last visit to England – a quirky memento of her own father, who'd served in the British army in Germany not long after the war. The book was very much a record of its time – advising troops to 'go easy on the schnapps' and explaining all Germans were raised with a 'deep-seated . . . desire to domineer over others'. 'When you meet the Germans you will probably think they are very much like us,' the book said. 'They look like us, except that there are fewer of the wiry type and more big, fleshy, fair-haired men and women, especially in the north. But they are not really like us at all . . . They have a streak of hysteria [and] you will find that Germans may often fly into a passion if some little thing goes wrong.'

Thankfully, Harald and his boat tour friends weren't too hysterical, and showed no signs of wanting to domineer over me just yet. In fact, I was already enjoying being back in Germany proper after a prolonged absence. The weather wasn't particularly welcoming, but everything was stereotypically efficient, and people were very friendly in a no-nonsense sort of way. 'You're a tourist?' an English-speaking passenger at the train station had asked. 'There's not much in Duisburg, but I hope you enjoy it!' Then, of course, there was the food, piled high in every train station bakery and convenience store: pretzels and bagels and *streusels* and doughnuts; *schnitzel* sandwiches and thick wedges of pastry coated with broken biscuits. I ate them all, and enjoyed them all, and then ate them all again. By the time I made it to the top of the Alps, I thought, I'd be able to turn around and roll back home.

The only problem with being back in Germany was the language. Living in the Netherlands, working often in Belgium and London, and spending long spells in English- and French-speaking parts of Africa, I'd got used to being able to make myself understood pretty much wherever I went. When in the Netherlands I usually spoke Dutch, but even when I didn't, a reported 90 per cent of Dutch people spoke English anyway, usually to an amazingly high standard. In Germany, though, the proportion of English speakers was far lower − 56 per cent − and it was still common to find onself in situations in big cities where no one understood a word of English. Trying to speak German didn't seem to help much − all my efforts to study flashcards and watch *Family Guy* with subtitles had apparently been in vain, and I often was forced to resort to saying Dutch words in a comedy German accent. Hideous compound words, clumsily stitched together like Frankenstein's monster, were best avoided altogether. I thought often of Mark Twain's famous essay on 'The Awful German Language', in which he critiqued the peculiarities of a language in which the rain through which a fishmonger's wife walks was referred to as 'he', the fishwife's male tomcat as 'she', and the wife herself had to be satisfied with being a mere 'it'. Thankfully, my guidebook for occupying British soldiers again offered some sound advice: 'The golden rule in trying to speak a language you do not know is to be as simple as possible. Take a two-year-old child as your model.'

The boat set off, its engines roaring loudly as we headed out of the Innenhafen towards the Rhine proper, passing through a deep concrete canyon. Near water level, the concrete docks were heavily tattooed with graffiti left by passing sailors: names and places which pointed to the strange internationalism of a harbour town: Mario, Ita, Władys and Manu; Riga, Warsaw, Omsk and Gdansk. High above us, the quayside was topped with modest factories and warehouses. It was all much more scruffy and ramshackle than the

Europoort in Rotterdam, which was like a well-oiled, heavily automated machine. Here there were no robot forklifts or artificially intelligent cranes, just tough guys with dented vans foraging in piles of greasy tools to find the right crowbar with which they could wallop a malfunctioning crane. Duisburg, it's fair to say, was not one of the most glamorous places in Europe. I sat choking on diesel fumes as a voice on the tannoy gave a detailed guide to the 1970s office buildings on the banks.

In Duisburg the good times ended abruptly with the outbreak of the First World War. In Britain and elsewhere, German industry suddenly was seen as something terrible; a producer of bullets, poison gas and even – according to popular rumour – margarine made from human corpses. Within a few years, the British royal family had changed their surname from Saxe-Coburg-Gotha to the less-Germanic-sounding Windsor, and dachshunds were being stoned to death in London on the grounds that they were 'German dogs'. Lord Northcliffe, owner of the *Daily Mail*, visited Germany and worried that 'every one of those new factory chimneys' along the Rhine and Ruhr was 'a gun pointed at England'.

During the First World War itself, the industrial heartland of the Ruhrgebiet largely escaped serious damage, but afterwards, as the victors sought reparations for the troubles they'd been caused, the region found itself firmly in the crosshairs. British Prime Minister David Lloyd George supposedly said he wanted Germany to be squeezed like a lemon, paying up 'until the pips squeak'. The harbours, mines and ironworks around Duisburg looked like a particularly juicy target. Others disagreed, but the pip-squeakers essentially got their way: under the terms of the Treaty of Versailles, Germany was ordered to turn over 60 per cent of its coal production until 1930, along with 90 per cent of its sea shipping fleet and half of all its river shipping. By the 1920s unemployment had soared, and inflation rocketed to the point where a newspaper cost 300 million marks. As tensions rose, Adolf Hitler promised to punish those who were 'responsible for the misfortunes of our nation'. 'Quite a few heads will roll,' he said.

The causes of the Second World War were many, but included the Nazis' desire to control not only the Ruhr and the Rhine, but also the rich coalfields of eastern France and Belgium. Hitler had long hectored anyone who would listen about his desire to see Germany modernised and industrialised, exhorting German youths to become '*hart wie Kruppstahl*', 'as hard as Krupp steel'. As the Rhineland became an epicentre of the conflict, many of its companies, along with German companies based elsewhere, played a key role supporting the Nazi military machine. Audi, Volkswagen, Bosch and BMW kept the Nazi war machine running smoothly, while the chemical cartel I. G. Farben established a plant at Auschwitz to take advantage of slave labour. Alfried Krupp kept a copy of *Mein Kampf* on his bedside table. Mass production and new technology enabled armies to batter one another on an unprecedented scale.

As the Allies stepped up their campaign against Hitler, the industrial importance of cities like Duisburg and Essen made them an obvious target. Bombing raids along the Rhine and Ruhr, Churchill said, offered an opportunity to 'cut Germany at its tap root'. It also helped that the region was easy to navigate. Radar wasn't widely available until late in the war, and for much of the conflict, pilots were forced to rely on paper maps, guessing their position based on hours travelled, the wind speed and the location of the stars. Cities such as Hanover, landlocked and miles from the English Channel, were relatively hard to find, but ones such as Cologne and Duisburg were easy to locate: Allied pilots could cross the Channel and then follow the moonlit Maas and Rhine right to them, as if following a well-lit footpath through a dark forest. Day after day, waves of bombers travelled along the Rhine from England, filling the skies like Hitchcock's birds. Fires swept through the cities. An American newspaper reported that British bombers 'flew so low the fliers could see by the light of the blazes they set fire engines scuttling about in the streets'. One raid even hit Alfried Krupp's palace east of the Rhine near Essen. With the water mains broken, staff were forced to put out fires using priceless bottles of Châteauneuf-de-Pape.

A suggestion from Noël Coward to bomb German rooftops with self-adhesive Union Flags was sadly rejected, and the damage done by the real bombs – including 12,000-pound behemoths known as 'small earthquake bombs' – was severe. In Duisburg, a total of 299 air raids destroyed 80 per cent of the city, leaving nearly 100,000 people homeless. As the Allied armies approached, Hitler made a terrible situation worse, ordering retreating soldiers to implement a scorched earth policy, destroying industrial works, waterways and ships. 'The enemy should find every bridge destroyed,' the Nazi newspaper *Völkische Beobachter* declared. The Rhine was blocked by hundreds of sunken barges. By the time the war ended, the once great cities of the lower Rhine were dangerously close to becoming, as George Orwell put it on a tour of the region, 'a sort of overcrowded rural slum'.

On the boat tour, we finally arrived at the Rhine itself, pulling out into the busy channel like a slow bus joining a motorway. After the confines of the Innenhafen, the river felt enormous and fresh, its banks sprinkled with muddy little beaches where children and dogs were swimming. We turned right, heading north. Desperate to escape the engine fumes and noise encircling my seat at the stern, I squeezed through the crowd to stand at the bow, where I met a German man of about seventy travelling with his wife and four other couples of a similar age. I introduced myself and he said his name was Peter, and his wife Sabine. He too was wearing a sand-coloured vest like a flak jacket, its pockets filled with maps and cameras and wallets. 'I worked for many years in Essen, in a shipping company, but I didn't go on the water much,' he told me. 'But now I've stopped working, it's a lovely day out, to come and see the habour.' He said something else which I didn't understand, and which his companions found utterly hilarious. I stood bewildered, hoping they weren't laughing at me. I opened my notebook and jotted a brief comparison with similar boat tours I'd been on in the Netherlands: 'In Germany, people laugh more.'

After another mile or so, we pulled off the main channel of the Rhine and into another harbour resembling a Rotterdam-style labyrinth of docks and canals. Even with a map in hand, I quickly lost track of where we were, but signs on the quayside suggested it was somewhere in Ruhrort – once a separate port from Duisburg, now amalgamated with it. In the distance, I could see the usual stacks of multicoloured containers, neatly piled like Lego bricks. High on one quayside, a giant Siemens wind turbine sat waiting for a ride. Around the corner was a recycling plant, with a crane lifting a massive tangle of cables from a barge. It looked like rusty spaghetti.

Compared to Rotterdam, the habours we cruised through were all pretty small – the biggest ship or crane I saw in Duisburg was perhaps a quarter of the size of the smaller ones in Rotterdam. However, there was still something impressive about it, given how far we were from the sea. As the crow flies, Duisburg lay more than 120 miles from the coast: further from the sea than Brussels, Paris or Milan. Yet thanks to the Rhine, Duisburg had the largest inland port in Europe. The small harbours were filled with cargo ships, tugs and bulkers, all jockeying for position like parents on the school run competing for parking spaces. On the riverbank roads, signs gave an indication of the true scale of the operation: turn left for dock number 3401, or right for 3590. *'Es ist wunderbar!'*, 'It's amazing!' said Peter, as I continued choking on diesel fumes and scribbling complaints in my notebook.

By time the Second World War ended, a region which had been the jewel in the German economic crown had been utterly ravaged. George Orwell, who toured the Rhineland in 1945, wrote: 'To walk through the ruined cities of Germany is to feel an actual doubt about the continuity of civilisation.' He continued: 'In the 300 miles or so between the Marne and the Rhine there is not such a thing as a bridge or a viaduct that has not been blown up.' The historian Robert Cole later put it even more succinctly: in 1945, he said, the Ruhrgebeit was 'a non-functioning pile of rubble essentially in a state of anarchy'. The Germans weren't the only ones who were suffering, of course – in the Netherlands and France the situation was also desperate. But the situation in Germany was arguably worst of all. In parts of the Ruhrgebeit, daily food rations were as low as 600 calories. 'Germans only talk about food,' wags said, 'while Americans only talk about music, culture and art. So everyone talks about what they don't have.'

Immediately after the war, the Allies' plan was to leave Duisburg and the rest of the Rhineland in ruins. The Brits, in particular, initially were keen to see heavy industry limited and nationalised, guaranteeing power-hungry industrialists could never again sponsor a war. Others simply wanted revenge. 'Why all this bosh about being gentle with the Germans after we have beaten them?' asked the British *Daily Express*, 'When ALL GERMANS ARE GUILTY.'

In time, though, the victorious Allies changed their tune. With the port of Rotterdam operating at less than half its usual capacity, the Dutch in particular were desperate to increase trade. Ignoring French fears that (as one correspondent wrote) 'to put Germany back on her feet was an invitation to have France's teeth kicked out for the third time in a lifetime', the Allies gave West Germany billions in Marshall Plan aid. Millions were spent removing debris from the Rhine and rebuilding Rotterdam. Many of those paying the bills for this work were uncomfortable about it, but as one British journalist wrote, Allied leaders ultimately decided they 'would rather have [West Germany's] citizens making money than guns'.

The West Germans themselves also transformed the way their economy was run. Under the leadership of Chancellor Konrad Adenauer, the currency was replaced and taxes slashed. To some, the policies sounded insane – the government said they'd end inflation by abolishing price controls, and end hunger by getting rid of rations. Hearing of the latest round of radical reforms, an American military commander reportedly confronted the West German economy minister Ludwig Erhard and said: '*Herr Erhard*, my advisers tell me what you have done is a terrible mistake. What do you say to that?' '*Herr General*, pay no attention to them!' an ebullient Erhard replied. 'My advisers tell me the same thing!'

Whatever the advisers thought, the strategy worked. Factories, mines and mills reopened, and within a matter of months industrial output had grown by more than fifty percent. Under a model which became known as the *Soziale Marktwirtschaft* or 'Social Market Economy', West Germans effectively split the difference between capitalism and socialism, rebuilding a dynamic free market while also investing billions in research and apprenticeships. Staff were trained intensively and developed a deep sense of loyalty to their employers, with whom they often stayed for a lifetime. Many firms were family owned, unions were consulted by managers on major decisions, and it was made harder to outsource production abroad. This philosophy would endure for decades, well after free-market doctrines became ascendant in Britain and America. 'The hire-and-fire principle does not exist here,' the chief executive of Siemens once said, 'and I never want it to.'

Some industrial facilities and companies were dismantled – the murderous I. G. Farben, for example, was broken up and several of its leaders convicted of war crimes. However, many got away lightly. Alfried Krupp was jailed for a while but then released, and quickly resumed his position as one of Europe's most powerful industrialists. West Germans were encouraged to produce as much as possible and export it far and wide. German car makers, in particular, became household names everywhere from Shanghai to Santa Fe. One car which Hitler had ordered, and which the Brits and Americans were convinced was worthless – the VW Beetle – became a phenomenal bestseller, with its cuddly, lovable image doing much to transform foreign perceptions of bloodstained West German industry. Within a few years of the war ending, West Germany's exports had trebled. For every new house which the French built, the Germans built eight. West Germany still faced some serious problems, but in towns like Duisburg, unemployment fell to almost zero. In 1948 a *New Yorker* correspondent who visited the Rhineland saw only 'smokeless chimneys rising above the twisted girders of silent factories'. Six years later the same reporter saw the wreckage had been replaced by 'blast furnaces and rolling mills . . . miles and miles of new one-family and two-family houses [belonging to] the best-housed workers in Europe'. Soon, West Germany's post-war economy was given a new nickname: the *Wirtschaftwunder* or 'economic miracle', also known as 'the miracle on the Rhine'.

In later years, a great deal of mythology sprang up around the *Wirtschaftwunder*. Like daydreamers reading a horoscope, people tended to see in the German story whatever they wanted to see. For those on the right of the political spectrum it offered proof that free-market policies could generate terrific growth, while for those on the left it proved that grand spending schemes like the Marshall Plan could lift people out of poverty. Outside Germany, the German economic model was often unthinkingly venerated by right-wingers the same way left-wingers unthinkingly venerated the Dutch social model, without actually knowing much about it. When I worked in politics in Britain, I soon learned that the best way to get a hearing for any industrial policy idea, however ill-conceived, was to say it was based on something already being done in Germany.

For many post-war Germans, though, there was only one reason they were rich, and it certainly wasn't a lucky 'miracle'. One steel-maker claimed: 'Marshall had nothing to do with it. This was a German miracle. We got back on our feet because we worked hard.' That was an overstatement, but there was little doubt that, in a country that was generally nervous about anything which smacked of patriotism, economic success was an unrivalled source of pride. As Herfried Münkler wrote, the logos of Volkswagen and Mercedes had replaced the Iron Cross as symbols of German patriotism, and Audi's famous slogan *Vorsprung Durch Technik* – 'Progress through technology' – had become a motto not just for that company, but for the whole country. German leaders tried to reshape Mediterranean economies on their own export-driven model, and German people took pride in their own efficiency. 'Why are Americans always boasting they work 60 hours a week, when we manage to get things done in 40?' a Duisburger once asked me.

The boat tour ended, and I walked back along the Innenhafen towards the train station. I was trying to be optimistic about Duisburg's future, but it was hard. The harbour may have been impressive in a low-key way, but the rest of the city was suspiciously quiet. Early on a Wednesday afternoon, there seemed to be perhaps ten people within a mile of me, and many of the modern offices were clearly empty. The city wasn't unpleasant, but it clearly wasn't thriving.

In Duisburg and elsewhere, the *Wirtschaftwunder* couldn't last forever. The decline of coal and steel businesses in the Rhine–Ruhr region had been precipitous, once mighty industries sinking as fast as a lump of iron ore tossed into a polluted river. The reasons for the decline were hotly debated, but it was essentially a familiar story: too much competition from abroad, and too little support at home. As steel production slumped, more than half a million miners were put out of work, and the Ruhrgebiet went from being one of the world's biggest coal producers to one of its biggest coal importers. In a globalised economy, Rhineland coal and steel was surplus to requirements.

From an economic perspective, all this may have been perfectly necessary and efficient. In cities such as Duisburg, however, mass lay-offs had a devastating social impact. Between the early 1960s and the mid 1980s, nearly a hundred and fifty thousand people left Duisburg in search of jobs elsewhere. A range of public and charitable schemes – ABIs and URPs; SCPs and UNSNRPs – were launched with bold promises of rehabilitating the job market, but had limited success in the face of the unstoppable juggernaut of globalisation. Ironically, some of the very industries which had helped spur European integration had become some of the first to collapse under the competitive pressures of a globalised world.

Germany being Germany, Duisburg wasn't really poor, of course. Parts of the city had been colonised by banks and insurance companies, and riverside car parks were full of gleaming Audis and BMWs. The Innenhafen had a lovely modern art gallery and a decent museum. Compared to deprived inner cities elsewhere, it looked like Disneyland. But there were also the unmistakable signs of low-level poverty. In the Netherlands, it was relatively rare to see homeless people, but in Duisburg I counted four inside the train station, and another five just outside. Statistically, Duisburg, along with its near neighbours Dortmund and Essen, was one of most impoverished places in Germany, and the unemployment rate (12 per cent) was more than double the average for Germany. For me, with a day job which often took me to desperately poor corners of the world, it served as a reminder that poverty was sometimes in the eye of the beholder, and could be relative: in a country where the average person earned more than €40,000, someone who earned €25,000 might feel like a pauper.

Predictably, as jobs had dried up, so Duisburg had also suffered ethnic tensions, with a large population of unemployed Germans sitting uneasily alongside a large population of (mostly Turkish) immigrants. Support for the centre-left Social Democrats, who'd long seen the Ruhrgebiet as an unassailable electoral stronghold, was collapsing. In 2015 an alarmist police report, leaked to the German press, claimed Duisburg included many 'areas of lawlessness' which were becoming de facto no-go zones for police. The city, one right-wing website claimed, was 'a volatile ethno-religious cauldron'.

Even to a grump like me, that sounded absurd. Yet it was also helpful to be reminded that the story of the German economic miracle was exactly that – a story, which included a large element of truth but also an element of myth-making. The British politicians whom I'd once worked for, for example, often seemed to forget that for much of the 1990s, the country whose economy they now venerated was seen as a place of excessive regulation and high unemployment; 'the sick man of Europe'. Things had improved markedly since then, but not for everyone: in 2017, the lowest-paid 40 per cent of German workers earned less in real terms than they did in 1997.

There were also good reasons why, looking at a place like Duisburg, a German finance minister might still find reasons to be nervous about the future. The challenges were partly political. Germany had long thrived in a world system based on free trade and mutual defence, but those principles were now being called into question. Donald Trump had horrified EU leaders by telling them that the Germans were 'bad, very bad' for selling too many cars in America, and repeatedly threatened to slap hefty taxes on cars imported from Germany. Brexit was another worry: the Germans sold more cars to Britain than they did to any other country, along with billions of euros worth of other products, thanks to the single market and customs union. There were also technical worries: despite setting ambitious targets for modernisation and innovation, German manufacturers were struggling to keep pace with foreign upstarts like Tesla, and lagged behind Silicon Valley in IT innovations. Car makers like Volkswagen were racing to increase their production of electric cars, but had to use batteries imported from suppliers in China. In a telling sign of change, in 2018 the Chinese car maker Geely bought a significant stake in Daimler, the parent company of Mercedes-Benz and (in the past, at least) a great symbol of German industrial prowess.

Perhaps even more worryingly, there were signs Germany might have been contaminated by the same kind of corruption (or at least sloppiness) which had afflicted other countries. Germans had long prided themselves on their decency and work ethic, but lately scandals at firms such as Volkswagen had begun to make those values look like a superficial lacquer prettying an otherwise inferior auto. Deutsche Bank had been accused of a startling array of financial misdemeanours, and Lufthansa had been undercut by budget rivals and crippled by strikes. Energy giants E.On and RWE were struggling, and Bosch was accused of helping VW cheat its customers. Several regional *Ländesbanken* had borrowed and lent recklessly, and quickly came unstuck when global financial markets imploded. For decades, the success of Germany – and of the Rhine–Ruhr region in particular – had depended on a widespread belief that German products embodied certain unshakable values: trustworthiness, discipline and precision. Now, though, those values looked like a thing of the past. As *Deutsche Welle* pointed out, the 'Made in Germany' brand had long been one of the country's most valuable assets, but now it sometimes seemed like a liability.

Most indicators suggested that the German economy was still in excellent health. However, as I wandered around the scruffy fringes of Duisburg, it occurred to me that a German industrialist might look nervously at the example of Japan. In many ways, the two countries' trajectories were strikingly similar. The Japanese, too, had seen their industries devastated by war and their moral authority shot to pieces, but then thrived as a high-tech exporter under the protection of an American military umbrella. Japanese GDP soared, and by 1991 many economists were predicting that Japan would overtake the United States as the world's largest economy by 2010. At one point, the grounds of the Imperial Palace in Tokyo were believed to be worth more than the entire state of California. Where Germany had its *Wirtschaftwunder*, Japan had its 'miracle economy'. But then the bubble burst. High-tech manufacturers elsewhere in Asia began to undercut the Japanese, and after years of rapid growth, the Japanese economy pitched into a vicious spiral of falling prices, job cuts, tightened purse strings, rising debts and insolvencies. In the space of few years, Japan went – as one journalist put it – 'from an economic Godzilla to little more than an afterthought in the global economy'.

The analogy between the countries obviously had its limits, and the fundamentals of the German economy looked strong. However, as I travelled around, watching the German car industry stumble and the banking system fray, it was easy to feel a little nervous that the Germans had had it too good for too long. If they lost their niche as high-end manufacturers, what would they do instead? And were recent troubles a minor blip or a sign of more endemic crisis? It was unlikely the economy would implode any time soon, but as a scholar once said, all revolutions seem impossible before they happen, but in retrospect they all seem inevitable. Walking back to the train station, I passed a north African-looking man shouting in English on the phone to someone: 'I was told come to Duisburg for job and house. But there's nothing here! No jobs! No factories! Only paperwork. It is place of devils!'

Leaving Duisburg, I continued my journey southwards, following the river about 25 miles to Düsseldorf. Several days in Duisburg had left me in a pensive mood, and I hoped my next stop might offer a welcome corrective: proof that Rhine cities could not only survive the slow fizzling of the *Wirtschaftwunder* but thrive. I'd been to Düsseldorf many times before, and always found it a bustling, attractive place that stood out from the surrounding industrial landscape like a supermodel in a supermarket.

I checked into a scruffy hotel in the centre and walked down to the riverside. A wide promenade was bustling with tourists and locals, cyclists and runners and businesspeople walking home. As in Rotterdam, the river felt busy and energetic; a natural focus for city life rather than an outdated water feature. The most prominent landmark was the Rhine Tower, the most popular annual event was the Rhenish Carnival, and the local paper was the *Rheinische Post*. Throughout the city, little signs were forever pointing the way back to the river, as if locals might get nervous if they ever strayed too far from it.

On a bad day, it would be easy to mock Düsseldorf for its globalist pretensions. Signs of affluence were everywhere: expensive cars, well-dressed people and shiny modern buildings. The Konigsallee (known as 'the Ko' to those in the know) felt like an even glitzier version of the Champs Elysée or Regent Street, with its brightly lit Louis Vuitton and Dior stores, and sharp-suited doormen keeping scruffs like me at bay. When I stopped to take a photo of one particularly fancy perfume store, a doorman shooed me away as if I was a dirty pigeon. After Duisburg, where dirty pigeons had outnumbered tourists, it all felt very odd. In other ways, though, the city served as a useful corrective to all the gloomy stories of decline I'd been hearing to the north. Although some heavy industries had collapsed, the Rhineland's economy was strong, and the car industry in particular remained a terrific success story, claiming to employ more than 200,000 people in North Rhine-Westphalia alone. Foreign fetishisation of the German economy sometimes went too far, but exports remained robust, debts relatively low and public finances healthy. In places like Düsseldorf, most economic indicators were at levels which a Greek or Portuguese finance minister would happily sell their grandmother to attain.

The sun came out and I walked south along the riverbank, almost jogging to keep up with a long train of barges. Passing under a massive bridge, I arrived at the MedienHafen or 'Media Harbour', a large harbour tucked in off the east side of the Rhine, nearly a kilometre long and as wide as a couple of football pitches. Old photos I'd seen had shown the area as a hive of heavy industry, but now the murky water was hemmed in not by warehouses and cranes but by daringly designed modern blocks which looked like the architects had been smoking something. One building was covered in giant plastic figurines, climbing and tumbling over the walls like a real-life Keith Haring painting. Others offered breezy open-plan offices for companies successful and aspirational: Nespresso, Regus, Bain. Where there must once have been burly stevedores lugging boxes, there were now Japanese and Mexican restaurants, a Levi's store and shops where the gullible could buy coffee tables which cost more than my car. A woman walked by with a ratlike Chihuahua on a bejewelled leash, teetering on heels which were high enough for the dog to run under.

The unrivalled centrepiece of the MedienHafen stood not far from the mouth of the harbour: the Neue Zollhof, a triptych of modern buildings designed by Frank Gehry. The three towers were similar in shape, but each was finished in a different cladding: one, white plaster; one, red brick; and one, shiny metal. The metal-jacketed one was truly eye-catching, a rippled wall of polished aluminium, studded with small windows and undulating like a mirrored shower curtain. I joined a small throng of tourists in front of it, and spent a happy few minutes taking photos of my reflection in the wall, warped as if in a funhouse mirror. I thought the building looked familiar and eavesdropping on two tubby Americans with a guidebook, I realised why – Frank Gehry had built a very similar building in Manhattan, close to the offices of an NGO I sometimes worked for. 'This Gerry guy made practically the exact same thing for two different clients!' the indignant guidebook reader exclaimed. 'Nice work if you can get it!'

The light was failing by now, and I resolved to stop being grumpy and do something fun. I followed the edge of the MedienHafen back to the main channel of the river, where a pair of hardy kayakers were bracing themselves to cross the water. I wished briefly I could join them, but opted instead for a less adventurous final stop: the riverside Rhine Tower, a local landmark which was unavoidable for someone writing a book about the river.

The tower (my guidebook said) had been built in 1981, primarily as a radio and television transmitter but also as a tourist attraction; it was a rocket-like concrete cylinder symbolising the rebirth of Düsseldorf. After paying an exorbitant entry fee, I rode 170 metres up in an elevator, accompanied by an attendant who had the doughy unhappiness of someone who had spent all day in an elevator. Eager to break the awkward silence, I asked him whether the view at the top was good. 'Yes, it's very good!' he said. 'On a clear day, you can see Essen!'

At the top, the view was indeed very good. I saw Essen. I also saw Duisburg, smoking heavily in the distance. In the other direction lay Cologne, about twenty-five miles to the south, glowing on the horizon like a forest fire. And between it all was the Rhine, glassy blue-black in the fuzzy evening light, winding its way through a carpet of busy streets, factories, hospitals, universities, warehouses and harbours. From above, one could clearly see how the river had shaped its surrounding towns and cities, which bulged from the channel like big beads on a thread. The harbours looked full and the promenades were crowded. I took a seat with a dizzying view and ordered an Irish coffee, realising a second too late that Irish coffee was the world's second most expensive liquid, after printer ink. Down below, streetlights flickered on along the riverside, and the barges set bright searchlights sweeping across the choppy waters. The sun dipped behind the Düsseldorf skyline, and I watched as the bend in the Rhine below me first darkened, and then glowed back to life.

6

God, Gays, Grapes and Grain
Cologne

A MAN IN a leather catsuit crawled down the middle of the road, while another wearing a muzzle and leash howled across the water at the twin-towered cathedral. Hours before Cologne's Gay Pride parade even started, the Deutzer Bridge over the Rhine was packed with thousands of people, many of them in various states of undress. Within moments of arriving, I'd been sprayed with champagne by a man in lederhosen, kissed by an elderly lady in a sailor's outfit, and hugged by a bearded man in a ball-gown. 'I haven't seen so many harnesses since I gave up horse-riding,' a passer-by said.

Cologne's Pride parade (also known as Christopher Street Day) had long been a major fixture of the Rhineland summer, attracting tens of thousands of people to drink and dance, protest and celebrate. This year, the mood was perhaps even livelier than usual. Just ten days before, the German parliament had voted to legalise gay marriage, and the mood in Cologne was celebratory. '*Danke!*' said the sign held by a man in hot pants and a cowboy hat.

Across Europe, gay rights had taken huge strides forwards in recent years. The Netherlands voted to legalise gay marriage in 2001, and was soon followed by a host of imitators. There were still serious problems with discrimination in some places, and countries where homosexual and transgender people were treated appallingly, but in many others the political turnaround had been remarkable. In Britain, for example, it had become almost as unacceptable for politicians on the conservative right to oppose gay marriage as it was for them to admire Fidel Castro. However, there were still some places in Europe where old attitudes and policies prevailed. Curiously, the Rhine, for much of its length served as a very rough boundary between pro- and anti-gay marriage countries.

To the west of the river, France, Belgium, the Netherlands, Luxembourg, Spain, Portugal and Britain all allowed full marriage. But to the south and east, Switzerland, Austria, Italy and Liechtenstein all had more restrictive rules, typically allowing same-sex 'registered partnerships', but not full marriage.* In Germany, gay couples could enter into a form of civil partnership but same-sex marriages remained (until the vote just before the parade) illegal, and it was impossible for a same-sex couple to jointly adopt a child. For a country which had worked hard to position itself as a moral leader, it seemed a jarring anomaly.

The reasons for this anomaly were partly a matter of simple politics. In the months leading up to the parade in Cologne, Chancellor Angela Merkel had been hailed as a hero by much of the European left for her strong stance in favour of refugees' rights. However, she remained at heart a pro-business conservative who depended on right-wing allies to remain in power, and who believed (as she once said) that 'man and wife, marriage and family, stand at the centre of our social model'. Another factor was religion. Among outsiders, there often was an assumption that Germany was largely a secular country. 'Germans are too busy making money to bother with all that churchy stuff,' one British friend said to me. The reality, though, was that the country was still strikingly religious: in 2010, 44 per cent of Germans said they believed 'there is a God', compared to 27 per cent of French people and 28 per cent of Dutch. Along the Rhine in particular, religion remained a powerful force in both politics and daily life.

In the sixteenth century, after the Reformation split Christianity between Catholics and Protestants, the general rule was that people living in a territory would usually follow whichever religion happened to be favoured by that area's ruler. Following this rule, the north and east of present-day Germany became mostly Protestant, while the south and west, along with the southern Netherlands, tended Catholic. Cologne in particular emerged as a major Catholic centre. In recent years, religious sentiment had been diluted by rising tides of immigration and atheism, but the Rhine

* After I finished my journey along the Rhine, the Austrian Constitutional Court ruled that same-sex couples should be allowed to marry by 2019.

region remained a relative stronghold of the Catholic faith. According to official statistics, in the eastern half of Germany 62 per cent of people said they didn't believe in 'any sort of spirit, God or life force', while in the Rhenish west only 17 per cent did. In each of the western ecclesiastical areas through which the Rhine flowed, between a third and two-thirds of population identified as Catholic, while in the north-east the equivalent figure was more like a twentieth. Travelling and working in the region, I often was surprised at the extent to which religion in general, and Catholicism in particular, remained a potent political force. Most people seemed intensely relaxed about Merkel (the daughter of a Protestant pastor) saying her faith was a 'constant companion', or that Germany's problem was not that it had 'too much Islam', but that it had 'too little Christianity'. The churches still played a significant role in German civic life, and were funded partly by special taxes collected by the government from everyone who was registered as belonging to a religion, regardless of whether they ever actually went to church. Like the Dutch, many Germans were still quietly but profoundly conservative in their attitudes to '*Kinder, küche, kirche*' ('children, kitchen, church'). However, the dividing lines weren't always clear. Politically, much of the Rhineland and the Ruhrgebiet often tilted leftwards rather than rightwards, and places like Cologne often seemed to exist in a state of constant, slightly uneasy balance. On the one hand they were open and cosmopolitan places where great fortunes had been made through international trade and cultural exchange; but viewed from another perspective, they were inherently quite conformist. Even Rhinelanders who weren't religious or didn't vote for Merkel's party often seemed quite traditional in their outlook, frowning on informality and eschewing debt or drama. 'We enjoy ourselves,' an acquaintance in Cologne once explained, 'but it only goes so far. Work hard, be careful with your money, get married and have children – that's what everyone really expects.' 'We're mostly Catholics here,' said another. 'We like to have fun, but then we feel bad about it afterwards.' There were also plenty of Protestants in the Rhineland, of course, but compared with places like Berlin, atheists often appeared to be in short supply. Travelling along the river, I was often reminded of an old joke from Northern Ireland, about the visitor who asked: 'Aren't there any atheists around here?' 'Yes,' came the reply, 'there are Protestant atheists and Catholic atheists.'

The odd tension between the German Rhineland's liberal, internationalist instincts and its less tolerant, more conservative ones was nowhere more evident than in Cologne, a city which was almost as famous for its boozy beer culture as it was for its towering cathedral. Today, though, it was clear which side in the culture war had the upper hand. Watching the Gay Pride parade pass by, my notebook quickly filled with a list of observations which could have been designed to disprove foreign clichés about Germany as a staid, humourless place: heavily tattooed older woman in a Wonder Woman costume; shaven-headed lady with no top on carrying a sign which offered 'Free Kisses'; man wearing nothing but a napkin-sized piece of cloth hanging from a string around his waist. A policeman in a 'Stop Homofobia' badge hugged a drag queen, and an elderly man and his wife proudly embraced their rainbow-shirted son and his boyfriend.

The event was, I belatedly realised, a celebration of pride not only for those whose sexuality didn't fit into a single catch-all category, but for many others who didn't feel quite accepted by society, and relished the opportunity to be who they were. 'I'm not weird' read the T-shirt worn by one awkward teenage girl, 'I'm limited edition'. I remembered the famous post-war photos of Cologne's ruined, broken-backed bridges collapsed into the Rhine, and thought – cheesily but truthfully – how wonderful it was that a place once so scarred by hatred could now be so filled with love and joy.

Leaving the parade, I walked down a spiral staircase from the bridge to the riverside, heading towards the city centre. From below, the procession of trucks and dancers was almost invisible, but the riverbanks echoed with the sound of Madonna and Macklemore. Inland, the small squares and narrow streets were filled with temporary bars and cocktail booths, food vans and stages playing live music. It felt a lot like Dutch King's Day, only with less orange and more rainbows. On one corner, a stall was doing a roaring trade in rainbow-striped flags, hats, neckties, T-shirts earrings, braces and sunglasses. A delighted-looking young German man bought one of everything and then stood by the roadside donning it all, swiftly converting himself into a walking set of traffic lights. A little further on, a stall offered spray-on temporary tattoos of the noted gay rights icon Mao Zedong. Further still, a small crowd had gathered to peruse a display of T-shirts for sale, each decorated with a different eye-catching slogan: 'Rubber', 'Leather', 'Woof'.

Cologne, like many German cities, was simultaneously beautiful and a little brutalist in style. In most Dutch cities, architecture was strictly segregated, with the historic cores kept completely unspoiled, and modern buildings confined to the fringes. German cities, though, were more like British ones – a jumbled patchwork of ancient beauty and post-war ugliness, with ancient cathedrals sitting incongruously close to gleaming fast-food outlets, and seventeenth-century townhouses sharing walls with hideous modern supermarkets.

Reading an American newspaper, I'd recently been assured Cologne was 'the most underrated city in Germany', but that didn't really seem to be the case. Lying close to borders with the Netherlands, France and Belgium, it wasn't exactly off the beaten track. The scenic riverbank was awash with postcard stands, tour groups and people hawking tickets for river cruises. Walking towards the cathedral, I passed a gaggle of tipsy thirty-something Englishwomen on a hen weekend, all wearing purple party hats and shiny makeup, drinking wine from paper cups and preparing to rampage through the city like glittery Visigoths or Vandals. 'Let's f***ing do this!' the pink-wigged ringleader cackled. Nearby, a big group of teenage punks in ripped denim jackets and mohawks stood loudly asserting their individuality by all dressing exactly the same.

It was, of course, the Romans who officially founded Cologne, building a fortified settlement here in about 38 BC and later giving it the catchy name of Colonia Claudia Ara Agrippinensium in honour of the emperor's wife Julia Agrippina. The settlement was easily reached by quite large ships, and a medieval visitor could have seen Italian merchants arriving with cargoes of oil and silk, Ottoman traders loading figs and raisins onto Rhine barges, and boats arriving from the north filled with herrings, furs and wools. Like a buttercup in the polder, the city bloomed. 'How glorious is this city!' the Italian poet Petrarch wrote in 1333. 'What a wonder to find such a spot in a barbarous land!' Later, it was damaged badly by conflict, but continued to thrill travellers arriving from the north. In 1839, a visitor called Joseph Snow described the river here as 'the centre of European civilisation'. Some others, though, disagreed. The libertine Casanova thought it an 'odious town', perhaps because he'd been frustrated in his efforts to have his wicked way with a young lady in a carriage bumping over the cobbled streets. 'We did all we could,' he wrote sadly in his journal, 'but that was almost nothing.'

Like many cities in the Rhineland, Cologne was damaged badly in the Second World War. Visiting in the spring of 1945, the writer Heinrich Böll saw people hiding under the ruins, in deep cellars left from Roman times. 'Cologne-on-the-Rhine is a model of destruction,' another visitor wrote in 1945: 'Recumbent, without beauty, shapeless in the rubble.' Soon, though, came a stunning resurrection. The river brought trade and tourists again. Within a generation, it was known again as a lively, prosperous place, with Christmas markets, a handful of good museums and – predictably – a fashion-friendly reconditioned river harbour, the Rheinauhafen, filled with the kind of people who used *FaceTime* as a verb and wore sunglasses indoors.

Continuing away from the river, I walked up through crowded, music-filled streets towards the mighty *Dom* (cathedral), pausing to pick up a takeaway *flammkuchen* – a kind of albino pizza apparently invented by someone who thought ordinary pizzas just weren't unhealthy enough, and would benefit from the addition of bacon and cream. Things were much quieter here than near the bridge, but the usual Gay Pride clichés were easy to find – drag queens in stratospheric heels, men in thongs, awkward teenagers trying to look relaxed. As I guzzled my creamy pizza, a passing woman in a 'Smile If You Feel Gay' T-shirt gave me a high-five.

Sadly, Cologne's reputation as a tolerant city had taken a serious battering in recent years, thanks to two terrible events which took place in late 2015. First, in October, a politician called Henriette Reker, who was running for Mayor of Cologne, was stabbed in the neck by a man opposed to her work with refugees. Then, a couple of months later, scores of women were sexually assaulted outside the cathedral on New Year's Eve. Reporting of the incident was often wildly inaccurate, but it was indisputable that crowds of young men, invariably described as 'North African or Arab in appearance', had attacked women who had gathered in the city's main square to celebrate the arrival of the new year. Police reportedly did little to stop the attackers, and even released a statement the following day saying Cologne's festivities had had a 'jolly atmosphere'. Initial reports suggested around 100 women had been attacked, in Cologne and elsewhere, but leaked police documents later suggested the true figure was more like 1,200. Several women were raped.

Months later, many of the details remained unclear, and only a handful of attackers had been convicted. Cologne's police chief had been sacked, and Henriette Reker – who'd survived the stabbing and been elected mayor while in hospital – was heavily criticised for issuing guidance implying women might be to blame if they failed to 'prepare' for the possibility that men might not be able to keep their hands to themselves. Angela Merkel's liberal policies towards refugees and immigrants – which saw an astonishing 1.4 million people apply for asylum in Germany between 2014 and 2017 – came under heavy fire. In the state of North Rhine-Westphalia, where Cologne stood, more asylum seekers were registered than in any other state, and the political reaction was predictably intense. Mainstream parties like the leftish SPD struggled to produce a coherent response, and support for right-wing parties like the AfD (Alternative for Germany) soared. Far-right politicians and bloggers had a field day. 'Cologne, a city where women can't walk safely on the streets,' the far-right website Breitbart called it. In the wake of the assaults, there were hundreds of attacks on refugee centres, sales of handguns spiked and German retailers reportedly sold out of anti-rape underpants. 'Yes, you should help refugees. But enough is enough,' one Cologne woman told the international news agency AFP: 'German culture is slowly disappearing.' The stickers I saw stuck on lamp posts all over Cologne were even blunter: 'Rapefugees not welcome'. I stopped to take a photo of one and right on cue, two women walked past me wearing burqas, completely cloaked in black apart from small letterboxes around their eyes. I nodded a greeting just as an elderly white man stopped to berate them. I couldn't quite keep up with his German, but he was obviously no fan of the Prophet's teachings, and made as if to grab at one of the women's coverings. The women, however, were clearly used to such things, and ignored him, continuing untroubled on their way. A few yards further down the street, a white German man who looked like a potato was shouting at his wife the way I shouted at my dog when she stole my socks. In Cologne, as elsewhere, the balance between tolerance and intolerance was clearly a delicate one.

Although I had other things I wanted to do, a quick visit to the *Dom* seemed unavoidable. Cologne's cathedral was the largest of its kind in Germany, and had helped cement the city's status as a religious centre. The cathedral had at one point been the tallest building in Europe, and still dominated the city centre and riverbank; a blackened heap of Gothic spires looking like a wax model of London's Houses of Parliament which had partially melted in the sun. I remembered visiting the *Dom* for the first time as a not-very-well-travelled nineteen-year-old and being astonished by the scale of it, and the fact that it dated from a time when producing a single square block of stone might take weeks of toil with a hammer and chisel. Today, well over a decade after my first visit, it still had a similar power to enthral. 'Goddamn that's a big-ass church!' hollered a Canadian in a baseball cap.

Construction of the cathedral had begun in the mid thirteenth century, but (as is often the case) the builders' initial enthusiasm proved bigger than their ability to finish the job. The building was the Berlin airport of its day, languishing half finished for centuries. In the 1880s, though, it was finally completed, an impressive 630 odd years after construction began. In a part of the world packed with grand religious buildings, it quickly became known as one of the grandest religious buildings of all, attracting visitors from across the Continent, including thousands who arrived by steamship along the Rhine. The building miraculously survived the Second World War almost unscathed, and was now the undisputed highlight of Cologne's skyline, looming over the city's inhabitants like a matriarch keeping a stern eye on her children.

Inside, it was stunning, of course. I'd been in dozens, perhaps even hundreds of big churches and cathedrals across Europe in recent years, but this was undoubtedly one of the most impressive. A forest of slender stone pillars held up an astonishingly high ceiling, surrounded by dozens of delicate stained-glass windows. At one end, a mighty organ stood propped against a wall, like a piece of heavy artillery, its dozens of long barrels pointed straight at the heavens. I marvelled again at the scale of it all, and rummaged in my notebook for a quote I'd copied down from the great Rhine poet Heinrich Heine: 'In those days, people had convictions. We moderns have only opinions, and it requires something more than opinions to build a Gothic cathedral.' On a weekday morning, it was packed with people – Japanese tour groups, Dutch holiday-makers, American backpackers, British weekenders – all raising their hands high and worshipping the camera functions on their smart-phones. Behind me, a middle-aged Dutch couple walked in the door and shouted with wonder the same words which a Dutch speaker can hear shouted at every beauty spot from Niagara Falls to the plains of the Serengeti: '*Wat mooi!*', 'How beautiful!' They were swiftly interrupted by a long parade of Italian sightseers who barged past in matching yellow hats, like McDonald's employees on a fire drill. A pair of Spanish backpackers waddled past with enormous round bags strapped tortoise-like to their backs. Then came a fat German couple, pushing rudely past me and stepping heavily on my toes. I began to think Brexit might not be such a bad idea after all.

Cologne wasn't always famed for its beauty. Early travellers' accounts of journeys along the Rhine were often notable for the complaints about the smell of Cologne. Samuel Taylor Coleridge, for example, wrote a grumpy little poem about how disappointed he was with the 'body-and-soul-stinking town'.

> The River Rhine, it is well known,
> Doth wash your city of Cologne;
> But tell me, Nymphs! What power divine,
> Shall henceforth wash the river Rhine?

In that context, there was something odd (or perhaps appropriate) about the fact that in modern times, Cologne's name had become synonymous with things which smelled nice. The fragrance in question was the brainchild of one Giovanni Maria Farina, an Italian who moved to Cologne in the early 1700s, changed his name to Johann and took a job with a family firm shipping goods up and down the Rhine. Impressed by the odour of the oils and fruit essences imported upriver from the Mediterranean, Farina opened a perfume factory, and named his most promising fragrance after his new home city on the river: 'Eau de Cologne'. Some of the ingredients he relied on were a little dubious – jasmine petals kneaded into pig fat – but the overall effect was refreshingly spritzy. Farina wrote to his brother that his product reminded him 'of a spring morning in Italy, of mountain narcissus, orange blossom just after the rain'. At a time when most rival fragrances were made with heavy natural stinks such as musk rat or musk ox, Farina's light, citrus-based scents proved hugely popular, attracting (if local legend was to be believed) the attention of customers including Napoleon, Goethe, Beethoven and a bevy of passing emperors, tsars and kings. Later, they were exported worldwide, often carried on cargo ships down the river. 'At last,' Voltaire declared upon smelling it, 'a fragrance that inspires the spirit!' Browsing the glitzy shops outside the cathedral, I thought about buying some, but when I saw the prices, decided I'd rather buy a private island instead.

Back near the bridge, the celebrations of Cologne's diversity were still in full flow, and the waterfront echoed with the sound of far-off whistles, dance music and cheering. I, however, had a far more important element of Rhineland culture to attend to: beer.

The pub I walked into turned out to be a classic of the genre, with all the ingredients of a German beerhall of cliché: heavy wooden chairs and beer-stained tables, dark wood-panelled walls, iron chandeliers, paintings of hunters and horsemen, and raucous, table-thumping laughter. The waiter who greeted me was burly and bald and moustachioed, and could easily have been cast as a German waiter in a Hollywood B-movie. A hundred or so patrons all looked to be having the time of their lives, and I thought again how strange it was that the rest of the world still insisted on thinking of Germans as joyless automatons who didn't know how to have fun. The misunderstanding arose, I think, simply because of how the Germans divided the worlds of work and leisure. In Britain, even formal meetings were punctuated by a steady flow of so-called 'banter' and quick wit. In Germany, though, such crossing of boundaries would be unthinkable. Relationships with work colleagues were kept formal, and personal relationships were binary, with people classified as either a good friend or mild acquaintance, with no other options in between. '*Dienst ist dienst und Schnaps is Schnaps,*' they said, 'Work is work and drink is drink,' and never the twain shall meet. This meant anyone who met Germans only at work would inevitably think they were all efficient robots, when the reality was that they were just as cheerful as everyone else. The beerhall in Cologne was, at lunchtime, no less lively or witty than a British pub on a Friday night, and jollier than any sedate Dutch café.

Like many beerhalls, this one had a simple system for ordering drinks: you didn't order them at all. Waiters paced around the room constantly, and whenever one of them saw an empty glass on a table they'd immediately swoop in and replace it with a full one, scrawling a thick black pencil mark on the customer's beermat to keep track of how many they'd had. There was no drinks menu to speak of – everyone automatically was served the same local *Kolsch* beer, meaning the whole experience had an air of surrendering to the uncontrollable. Thankfully, the beer turned out to be very good indeed; light and sweet, like an Australian lager, but nice. I ordered something which I didn't understand from the menu and it arrived almost immediately: a giant curved dam of white sausage, holding back a mountain of fried potatoes and red cabbage. Dutch cuisine suddenly looked featherweight in comparison. I sat and ate, and drank, and drank, and drank, and black marks accumulated on the beermat like bars on a prison window.

Outside Germany, the country's fondness for beer is often treated as little more than a crude cultural stereotype; the moustachioed beer-drinker or pigtailed barmaid acting as the local equivalent of a cowboy for the US, a stoned liberal for the Dutch, or a top-hatted gentleman for the English. However, there was little doubt that beer formed one of the soggy bedrocks of Rhineland culture, and I was glad of an excuse to learn more about it. 'You're a Brit writing a book about Germany,' one German friend said. 'So I guess there'll be a big section about beer?' Yes, I replied, there will indeed.

The German love of beer may often have been exaggerated, but it was also very real. In one legal case at the European Court in Luxembourg, lawyers for the German government even argued beer wasn't simply a drink consumed for pleasure, but a key component of a balanced diet. Beer was sold in vending machines in railway stations and shopping malls, served in the cafeterias of corporate headquarters, and – according to brewer and historian Horst Dorbusch – 'many German physicians counsel expectant mothers to have a moderate amount of brew every day'. On average, Germans drank roughly 50 per cent more beer in a year than the British, Belgians or Dutch. Reading the figures, I thought it was a miracle the Germans managed to get out of bed at all, let alone run one of the world's most productive economies.

These days, German beer is often associated in the foreign mind with Munich or Bavaria – home to many well-known breweries and the famous Oktoberfest. However, a west German beer-lover could make a strong argument that beer was a quintessential product of the Rhineland. The region's Germanic tribes had helped cultivate Roman appetites for beer, its monasteries had helped refine and popularise German beer recipes, and the Rhine had served as a major shipping route for the completed product. Breweries in the Rhineland provided the golden fuel for some of the country's biggest carnivals and events, and there was a sparky rivalry between the cities of Düsseldorf and Cologne over whose beer was best. For me, well-equipped with an Englishman's prejudices about Germany, the lively beerhalls also offered a helpful corrective to the deeply rooted assumption that all Germans were sensible and unadventurous. In the Rhineland, as Walter Benjamin once wrote, 'the ale-house is the key to every town, [and] to know where German beer can be drunk is geography and ethnology enough'.

The world's first beer was probably brewed not in Europe but, ironically enough, in the Middle East or the Caucasus. The ancient Sumerian epic of Gilgamesh told the creation myth of 'the wild beast Enkidu' who became human after drinking beer. 'He drank of it seven times,' the ancient texts said: 'His spirit relaxed and he started to talk in a loud voice.' In Europe, the tribes of present-day

Germany and the Low Countries began to hit the bottle sometime around 1,000 BC. Working over fires in forest camps and villages, Germanic brewers – usually women – began brewing beers based on bread, mashing half-baked loaves into jugs of water, which would then be left to ferment into a thick, sour, alcoholic porridge. Just like modern beers, tribal brews were available in many different styles, and often were improved by the addition of delicious flavourings such as honey, tree bark or ox gut.

By the time the Romans arrived, beer was already popular throughout the Rhine region. Beer, Tacitus noted, flowed heavily at tribal meetings and banquets. As wine-drinking denizens of a Mediterranean civilisation, the Romans were naturally appalled at the idea of drinking barbarian beer-mash. Tacitus implied that the tribes' love of beer might well be the cause of their 'customary laziness', and suggested their alcoholism could be turned against them. 'If we wanted to make use of their addiction to drink, by giving them as much of it as they want, we could defeat them as easily by means of this vice as with our weapons,' he said. In time, however, the Romans gradually came to see the appeal. At first, they bought beer from local Germanic women who brewed in the traditional way, but soon they began brewing their own, adapting the tribes' bread-mashing technique by grinding the raw grains directly. The growing esteem in which the Romans held the tribal drink was reflected in the name they gave it: *cerevisia*, a gift from the goddess of agriculture, Ceres.

When the beer-drinking Germanic tribes finally saw off the lily-livered, wine-drinking Romans, beer's primacy as northern Europe's drink of choice seemed assured. In the eighth and ninth centuries, the Emperor Charlemagne turned out to be something of a real ale fan, ordering each of the estates which made up his vast territory to maintain its own functioning brewery. After Charlemagne's death, when his descendants divided his empire, the liquid boundaries of the continent became clear. Roughly speaking, to the west of the Rhine, the people of present-day France retained a more Roman way of life, and enjoyed wines, while to the east of the river, the Germans stuck with beer. In the rural villages of the Rhineland, beer was a staple, enjoyed by farmers with hunks of bread dipped in it like soup.

In time, many monasteries began running their own breweries and pubs – the ancient equivalent of a church having a pub and microbrewery out the back. Under the monks' careful supervision, brewing became rather less like a child's attempts to bake a cake, and rather more scientific. The monastery at Saint Gall, near where the Rhine flowed into Lake Constance, built a massive brewery and became perhaps the largest and rowdiest hotel bar in the whole of Europe, with hundreds of monks and serfs tending fields of grain and hops. Even the Islamic Saracens, who invaded Europe from their caliphate in northern Africa, were recorded stopping at Saint Gall to enjoy a brew. The Saint Gall brewery eventually expanded to fill around forty buildings, but no storage cellars were needed – the beer always sold out as soon as it was ready. Exempt from taxes and enjoying free labour, the monasteries made handsome profits from their brewing operations, but also gave beer away to poor visitors, a tactic which today's vicars, struggling to attract worshippers, might do well to consider. At Saint Gall, each monk was allocated a ration of at least five litres of beer per day.

In time, though, the monks' beer monopoly began to weaken, and the brewers' foamy baton passed to the new merchant class: the shippers and traders who'd quietly been growing rich from the Rhine, and who now began to trade in beer as well as wine, wool, timber, amber and olive oil. Canny merchants began selling German beers throughout Europe, with barrels and flasks shipped downriver to Wijk bij Duurstede and Utrecht. However, the stuff they sold was still very different from what a modern European would think of as beer; often made from beans or peas rather than grain, it was flavoured with salt or hard-boiled eggs. In time, though, standards rose, thanks partly to the famous *Reinheitsgebot*, or beer purity law, which said beer should include only three ingredients: hops, water and barley.* When Martin Luther stood trial in 1521 on charges of defying the Catholic Church, he allegedly asked for only one drink to sustain him during the ordeal: a cask of crisp Einbecker beer. 'Strong beer,' Luther supposedly wrote, 'is the milk of the old.'

Germany's fractured political system meant regional rivalries over

---

* *Rein* means 'clear', so the phrase *Reinheitsgebot* has nothing to do with the river Rhine.

booze had long been fierce. In the fourteenth century, for example, beer-makers in the towns neighbouring Dortmund were known to hire snipers to shoot holes through barrels of Dortmund beer being brought along the river. If caught, the gunmen were at least assured a happy death: they were usually drowned in barrels of beer. Along the Rhine, the main distinction today is between beers brewed with yeasts which work their magic at the top of the fermenting tank, and those which thrive at the bottom. In Cologne, the general preference is for lighter, more lagery bottom-fermented beers. Down the river in Düsseldorf, though, most brewers were apparently aficionados of the *Alt* (old) style, where yeasts fermented at the top of the tank, creating maltier and fruitier brews. To an outsider, the whole debate appeared arcane; like arguing about whether tea tasted better if it was stirred clockwise or anti-clockwise. But to residents of the Rhineland, the top–bottom debate was a serious business. The rivalry between the two beers – Cologne's more modern *Kolsch* and Düsseldorf's old-school *Alt* – had been brewing for decades, and inevitably spilled over into other rivalries which existed between the neighbouring cities. Breweries ran adverts poking fun at the foolish techniques used by their rivals up- or downriver, while bars pointedly refused to include non-local beers on their menus. My own preference was for the *Alt*, caramel-coloured, and darker and smokier than the *Kolsch*; a kind of Düsseldorf Coca-Cola to Cologne's lemonade. But on trips to Cologne, I was always careful not to say so. 'You'd have to be very brave or very stupid to order an *Alt* in Cologne,' one German acquaintance warned. He'd clearly failed to consider the possibility that I might be both.

The next day, I awoke to the sound of an army in full retreat. Outside my hotel window, dozens of trucks lined the narrow streets, loading Gay Pride detritus including portable toilets and stages. A few street sweepers were collecting a last few scraps of litter, but before breakfast-time the streets were already largely spotless. My plan was to continue south along the river towards Bonn, but first there were a couple of other sights in Cologne I wanted to pay a brief visit to.

First was the Heinrich Böll Platz, named after one of the city's most famous sons. Böll, like many other great German writers, never quite became a household name outside Germany, but was undoubtedly one of the giants of twentieth-century literature; a Nobel-prize winner who drew on his experiences as a soldier in the Second World War to write tales which poked sharply at the moral dilemmas and contradictions faced by his generation. Böll had played near the Rhine as a boy, and often described the river lyrically in his works – writing, for example, of the winter 'ice floes as big as football fields, white, covered with a thick layer of snow . . . [on which] the only passengers were the crows being carried by the ice floes toward Holland, calmly riding on their huge, fantastically elegant taxis'.

Continuing south along the river, I walked past a row of half-timbered restaurants and under the big bridge over which the parade had crossed. A footbridge led on to a small artificial peninsula which jutted into the river, and which was home to the Schokoladenmuseum or Chocolate Museum. I'd done the museum tour once before and wasn't inclined to repeat it, but did stop to buy four big bars of ruinously expensive chocolate – one for each of my parents, one for my sister and one for my wife. By the time I'd walked back to the city centre, fifteen minutes later, I'd eaten them all.

The weather was fine, and I sat for a while in the sushine outside a pretty half-timbered restaurant reading Böll and looking out across the sparkling water. Joggers jogged past, cyclists cycled and rowers rowed. The atmosphere was holiday-like, and, feeling indolent, I ordered a mid-morning drink; a Johannisberg Riesling, served in a glass that resembled a goldfish bowl. Like beer, wine had for centuries been one of the Rhineland's greatest exports. It was produced in many different places in Germany, but one of the most prolific was the region to the south of Cologne, around where the Rhine met the rivers Moselle and Main. There, the low hillsides along the riverbanks were carpeted with rows of leafy vines, and it was hard to walk more than a few minutes without being tempted by a bottle.

Not long before my visit to Cologne, I'd spent a happy day exploring the world of Rhine wines in Wiesbaden, south of Cologne, at a local wine festival. The historic *Markplatz* in the lee of the rust-red cathedral had been taken over by dozens of circular tent-topped bars, each representing a different vineyard or region, and the gaps in between them were crowded with trestle tables and benches. By midday, the benches were already well stocked with patrons. As far as I could see, they were divided into two groups: the serious tasters, standing at high round tables, carefully rolling small sips of wine around their tongues and comparing notes; and the serious boozers, sitting at the trestle tables and guzzling as quickly as they could. Around the edges of the square, stalls offered enticing regional produce: hams, dried sausages and pungent cheeses. The weather was warm and it all felt amazingly civilised, a sharp rebuke to those (including me, on grumpier days) who assumed German cuisine was all about sausages and schnitzel, and who remained oblivious to the amazing breadth and diversity of local cuisine. For me, it also made a welcome change from the Netherlands, where public events usually were dominated by thumping music, deep-fried food and plastic glasses of Heineken.

Picking a bar at random, I ordered a glass of Riesling and then stepped next door to collect a Roman-style platter of ham, roasted peppers, grapes and cheeses. The wine proved to be very sweet, with a sharp aftertaste of nail polish. The ham was delicious. To my left, a young boy tried a sip of Riesling diluted with water. '*Lecker!*' he pronounced to his father, 'Delicious!'

Like many things, it seems likely that wine arrived in Germany with the Romans. As towns like Koblenz and Cologne grew into important military and trading centres, so Roman farmers planted the surrounding hillsides with vines imported from the Mediterranean. At first, the wines produced in the Rhineland don't seem to have been a great success – Tacitus didn't mention them in his famous accounts of German life, and neither did Caesar in his reports of visiting Germany. This was partly because of the region's cool climate, but also because the Romans were keen to preserve their Mediterranean monopoly on wine-making. Cicero once reported that a decree issued by the Roman Senate had prohibited wine-making in the outer provinces of the empire for purely economic reasons. 'We, the most just people, do not allow people outside our frontiers to plant the olive-trees and the vine for one reason: so that our own olive-trees and vineyards have higher value,' he wrote. 'We are clever, but we are not just.'

In time, though, Roman opposition to wine-making in the north was watered down. Vineyards were planted across the hillsides along a long stretch of the middle Rhine, tended by serfs and prisoners of war captured from across the river. Rhine cities like Speyer became major centres of the wine trade. While the quality of German wines remained fairly low, it was improving, and although beer was still far more popular, the idea of a rich Roman drinking wine from Germania was no longer as absurd as it once had been. Like the wines themselves, German wine-making was improving with age.

After the Romans retreated from the Rhineland, the vineyards stayed behind, of course, and thrived well into the reign of Charlemagne. Although also known as a beer lover, the Holy Roman Emperor was a man who liked to mix his drinks. According to legend, he once stood in his chateau by the Rhine in Ingelheim and, seeing that the snow had melted on the hills of Johannisberg but not on the other hills, deduced that the climate across the river was warmer than elsewhere. He ordered many vines to be planted there, and these soon spread to the surrounding areas. As with beer, monks and monasteries became major producers, making their own wine for use at Mass. Inevitably, the monasteries soon were producing far more wine than they needed and began selling it elsewhere, via the Frisians and the Hanseatic League. Barges filled with heavy barrels of wine were a regular sight on the Rhine, rushing downstream to Wijk bij Duurstede or the coast. Growers experimented with many varieties of grape, but the most successful were Rieslings; white grapes which thrived on the cool, stony hillsides of the middle river. Chilly weather sometimes meant it was hard to get wines to ferment, so makers adopted a special shape of bottle: tall and slender with an unusually long neck.

In subsequent centuries the Rhine wine trade waned somewhat. Cold spells often killed off grape harvests, and the growing population of the Rhineland meant many vineyards were razed and converted to housing, agriculture or industrial land. However, growers soldiered on, and some German wines became very popular abroad, including *Liebfraumilch*, a white wine originally grown in vineyards near a church, the *Liebfraukirche*, in the city of Worms. Rhine wines evolved from an international laughing stock into something more like a Spanish car – not what you'd buy if you had money to spare, but actually pretty decent.

However, German wines were never quite as popular as French, Italian, Spanish or even South African wines – partly because their quality was genuinely lower, and partly because they had a reputation for being harsh and cheap. ('The Germans are exceedingly fond of Rhine wines,' Mark Twain wrote. 'One tells them from vinegar by the label.') It also probably didn't help that many of the wines had names which could tie a non-German tongue in knots; combining the unpronounceable name of the town where the wine was produced with the unpronounceable name of the vineyard and the unpronounceable name of the companies which had shipped it. Looking at the bottles of *Huxelrebe* and *Trockenbeerenauslese* on sale in Cologne and Wiesbaden, it wasn't hard to see why simple old Blue Nun and Black Tower had become popular abroad.

I finished my Riesling and ordered a *Spätburgunder* pinot noir; thick, velvety and blackberry-flavoured. To my right, a pair of older German men were working their way steadily down the wine list, one drink at a time, like pilots completing a pre-flight checklist. One of them took a tiny sip of rosé and agreed with his companion: '*Lecker!*' A tipsy Frenchman wobbled past, wearing a stained brown T-shirt which read: 'Wine Improves With Age. I Improve With Wine.' I flicked idly through a regional newspaper someone had left on the table: climate change and environmental damage, Merkel and Trump, refugees and nationalists. The Rhineland, like everywhere else in the world, was not without its problems these days, and in places such as Cologne, it didn't always seem that the forces of tolerance had the upper hand. Yet despite what the doom-mongers said, and as events like the Gay Pride parade and the wine festival showed, the region remained a hotbed of what the Germans called *gemütlichkeit*: warmth, solidarity, hospitality and good cheer. Sitting in the sun in the marketplace, overlooked by yet another glorious cathedral, with a smooth glass of red at my elbow, life seemed very fine indeed.

7

Cold War Blues

Bonn and Königswinter

THE SECRET NUCLEAR bunker was surprisingly difficult to find.
Heading south from Cologne, the Rhine valley looked increasingly like pages of a Brothers Grimm story book. The river was
wide and flat and grey as always, but the land surrounding it swelled
with gentle hills, rising up from the water like waves. German beer
culture had begun to give way to wine, and the gravelly hills were
carpeted with long parallel rows of vines. It looked as if the whole
valley was upholstered in yellow-green corduroy.

Heading away from the river I quickly got lost, and stopped to
ask a bearded vineyard worker for directions. He paused from retying
some vines and answered my question. *'Ja, ja*, the secret thing is
up that way!' I followed the lane further uphill, through a pretty
forest of beech and sycamore, and eventually found what I was
looking for: an unremarkable little concrete building half hidden
in the trees, which looked like somewhere a farmer might store
his tractors. I thought I'd come to the wrong place, but checked
my map and realised yes, this was it: the hidden entrance to a top-
secret military installation.

Inside, the bunker proved to be all the things one would expect
a nuclear bunker to be: grey, gloomy and eerily cold. I hadn't phoned
ahead to arrange my visit, but in an exceptional stroke of luck, a
group of German history buffs was about to begin a tour of the
bunker, and I was allowed to tag along. Together, we shuffled down
a long concrete tunnel about the size of a subway, burrowing deep
into the hillside between the vines, led by a grey-haired guide with
a short stature which must have come in handy for someone who
worked in a bunker. My rudimentary German struggled to keep up
with his commentary, but there was no mistaking the key phrases:
'Atombombe', 'Nuklear', 'Kommunistisch' and *'Dekontamination*'. The

passage twisted and turned, passing through thick steel doors which looked like they belonged on a submarine. Pausing to take a photograph, I leaned accidentally on a big mushroom-shaped button fixed to the wall. No one noticed, but I briefly feared I might have destroyed Vladivostok or Minsk.

For someone of my generation, raised to see Germany as a land of beer festivals and art galleries, and schooled to believe German history began in 1914 and ended in 1945, it was hard to appreciate why such a bunker might ever have been necessary. However, until relatively recently the Rhineland had remained one of the world's most heavily militarised zones; a place where nuclear war was just as likely to break out as it is in North Korea.

After the defeat of the Nazis in 1945, the victorious Allied and Soviet powers divided Germany into four zones of occupation: roughly speaking, a British-run north-west, an American south-east, a French south-west and a Soviet north-east. ('The British and the French got the coal, the Russians the wheat fields and we got the scenery,' one American officer explained.) In theory, the wartime Yalta and Potsdam agreements had laid the foundations for a delicate balance of powers which would bring peace to mainland Europe. But in practice, like squabbling children trying to share a birthday cake, the occupiers soon fell out. In the east, the Soviets established a communist client state – the ironically named German Democratic Republic (GDR) – while in the west, the British, French and Americans united to create a pro-capitalist Federal Republic of Germany (FRG), better known as West Germany. Germany, the country which Bismarck had united barely seventy years previously, was thus cleaved in two parts: one where almost every home eventually had a washing machine, and one where it was sometimes forbidden to even print the words *washing machine* in the newspapers.

Outside Germany, public attention naturally focused on the places where the divide between the Cold War superpowers was starkest, along the Iron Curtain. Berlin, in particular, assumed huge symbolic status as a divided city. ('Berlin is the testicles of the West,' the Soviet leader Nikita Khrushchev was supposed to have said, 'and when I want the West to scream, I squeeze on Berlin.') The Rhine and its major cities – Bonn, Cologne, Düsseldorf, Mainz – lay firmly in the western half, on the happier side of the Iron Curtain. However, just as it had in previous conflicts, the Rhine played a critical role.

Based on the bitter experience of the Second World War, the Allies assumed that if a Soviet assault on Europe occurred, it would probably take the form of an overland invasion, with tanks racing across the flat plains all the way to Paris and Brussels. As the industrial heartland of West Germany, and home to the West German capital of Bonn, the Rhine region would also be a key military target. Ports like Rotterdam, meanwhile, would be crucial for enabling NATO reinforcements to flow into Europe. The Western powers' 'Emergency Defence Plan' for Europe, written in 1951, planned for 'a defence along the Rhine River'. Similarly, a secret NATO strategy document written in the mid 1950s said that in case of war in Europe, one of the most important objectives would be 'to hold the Rhine River bridges'. While pawns like Hannover and Frankfurt could, at a pinch, be sacrificed to the Soviets, 'final positions astride the Rhine–IJssel line had to be held at all cost'. Centuries after the Romans left, and years after the bridges near Arnhem had fallen, the Rhine was once again a kind of final frontier; a barrier preventing enemy forces from reaching the 'civilised' heartland.

As the Cold War heated up, the middle Rhine region became rapidly militarised. Most foreign forces were concentrated in two places: the so-called Fulda Gap, a corridor of lowland through which it would be easy to drive Soviet tanks; and the area around the middle Rhine, where dozens of American and British military bases were built at places like Karlsruhe, Mannheim, Worms, Mainz, Wiesbaden and Rheinburg. Even in an era of fantastical military spending, the scale of operations was astonishing: in parts of Rhineland-Pfalz, it was estimated that American military spending accounted for up to 43 per cent of GDP. Some West Germans were bitterly opposed to NATO, but most were in favour, and the presence of thousands of foreign troops had a profound impact on the national culture. Some West Germans thought American consumerism was almost as unappealing as communism, but others who had recently been schooled to see America as the great enemy now came to see it as a shining city on a hill, bursting with lust-worthy Cadillacs and blue jeans, milkshakes and Marlboros, Wild West movies and pop songs. The nineteenth-century novelist Karl May's fanciful adventure stories about the American West sold tens of millions of copies, and were made into a series of astonishingly popular movies.

The American influence dominated, but the British influence was also strong, thanks to the British Army of the Rhine, which sent thousands of young soldiers and their families to live in drab prefab homes in suburbs of towns like Duisburg, Essen, Düsseldorf and Cologne. The newspaper *Die Welt* was based on the British *Times*, and the German electoral system was inspired in part by the British one. Sadly, British efforts to teach Rhinelanders to play cricket were rather less successful.

Less amusingly, dozens of nuclear weapons were also shipped to the Rhineland. Secret NATO war plans said that 'If the Soviet ground forces penetrated to the Rhine, a maximum Allied effort . . . with all forms of atomic support was to be made to hold onto that line'. To defend Europe 'from behind the Rhine', another confidential report said, 'we will use atomic weapons plentifully'. Needless to say, the results would have been devastating. In 1979, a Soviet 'war game' called 'Seven Days to the River Rhine' forecast a West Germany studded with red mushroom clouds and cities including Bonn, Düsseldorf, Cologne, Brussels, Antwerp, Haarlem and Amsterdam destroyed. In the event of a full-blown war, President Eisenhower said, 'there just aren't enough bulldozers to scrape the bodies off the streets'.

Inside the bunker, our group continued its slow march towards the centre of the earth, the temperature dropping as we moved further from the sunlit vineyards. The tunnels, the guide explained, originally were constructed for an unfinished railway project before the First World War, and then in the 1960s massively extended. The expansion project produced an impressive piece of architecture: an underground city where the West German government could shelter in case of a Soviet attack, protected by a thick layer of rock and concrete. From the outside, the facility was all but invisible, but inside were offices and accommodation for thousands of people, as well as a television studio from which the chancellor could assure everyone that radiation sickness wasn't as bad as it sounded. The bunker was finally sealed in the 1990s, after the Cold War ended, with only a small section kept open as a monument to the follies of a previous generation. 'Are there still bunkers for the chancellor now, somewhere else in Germany?' I asked the guide. 'There's still . . . something,' came the cautious reply.

Walking further, we came to one of the communications rooms, where a swivel chair stood before a *Star Trek*-style console of lights, buttons, switches and TV screens. Around the corner was the chancellor's suite, with salmon-coloured sofas, retro TV screens and orange plastic lamps which gave it the unmistakable air of a 1960s groovy student apartment – less *Doctor Strangelove* and more *Austin Powers*. Nearby, a flyer pinned to a wall advertised film screenings to entertain bored bunker workers: *Marathon Man*, *Beverly Hills Cop* and – of course – *War Games*.

A few minutes later, we reached the end of the tour, a huge iron grate blocking us from exploring any further. Beyond the grate lay nothing but darkness. The bubbly amateur historians fell silent, and all eyes turned to a big black-and-white photograph hanging prominently on the wall: a monstrous mushroom cloud, boiling over some ruined atoll. The group shuffled off and I stayed behind for a few minutes alone, looking down the tunnel and thinking how lucky I was to live in an age when a nuclear war was about as likely in the Netherlands as a skiing championship. The yellowish light overhead flickered a little, and I turned and walked quickly back towards the daylight.

Back down in the valley, I boarded a little train heading towards Bonn, where I'd left my bike and baggage at a hotel. The journey was a delight; the train hurtling through a series of pretty riverside towns, each with near identical church, high street and scenic riverside walkway. In a few places, the train line passed so close to the water that a commuting angler could almost have cast a line out of the carriage window. In the Netherlands, even corporate titans thought themselves lucky to have a tiny garden, but here the houses were well spaced and almost everyone had their own little patch of wilderness fenced off beyond the back door. The river, though, was as busy as always, with cargo and ferries racing the trains to Basle and Rotterdam. Across the aisle, a young backpacker spread his damp clothes across the seats to dry, until the whole carriage looked like a teenager's bedroom. Down the carriage, a young woman sat simultaneously eating a takeaway pizza, listening to dance music on a loudspeaker and noisily talking on the phone to her boyfriend. I silently wished a missile would land on us all.

After half an hour I arrived in Bonn, another city which I knew quite well and liked very much. With its leafy streets and pavement cafés and colonnaded houses which looked like embassies, it retained the slightly aloof air of somewhere used to being taken seriously. The main bookshop was almost as big as a football stadium, and the city hall looked like a wedding cake. I wandered the cobbled streets for a while, happy to be back on familiar turf, enjoying a chocolate ice cream which was called, for some reason, a Nogger. It was a typical summer's day in northern Germany: grey and cloudy, with an 85 per cent chance of rain.

Like so many cities on the Rhine, Bonn was essentially founded by the Romans, who built a great fortress – the Castra Bonnensia – intended (as one nineteenth-century writer put it) to 'overawe the barbarians' on the opposite side of the river. Later, when the Romans left, it morphed into an important religious and political centre. Bonn's university was, for a while, considered among the best in the world: when the University of London was founded, it took as its model not nearby Oxford or Cambridge, but Bonn. Among those who studied there was Karl Marx, who quickly made a name for himself as a sword-fighting, heavy-drinking hell-raiser well known to the city police. According to the official Certificate of Release issued when Marx left Bonn, his academic record was 'excellent', but he'd also 'incurred a punishment of one day's detention for disturbing the peace by rowdiness and drunkenness at night'. I remembered my own days as a student, and felt glad no one had been asked to write such a report about me. Resisting the siren song of a riverside pub, I walked instead to the Beethoven Haus, a big old red townhouse sandwiched incongruously between a shoe shop and a Jack Wolfskin camping store. Ludwig van Beethoven was born here, little more than a stone's throw from the river, in

1770; he was christened in the solidly built St Remigius Church, which I'd passed on my way through town.

Beethoven's father was a singer who was determined to make his son into a child prodigy along the lines of Mozart, and while his early efforts at pushy parenting fell a little short, by his teens young Ludwig's skill was clear. Beethoven thrived as a member of Bonn's city orchestra and eventually got himself sent to Vienna to study with the mighty Mozart, who allegedly told friends 'this young man will make a great name for himself in the world'. Returning to Bonn, Beethoven became a private music tutor and composer for wealthy families. The city was at that time a key outpost of the great German musical hub down the river at Mannheim, and Beethoven was deeply influenced by this middle Rhine style, including innovations such as the jiggling riffs which were said to reflect the flavour of the French Revolution, and the explosive musical happy endings known as 'Mannheim rockets'. Relocating again to Vienna, Beethoven continued to thrill with his skill, even as encroaching deafness limited his career as a virtuoso. ('If only I were rid of my affliction I would embrace the whole world,' he said.) As a child, Beethoven reportedly enjoyed hanging around the river toll booths on the Rhine in Bonn, and once travelled with his mother all the way down the river to Holland. Although his work was never influenced by the river in the way that other composers like Richard Wagner's was, Beethoven still had a deep affection for it. Later in life, in letters to friends and supporters, he referred often to the Rhine, and looked forward to returning to 'the Rhine country which is ever dear to me'. 'I shall count it the happiest experience of my life when I shall again . . . greet our father Rhine,' he once wrote. Like many sons of the Rhineland, Beethoven was also a lover of the region's red wines, which he believed 'necessarily and beneficial' for his rapidly ailing health. His doctor recognised that he had 'a liking for spiritous beverages', but generally thought this was no bad thing, as it helped 'aid his stomachic weakness', and he encouraged Beethoven to drink red wine as if it were a tonic. Early in 1827, Beethoven wrote from his sickbed in Vienna 'a very important request' to one of his regular suppliers of booze. 'My doctor,' the composer said, 'ordered me to drink very good old Rhine wine [but] to get it here, unadulterated, is not at all possible even by paying the highest price.' He went on to explain that he was just about to undergo an operation, and 'the sooner . . . I receive the Rhine, or Moselle, wine, the better it will be for my present state'.

Perhaps not coincidentally, Beethoven died from cirrhosis a few weeks later, in March 1827. Now, almost two centuries later, he'd been adopted with customary German tourist-board gusto as a proud son of Bonn; celebrated in a museum, in a Beethoven square, and with a greenish-bronze statue which (on the day I visited) was surrounded by a temporary fairground, complete with doughnut sellers and bars playing loud dance music. The bard of Bonn stared severely down at a beer stand, the beat of a Justin Bieber song thudding off the wall behind him, and I thought it was probably just as well he'd gone deaf.

With an hour or so to kill, I set out on a long amble along Bonn's lovely tree-lined river promenade. Cyclists and runners sped past, tour boats docked and departed, and some students conducted an in-depth riverbank study of the effect of a crate of beer on their ability to revise for a philosophy exam. The river itself was stately and bullet-coloured, and about as wide as the Thames in London. I soon realised I was inadvertently following one of the signposted tourist trails of which Germans were so fond – this one designed to teach idle wanderers about the wonders of the solar system. In the space of a mile or so, I rocketed past small sculptures of Mars and Venus before arriving in a blaze of glory at the Sun, a wrecking ball-sized sphere of yellow-painted concrete plonked on the river-bank. 'It's the centre of the universe!' a passing mother explained in German to her son. In a strange way, her comment was more accurate than she might have realised. At the time of my tour, Bonn was a sedate place, but it was once if not the centre of the universe, then at least one of the most important cities in the world.

Bonn was abruptly thrust onto the world stage in May 1949, when the West German Parliamentary Council (the forerunner to the modern Bundestag) voted that it should become the capital of the new Federal Republic of Germany. It was in many ways a strange choice – Bonn was, in the late forties, a sleepy little city used to being overshadowed by its bigger, brasher neighbours. However, like many a candidate running for high office, it benefited from the weaknesses of its rivals. Frankfurt was run by socialist local government, while Berlin was partly under communist control, and disliked by many westerners because it was what one observer called a 'colonial frontier city on the edges of the Slavic wilderness'. In that context, Bonn emerged as a compromise choice; an attractively modest little city which was centred not on a statue of some great military leader, but of Beethoven. 'Bonn was a beginning, a city without a past,' Chancellor Konrad Adenauer said. The *Hauptdorf*, others called it, the 'Capital Village'.

The coronation as capital was a boon for Bonn. In the first four years, the city's population reportedly increased by more than half, from 90,000 to 140,000, including many refugees from the Soviet-dominated east. However, some new residents received a hostile reception. 'The Bonners talk about these people as if they were immigrants and not fellow Germans,' a visitor reported in 1954. 'Our schools are jammed with their children,' one local complained, 'and their young people are already marrying our sons and daughters. In a few years, the pure Catholic character of our region, the whole cultural and religious structure of our beautiful Rhineland, will be destroyed by those Protestants from the east.'

Like an African dictator converting their home village into a sparkling metropolis, the West German government spent a fortune building the trappings of a world capital. Grand ministries and debating chambers sprung up on the banks of the Rhine, including a riverside defence ministry which became known as the 'Pentabonn'. Yet the city never managed to shake off its reputation as an innocent country bumpkin which had accidentally wandered onto the global stage at a crucial moment in history. The Rhine provided a scenic backdrop, but diplomats and officials posted to Bonn often thought it unbearably dull compared to the likes of swish, cosmopolitan Paris, Geneva or Vienna. Bored British diplomats took to referring to their embassy in the city as 'Her Majesty's only mission in a cornfield'.

Getting tired, I stopped for coffee at one of the many riverside bars, taking a seat with a fine view down the river towards the forested hills in the distance. My book was one I'd bought second-hand: the spy thriller *A Small Town in Germany*, by John Le Carré. In the 1960s, Le Carré (then known by his real name, David Cornwell) lived for a while in Bonn, working as an unusually curious 'diplomat' in the British Embassy. This, his fifth novel, published in 1968, was a tangled tale of stolen files and defecting diplomats, in which Bonn provided not only the backdrop but a key supporting character. Le Carré's description of the city helped establish many of the tropes of the modern espionage thriller: gloomy bridges and thick river mists, lamp-lit cobbled streets and morally dubious heroes. The story itself wasn't entirely to my taste, but the book offered a compelling portrait of the city, and of the tensions between generations in a nation haunted by its past. Sitting with my coffee by the river, in the age of Brexit, I winced when I read Le Carré's description of the post-imperial angst of British expats hanging out the bunting of 'small flags of the commonwealth, creased by storage and diminished by secession'.

By the time Le Carré lived there, Bonn had become an epicentre of the Cold War; considered an outpost of western 'civilisation' in the same way that Utrecht and Cologne had been centuries before. As West Germany's reputation recovered, it also became a regular stop on the global power trip circuit, hosting a rotating cast of presidents, prime ministers and royals. Ronald Reagan, for example, came and quoted Schiller and Heine in the modern parliament building by the Rhine, arguing 'the soil of Germany . . . is of vital concern'. 'If we construct our peace properly,' the president said, 'it will endure as long as the spires of Cologne.'

In the riverside suburb of Plittersdorf, more than 400 homes were built for American diplomats, soldiers and spies, all designed 'in the southern California style', arrayed around a US post office, tennis courts, church, bowling alley and baseball field. According to a journalist who witnessed the opening of the new US Embassy in 1951, diplomats were assured by the architect that they could 'shop and do their laundry . . . without ever having to come into contact with a single German'. West German attitudes to their American allies remained conflicted: in 1982, 250,000 people joined anti-nuclear protests in Bonn. Yet for the most part, Rhinelanders remained firmly in the western sphere; enthusiastic producers and consumers of the latest consumer goods. People generally viewed the Americans as a kind of cheerfully reckless cousin or uncle: a little trying at times, but generally nice to have around.

Leaving Bonn, I took the ferry south along the river to Königswinter. The boat was busy, and for the first time since leaving the coast I wondered whether my Dutch friends' warnings that Rhine cruise ships were essentially mobile retirement homes might be right: of perhaps sixty people on board, I was by far the youngest. Yet despite my ageist prejudices, the people were lively and intelligent, and the atmosphere jolly. At 10.30 a.m., several passengers were already ordering their second beers of the day, and the air was abuzz with the chatter of people enjoying the highlight of their year.

A significant proportion of the travellers were Dutch, and I fell into conversation with four Amsterdammers in matching baseball caps, who were astonished to meet an Englishman who spoke Dutch travelling along the Rhine alone. 'But . . . where are all your friends?' one woman asked, clearly unconvinced of my sanity. 'We're taking the boat all the way from Cologne to Koblenz!' interrupted her husband, excited to have a captive audience. 'Let me tell you, we've been here so many times. I remember the first trip, back in '86, the weather was dreadful, and Eve had forgotten her rain-coat . . .' I suddenly got the feeling it was going to be a very long voyage.

A lot of stories later, I bid my new friends farewell and disembarked, joining a great wave of grey heads sweeping into the riverside town of Königswinter. This turned out to be touristy but pleasant, with a fountain in the main square and a tiny library in a red British phone box. The star attractions, though, lay beyond the town, amid the cluster of steep, forested hills which rose from the river. From the waterfront, I could see three dramatic hilltop castles – the cuboid Petersberg, the Disney-style Drachenburg and the ruined Drachenfels, whose jagged silhouette poked through the treetops like a broken tooth. Most visitors rode a little train up to the castles, but I rashly opted to walk. As mountains went, the 'Seven Hills of Königswinter' ('Seven Hills' is a misnomer; there are actually far more) weren't terribly intimidating – little more than three hundred metres high at their tallest. However, for travellers like me, heading south along the river from the low-lying

Netherlands, they looked Himalayan. On the boat, the Dutchman had warned me: 'Take it easy up there! You'll get tired quickly, because the air is thinner so high up.'

The path was steeper than I'd expected, and I was soon wheezing like a steamship, searching desperately for excuses to stop and take a photo or consult my map. There were only three other people making the hike: a pair of young Muslim women sweating in thick headscarves, and a teenage boy in an electric wheelchair, putting his machine to the ultimate test as he grinded his way uphill. It all seemed like some kind of metaphor for the ascendancy of modern Germany, but I wasn't quite sure how.

Finally topping the first hill, I stopped briefly at Drachenburg – a glorious Gothic fantasy of red stone and grey slate, overlooked by towering redwood sequoia trees. The castle was built in the 1880s by Stephan von Sarter, a Bonn innkeeper's son who deftly rode the wave of rising prosperity in the Rhineland, made a fortune speculating on the stock exchange, and then made another helping to finance the Suez Canal. Like many Germans of his era, Sarter depended on the rapid industrialisation of the Ruhrgebiet to make him wealthy, but was also disturbed by the way in which his country was becoming greyer, dirtier, noisier and more polluted. In middle age, feeling flush, he commissioned a private rural retreat: a bewildering mish-mash of towers, spires, stained glass and steeples which deliberately harked back to the times when Germany had been an idyll of nature, romance and chivalry. The location he chose was spectacular, but the overall effect was a little bizzare, as if the Houses of Parliament had been airlifted from London, colourfully decorated and then dropped on a forested hillside.

Stephan Sarter died without ever actually living at Drachenberg, and the castle's subsequent history was almost as colourful as its décor – it served at various times as an elite Nazi college for boys, a Catholic boarding school, a US military facility, a home for war refugees, a training centre for German railway staff and a tacky unfinished amusement park. Now, after an enormously expensive renovation project, it had been restored to its former immodest glory, of which Dumbledore would surely approve.

I didn't stay long, but wandered through the sumptious dining rooms for a while before climbing a turreted tower to the roof, from where the view was literally jaw-dropping: two other castles peeking over the green-clad hills, Bonn in the distance and, of course, the river, snaking its way northwards like a bottle-green serpent.

I walked downhill through the forest, back towards the Rhine. After an hour or so I arrived in Rhöndorf, another fine little river town filled with suburbanites living what might be called the German Dream: two Volkswagens on the drive, fir trees in the garden and a basketball hoop out front. I paused to take a photo of an unremarkable villa, and a passing German hailed me in some strange hybrid of pride and envy: 'Beautiful, isn't it!' I walked around for a while, using a map I'd sketched on a napkin, until I found the particular house I was looking for: a big white villa which slotted into the steep hillside like a dropped block in Tetris. In front, a big sign announced the name of the statesman who'd once lived here: Konrad Adenauer.

Adenauer, it must be said, was not one of history's most flamboyant figures. As his biographer Anthony Nicholls wrote: 'of all the statesmen who shaped the destinies of Europe . . . Adenauer was one of the least colourful'. Sombre and black-hatted, gaunt and reptilian, he was a devout Catholic who lived modestly and had none of the panache of Churchill or grandeur of de Gaulle. Yet there was little doubt he was one of the most significant figures in German history: chancellor of West Germany for fourteen years, his iron discipline helped him rebuild shattered cities, kickstart the *Wirtschaftwunder* and restore his country's reputation abroad. He was also another quintessential Rhinelander, who did more than anyone else to make the region around Bonn an unlikely lynchpin of what was then called 'the free world'.

Adenauer was born in Cologne in 1876, the son of a minor Prussian official. After studying law and marrying well, he became mayor of Cologne in his early forties, towards the end of the First World War. As mayor, Adenauer was faced with a range of post-war challenges, including serious food shortages and revolutionary disturbances, but handled these skilfully. He was no great orator, but obsessed over detail and bulldozed anyone who disagreed with him using a lawyer's meticulous argument. He oversaw the reopening of Cologne's university and opened grand buildings and parks. That steady progress abruptly ended, however, in 1933, when the Nazis – annoyed by Adenauer's independence – removed him from his post as mayor. Over the following nightmare years he was arrested several times before being exiled to Rhöndorf, where he watched from afar as his beloved city was largely destroyed. In the spring of 1945, Adenauer emerged to find an American army jeep waiting outside, bearing two officers who asked him to return to Cologne and take charge of rebuilding the city.

As mayor, Adenauer spoke out against the Allies' policy of dismantling German industry along the Rhine and set about rebuilding Cologne with gusto, but a little too much gusto for the British, who abruptly dismissed him after he refused to cut down the city's trees for firewood. Unbowed, he threw himself into building up his Christian Democratic Union (CDU) party and crafting a 'social market economy' which balanced the best of pure capitalism with the best of social welfare. Adenauer's approach was dismissed by the rival Social Democrats as 'the fat propaganda balloon of private enterprise filled with putrid gases of decaying liberalism', but those putrid gases rose quickly, and in September 1949 Adenauer became the first democratically elected chancellor of post-war West Germany. He secured the job by a majority of one vote – and that vote, he was fond of telling people, was his own.

As chancellor, Adenauer fought fiercely against plans to strip Germany of its industrial capacity, and won control over foreign policy. He paid millions in Holocaust compensation to Israel and banned anti-Semitism. At home, he could be utterly ruthless – backing the arrest of journalists accused of violating national security, for example, and collecting damaging intelligence on his rivals. Critics accused him of being a 'democratic dictator', while people in Cologne joked that CDU stood for *Conrad der Unsterbliche*, Conrad the Immortal. However, as Adenauer's rivals floundered, he came to seem like the ultimate safe pair of hands; a stern father figure who could force the Germans to behave themselves. John F. Kennedy, visiting Bonn not long before his own assassination, paid fulsome tribute to the new Iron Chancellor. 'Already he lives in the history he helped to make,' Kennedy said.

Adenauer's political career ended, as all political careers do, in a form of failure. Like a star athlete refusing to retire, Adenauer clung to power a little too long, refusing to accept anyone else could fill his shoes. In Bonn, people liked to tell of the time when Adenauer supposedly asked a small boy what he wanted to be when he grew up. 'I'd like to be chancellor of West Germany,' the eager child replied. 'But that is impossible!' Adenauer said. 'I already have that job!' He was eventually shoved into retirement in the autumn of 1963, but his reputation endured; his name adorning streets and aeroplanes, T-shirts and charitable foundations, bottles of Riesling and packets of Darjeeling tea. The old man himself, though, cared little for all that, focusing instead on tending the roses in his garden by the Rhine. He died at home in April 1967. Born twelve years before Hitler, Adenauer ended up outliving him by two decades.

Leaving Adenauer's house, I walked back down to the river. The weather was still marvellous, and I was delighted to find Mediterranean scenes: a couple of small beachy areas, children swimming in the harbour, and a lively wedding party toasting a happy couple by the water. Young women in bikinis ran across a patch of parkland, and young men dived daringly from a pier into the water. Adenauer's home town clearly wasn't quite as austere as its most famous resident.

Looking south, I saw what I thought was the little green island of Nonnenwerth, hulking in mid-stream like a leafy green battleship. I remembered reading that this was a favourite retreat of the composer Franz Liszt, who arrived by ferry, dragging a piano with him, in the summer of 1841. Liszt had hoped to find some peace and quiet, but was sadly disappointed. He was recognised almost as soon as he arrived, and over the following days dozens of sightseers came, including more than three hundred members of the Cologne Philharmonic on a steamship, asking Liszt to come and play a benefit concert for the cathedral. Nevertheless, the picturesque location clearly did some good – it was on the island that Liszt composed *Die Zelle im Nonnenwerth*, accompanied by lyrics telling of its cloister cell 'which is held embraced / by the Rhine with loving concern'.

After a short stroll on the sand, I caught a ferry back towards

Bonn. Big signs on the riverbank told passing ships the distance to Lake Constance, rowers flitted quickly across the water, and young couples canoodled on muddy little beaches. 'It looks just like the Norwegian fjords,' I heard a Belgian passenger tell his wife, implausibly. The decks were already crowded with holidaymakers, but we stopped to collect even more in Bad Godesberg, just across the river from Rhöndorf. I thought I recognised the name and thanks to Google, I realised why. In 1938, Hitler and Neville Chamberlain met at the town's Hotel Dreesen for talks at which the British prime minister failed to prevent the Nazi takeover of Czechoslovakia, dismissing it as 'a quarrel in a faraway country, between people of whom we know nothing'. Later, after that faraway squabble blew over, the town became a popular evening retreat for visiting statesman who wanted to escape the confines of Bonn. One evening in the 1990s, a drunken Boris Yeltsin was reportedly seen hiding under a table in one of the town's restaurants, after being caught by a journalist drinking too much vodka at the height of a Russian government campaign aimed at discouraging people from drinking too much vodka.

Approaching from the south, Bonn's southern frontier was marked by a hefty skyscraper, the former meeting place of the German parliament, or Bundestag, built in the 1960s as a giant democratic middle finger sticking up at the authoritarians in the east. Peeking through the trees on the riverbank, I caught a glimpse of the Villa Hammerschmidt, the official Bonn residence of the German president, which looked rather like the White House in Washington DC. Nearby was the Palais Schlumburg, the official residence of the chancellor. I'd visited this on foot a year or so previously, and (given the current of debates about terrorism in Germany) been surprised to find it deserted. Security cameras watched me as I peeked over the walls, but the main fence was less than two metres high and smooth-topped; had I felt so inclined, I could easily have hopped over and dropped in on Merkel for a cup of tea.

In some ways, Bonn's blandness was symptomatic of the way Germany's political centre of gravity had shifted from the Rhineland to Berlin in recent years. The full story of what happened is long and complicated, but a key turning point came in the late 1980s, when Soviet leader Mikhail Gorbachev introduced his famous policies of glasnost and perestroika, and eastern Europe began inexorably to spin out of the communist sphere of influence. On 9 November 1989 – the original '9/11' – an official called Günter Schabowski gave a boisterous press conference in East Berlin. Struggling to make himself heard to a room full of noisy reporters, Schabowski read out a decree summarising some new visa rules. It was fairly dull stuff, but read out of context, and clumsily phrased, the changes made it sound as if East Germany's own borders would open. When a reporter asked when the change would happen, Schabowski replied, 'As far as I know, now, immediately.' People watching on television rushed to the Berlin Wall, and border guards – who had heard the same garbled announcement – let them cross. Within hours, Germans on both sides began taking hammers to the concrete. Thanks to a slip of the tongue, the Berlin Wall had fallen.

In the following months, attention again naturally focused on the places where the most dramatic action was taking place – in Berlin and along the crumbling Iron Curtain. However, Bonn again played a crucial supporting role, as the setting for a series of meetings and summits at which leaders hammered out what they grandly called the 'New World Order'. Perhaps the most exciting was the visit in 1989 by Gorbachev, who told a banquet in Bad Godesberg that he wanted to 'reverse the process that has made Europe the most militarised region in the world'. Walking around Bonn after dinner, Gorbachev was mobbed by local admirers who followed him around cheering, 'Gorby! Gorby!' 'He could be an American . . . the way he does public relations,' one onlooker marvelled.

Of course, such high jinks were merely the beginning of a long process of change. Chancellor Helmut Kohl – another son of the Rhine, born in Ludwigshafen – skilfully negotiated a series of agreements to make peace with the Soviet Union and begin reuniting Germany. It seemed fitting that after his first landmark meeting with Gorbachev, the first three congratulatory phone calls which Kohl received came from Prime Minister Ruud Lubbers of the Netherlands, the Nazi-hunter Simon Wiesenthal and Prince Louis Ferdinand of Prussia, a descendant of the eighteenth-century rulers who'd done much to unite Germany the first time round.

'That the head of the House of Hohenzollern would congratulate me on German unification is quite normal, isn't it?' Kohl said.

The Americans also strongly backed reunification, further cementing the friendly geopolitical alliance between Germany and the United States. Others, though, were less enthusiastic, worried that a reunited Germany would dominate the rest of Europe. Notoriously, Margaret Thatcher (whose home town of Grantham was bombed by the Nazis during the war) told a dinner with EU leaders in 1989: 'We beat the Germans twice, and now they're back.' Thatcher wasn't alone in her scepticism. The Dutch were wary of recreating the behemoth which had menaced them in the past. The French, meanwhile, worried an empowered Germany might derail European unification. Others were even more zealous: Israeli Prime Minister Yitzhak Shamir said that given 'the German people decided to kill millions of Jewish people', there was a risk that if a reunified Germany became 'the strongest country in Europe . . . they will try to do it again'. For the government in Bonn, the lack of support was hard to swallow. The public, however, were united. From November 1989 onwards, crowds in Bonn and elsewhere began chanting '*Wir sind ein Volk*', 'We are one people'.

Meanwhile, Kohl and Gorbachev continued their slow-motion, high-stakes chess game. In the summer of 1990, with the Kremlin on the brink of insolvency, the West Germans agreed to bail out the Soviets with a loan in exchange for an easy ride on reunification. On 3 October 1990, East Germany was officially dissolved and its constituents absorbed, along with West Germany, into a single reunified country. New *Länden* (German states) were created in the east, and extra income taxes introduced to cover the cost of reunification. Like a Trotskyist erased from photographs of a revolution, East Germany largely vanished without a trace, unlamented and uncommemorated. '*Jetzt wächst zusammen was zusammengehört*', Willy Brandt famously said; 'Now what belongs together is growing together'.

Around the Rhine, thousands of military personnel and diplomats began packing their bags. Between 1989 and 1996 the US military budget for Germany halved. Some major bases stayed open, but many were dismantled or abandoned. Vast car parks outside cities like Karlsruhe were filled with long rows of trucks and jeeps waiting export. To the relief of many, thousands of nuclear weapons were also exported: across Europe, the number fell from around 4,000 in 1990 to about 480 by the 2000s. The bunker south of Bonn was closed. A region which had once been a potential ground zero for a third world war was at peace again.

In Bonn, the end of the Cold War meant the city's fifteen minutes of fame were over. In June 1991 parliamentarians held a passionate ten-hour debate about whether the capital should stay in Bonn or move elsewhere. In the end MPs voted 320 to stay in Bonn and 337 to relocate to Berlin. Government departments and embassies began packing boxes and convoys of trucks headed east. 'It kind of reminds me of [the fall of] Saigon,' one anguished American diplomat said.*

To atone for Bonn's loss of status, the new federal government pledged billions for redevelopment. The UN arrived in 1996 and filled several big riverside buildings which loomed over their German neighbours – a ready-made metaphor for the declining power of nation states. Most agreed there was little evidence the change had boosted either centralisation or militarism. If anything, the opposite occurred: visiting Berlin, with its checkpoints and walls and memorials, people were more acutely aware of Germany's anguished history than if they'd gone to twee little Bonn or bustling Frankfurt. 'Bonn's a bit dull,' one friend who often worked in Germany told me. 'But when you go to Berlin, you get to see everything: pride, shame, sadness, optimism. It's German history in microcosm.'

In Bonn itself, optimists claimed the loss of capital city status had lightened the local spirit, helping the city lose some of its government-induced greyness. Personally, I wasn't quite sure that was right. I always loved visiting Bonn: there were good museums and beerhalls, the long riverside promenade was perfect for running in the mornings, and the people epitomised Rhineland hospitality. But I also often found the atmosphere a little deflated. As Berlin boomed, there seemed something slightly tragic about Bonn's defiant claims to be a great world city, long after everyone had packed up

---

* Remarkably, the politician who gave perhaps the most influential speech in the relocation debate was one Wolfgang Schäuble, who twenty-five years later was still reshaping Europe as Germany's all-powerful finance minister.

and left. Parts of the old city were beautiful, but tall weeds sprouted between the flagstones on the riverbank, and there was so much graffiti that I wondered whether the city government had given the decoration contract to a street gang rather than the usual house painters. In the summer, Bonn could be delightful, but in the winter, I often thought Gorbachev's glasnost and perestroika had destroyed it almost as effectively as any nuclear strike. Others, though, disagreed. The *Lonely Planet* guide I flicked through in a bookshop was succinct if a little prim: 'Bonn is doing just fine, thank you.'

It was evening by now, and with the sun sinking towards the river, I walked back towards the old town. Two young men sat sharing a crate of beer on a pontoon, while a child stared open-mouthed at a fat man driving a fancy speedboat perilously close to the shore. 'He's the captain of that boat,' the little girl's mother explained. 'He must be very rich!' Near the Kennedy Bridge, I stopped for dinner at another tourist-friendly pub, where I ordered a schnitzel the size of a frisbee. On the television in the corner of the bar, Angela Merkel was grimacing through a photo call at a G20 summit in Hamburg, while rioters outside showed how much they hated western capitalism by smashing into department stores and stealing the products of western capitalism. 'For Merkel,' the announcer intoned, 'the summit has been a disaster. Germany has been humiliated.'

For the Germans, that day's headlines were an unusual setback. For many Europeans, following Donald Trump's election to the American presidency, the Germans' post-war rise seemed complete. 'Isn't it great to see peaceful transfer of power of leadership of free world?' an American friend once texted me as we both watched the live footage of Barack Obama handing over office to Donald Trump. 'From Obama to Merkel, without a single shot being fired.'

The German ascendancy had been a slow one. In the years following the end of the Second World War, West German leaders fought a determined campaign to regain some moral authority from beneath the ashes of Auschwitz, Buchenwald and Spandau. A succession of chancellors made grand, photogenic gestures of atonement. It was a slow process, with downs as well as ups, and many people were rightly furious at how easily some Nazis resumed their old places as pillars of the establishment. Incredibly, one Nazi officer who'd been standing next to Hitler when he survived the famous briefcase bomb assassination plot, Adolf Heusinger, was elevated to serve as Adenauer's military adviser and eventually became chairman of NATO's Military Committee in Washington DC. Overall, though, the rehabilitation efforts were strikingly successful. By the early 2000s, when I first started visiting Germany, it had finally become a normal country, where the young were not expected to account for the failings of their grandparents, and history was generally just that: history.

More recently, Angela Merkel had made a concerted effort to position her country as not just an economic exemplar to the world, but a moral one too, setting Europe's agenda on refugees and climate change, and resisting populism. To call Merkel 'the leader of the free world' was hyperbole, but she was clearly the leader of a certain centrist European worldview, combining economic dynamism with tolerant humanitarianism. Some seventy years after Auschwitz, Germany had come full circle: from moral pariah to conscience of a continent.

In other ways, though, it wasn't hard to see Bonn's decline into provinciality as a metaphor for broader unease about Germany's global stature. The more time I spent in the country, the more I thought there was also something a little stunted about Germany's political development. In many ways, of course, the country was a big fish in the geopolitical pond. German forces had fought in Afghanistan, and defence spending was set to increase sharply. In international development circles, Germany's development ministry was considered a global leader. In contrast with some of their British counterparts, German MEPs always seemed deeply at ease in a European parliamentary system which was based on political group-ings rather than parties, mind-numbing committee work and endless capacity to compromise.

Yet on the world stage, the Germans often lacked confidence; perpetually worried about what others would think if they acted too assertively. In 2011, for example, they joined Russia and China in abstaining on a UN Security Council vote for air strikes in Syria; while seven years later they said air strikes were 'necessary' but declined to actually participate in them. Armed interventions abroad remained exceedingly rare, and German leaders rarely displayed the swashbuckling swagger of their French or British counterparts. In the early twentieth century, Germany still often seemed, as the author Michael Wise put it, 'an economic giant but a political pygmy'.

In many ways this pacifist outlook was understandable – admirable, even – given their history. But there was often tension between what Patrick Keller described in *Der Spiegel* as Germany's 'strategic interest' in protecting a liberal international order, and its 'political will' to do so. The contrast with the neighbouring Dutch – breezily confident of their place in world, and their ability to shape it – was stark. Overall, the German government often looked like a new driver at the wheel of a powerful Porsche; afraid to put their foot down for fear of the horrors which might result. The prevailing attitude to entanglements overseas was perhaps best summarised by the FDP statesman Hans-Dietrich Genscher, who once said: 'I will be happy to give anyone in search of adventure the phone number of the French Foreign Legion.'

Back near Beethoven's house, I sat watching the bustle on the riverbank. I flicked through my notes for a while, trying to brush up my still terrible German-language skills – a task which had become easier now I'd remembered a single word, *bitte*, could be used to mean everything from 'please' to 'go ahead', 'you're welcome', 'I beg your pardon?' and 'yes, I definitely would like another cocktail'.

With dinnertime approaching, I wandered through the city centre and found two restaurants I liked the look of; one German and one Italian. I couldn't decide which one was best, so opted to eat at both: a pizza in one, followed immediately by a giant sausage and potatoes next door. Afterwards, I felt proud that I'd done my bit to support the German economy, even if I could hardly walk. I rolled down the street in the direction of my hotel, and was intercepted by a man holding a menu, trying to tempt passers-by into his restaurant. 'Why don't you come in and try our chocolate pudding?' he asked. '*Bitte*,' I replied, 'Yes, please.'

8

The Romantic Rhine

Koblenz to Rüdesheim

Fᴏʀ ᴀ ᴍᴀɴ who had been dead for nearly a hundred and thirty years, Kaiser Wilhelm looked in surprisingly good health. Wearing a plumed helmet and sitting high on a prancing horse, he commanded a sweeping view over the Rhine in Koblenz, staring sternly across the water towards the mighty fortress on the opposite bank. In front of him, at the base of the statue, a small crowd of sightseers took selfies and posed for photographs on the steps, as tour boats on the river slowed to get a better look. The only one who wasn't impressed was my dog, Blackie – who, following a complex series of dog-sitting failures and train transfers, had joined me for a few days walking and boating along the river. She sniffed the granite, peered up at the Kaiser and his horse, and carefully peed on the stones.

Rounding the front of the statue, it quickly became apparent why it had been built where it had. A row of flagpoles led to a sharply pointed spit of land which jutted out into the grey water like the bow of a battleship: the Deutsches Eck or 'German Corner', where the Rhine met the Moselle at a great Y-shaped junction. As well as being an important river confluence, the corner was also roughly the point where the industrialised lower Rhine gave way to the picturesque 'Romantic Rhine' of tourism, cliché and legend. North of Koblenz, the channel was littered with factories, harbours and staid modern architecture, but for a long stretch to the south there were almost no bridges and few modern buildings, and the river looked largely as it would have a century previously; lined with castles, churches and forests. It was here more than perhaps anywhere else that the Rhine became a true symbol of Germany; the legendary lifeblood of the country.

With the dog trotting contentedly behind me, I walked along the river, passing tourist booths selling T-shirts and fishermen casting long lines into the current. In many ways, Koblenz was another archetypal Rhine city; a smallish place with a charming old centre and a dreary modern shopping zone, all neatly hemmed in by low hills and water. I suspected most non-Germans would struggle to locate it on a map, but it was attractive, and had a sense of historic grandeur which made you feel you might bump into a pope or an emperor around every corner.

Like so many other cities in the region, Koblenz had often found itself at the crossroads of history: as a major Roman trading centre, as a Frankish royal seat, as the capital of the Prussian Rhine Province, and as the scene of heavy fighting during the Second World War. By the twenty-first century it had become best known as the gateway to the castle-filled middle Rhine, but was also a significant commercial centre; home to companies shipping car parts, paper, beer and petrol up and down the Rhine, and along the Moselle into Luxembourg and Belgium. My last visit had been in 2016, when the city had briefly the hit headlines by hosting a conference of far-right nationalists looking forward to their own supposedly inevitable election triumphs. Marine Le Pen had pledged to 'free ourselves from the chains of the European Union', while Geert Wilders, on a visa-free trip over the border from the Netherlands, had declared in fluent German that 'Europe needs a strong Germany, a self-confident Germany, a proud Germany'.

For non-racist visitors, Koblenz's main attraction lay opposite the Deutsches Eck and Kaiser statue, in the form of the terrific Ehrenbreitstein fortress, a great hulking pile of stone which dominated a clifftop above the Rhine. It wasn't the region's most attractive building, but was wonderfully intimidating; sometimes known as the 'Gibraltar of the Rhine'. I'd visited it once before, a few years previously, on an icy November morning when the city was deserted. Then, sneaking away from a boring work conference, I'd spent a frigid afternoon tramping up and down looking for the path which led up to the fortress, cursing its impregnability and vowing to make sure my next business trip was to balmy Italy or Portugal rather than frosty Germany. Today, I resolved not to make a similar mistake but to breach the cliffs the easy way: by cable car.

Carrying my dog, I boarded the cable car and was soon sliding alarmingly high and fast over the river. Opposite the statue of the

Kaiser, a large riverbank park contained dozens of brick-like white holiday caravans – filled, no doubt, with Dutch families happily barbecuing imported Dutch food and spending as little money as possible. We rocked a little in the wind, but my dog was again utterly nonplussed by the experience; no more afraid of the swaying glass cubicle than she had been of a dustbin we'd seen a few minutes before boarding. I'd found her as a tiny foxlike stray on a beach in Malawi some months previously and brought her back to the Netherlands with me, in a triumph of bribery over bureaucracy. I'd assumed she'd despair of life in a chilly Rotterdam apartment, but she loved it, gleefully chasing ducks up and down the river Rotte, eating green *erwtensoep* for dinner and surviving the chilly Dutch evenings by sleeping atop a hot-water bottle. The only problem was her tendency to mistake window cleaners' hoses for snakes, and stand barking furiously at them in the street. Now, she became probably the first Malawian street dog ever to ride a German cable car. Her verdict was again swift and unambiguous: after taking a quick look at the view from the enormous curved windows, she curled up to sleep on the floor.

After a few minutes' ride, we arrived at the top of the rock and departed, following a large group of French schoolchildren accompanied by a tour guide dressed for Dickens, in a top hat and tails. Inside the fantastically thick walls, the fortress was strangely hollow, with an open, geometric shape which looked more like the star-shaped Portuguese and Omani forts of East Africa than the crumbling grey piles one usually saw in northern Europe. A vast sandy-floored parade ground was surrounded by neoclassical buildings plastered in buttercup yellow, and a wooden hut selling beer was tragically closed. I paused on the thick ramparts and childishly aimed an imaginary cannon, sinking a passing barge in a great plume of water just before it turned the corner into the Moselle. The dog, perhaps sensing I was distracted, took the opportunity to make a break for freedom and sprinted away across the gravel and into a little café, where I found her staring happily at a row of *bratwurst* on the grill.

Like many such fortresses in the region, Ehrenbreitstein had an impressively swashbuckling past. The history of the region around

Koblenz has enough twists and turns to make an acrobat dizzy, but it's probably sufficient to say that under the Romans, Koblenz was yet another of the Rhine's great military and trading hubs – the city's modern name probably comes from the Latin *confluentes*, or confluence. Caesar built one of the first ever bridges across the river here, using enormous logs from the surrounding forests, and just outside the city stood a shrine to Mercury, the Roman god representing the people who played such a pivotal role in the region's fortunes: merchants and tradesmen, travellers and transporters. Later, after the Romans packed their bags, Koblenz remained important; a Frankish royal seat in the sixth century, it was given to the arch-bishops of Trier in 1018. Later still, this part of the Rhineland became the focal point of a prolonged tug of war between French and Prussian★ forces, both of whom were determined to control the great river. In 1814–15 the great powers assembled at the Congress of Vienna to agree the reorganisation of Europe after the Napoleonic Wars. The outcomes included a fiendishly complex series of land swaps in places such as Modena and Lauenberg, but one of the most significant was that much of the Rhineland fell decisively under Prussian control. The area around Koblenz became a major strategic concern – a bottleneck for river traffic, the site of several key bridges, and a natural defensive barrier lying roughly a hundred miles from present-day France, Belgium and Luxembourg. The fortress at Ehrenbreitstein was enlarged and strengthened by the Prussians, forming the keystone of a ring of fortifications around Koblenz. The fortress became a by-word for toughness, even earning a mention in Herman Melville's *Moby Dick*, where Father Mapple's preaching pulpit was compared to 'a self-containing stronghold – a lofty Ehrenbreitstein'. Ironically, though, all the building work turned out to have been in vain; the long sloping access ramp at the rear of the fortress, coupled with improvements in weapons technology, meant it was rendered somewhat obsolete not long after it was completed, an outdated MiniDisc player in an iPhone world.

★

★ Prussia, for those who weren't paying attention in school, was a vast, powerful kingdom which stretched across much of northern and eastern Europe, dominating the region's politics and eventually forming a large part of modern Germany.

The dog and I walked briefly around the fortress's thick walls. On the western side, the steep drop down to the river was shielded by a railing decorated with the obligatory 'love locks' left by couples who thought the perfect symbol of undying affection was rusting theft deterrence. The view from the front parapet was easily the best I'd had since Königswinter: the Rhine and Moselle laid out like lines on a map; the lumpy spurs of the Eifel, Taunus, Westerwald and Hunsrück mountains; and Koblenz itself, looking like a child's toy town dropped on a rumpled green bed-sheet.

I bought a pretzel to share with the dog. Nearby, a school group was doing target practice with real bows and arrows, aiming at a life-sized model deer. I found it hard to imagine a school outing doing the same thing in another country, but they seemed to be having terrific fun, and the next generation of hunters looked ruthlessly accurate. 'Try to hit the heart!' their female teacher cried. The dog barked, and I turned and ran before the children had time to take aim.

The Germans weren't always so united in their purpose. For much of the 1800s, Germany was as fractured and fragmented as a dropped plate; divided into hundreds of different territories and fiefdoms. The country wasn't entirely disunited, and people did feel a certain kinship with one another, but a Bavarian Catholic farmer could have been forgiven for wondering what he had in common with a Lutheran pastor in Bonn, a Protestant trader in Cologne or a Jewish boatman in Mannheim. 'What are the Germans?' the nationalist Friedrich Karl von Moser famously asked in 1766. 'What we are . . . is a puzzle of a political constitution, a prey of our neighbours, an object of their scorn . . . weak from our divisions, strong enough to harm ourselves [but] powerless to save ourselves.'

As the nineteenth century progressed, the different states and territories began the slow process of integration, the Rhine helping to drive it as merchants and shippers formed customs unions and reduced barriers to river trade. As the process continued, however, it quickly became clear that legal and diplomatic treaties would not on their own be enough to build a country. In order to be truly united, people needed not only the physical trappings of a nation state – borders, flags and coins – but also something less tangible: a distinctive national culture, with literature, music, myths and legends which encapsulated what the country was and what it stood for. In 1808, Johann Gottlieb Fichte delivered his famous '*Reden an die deutsche Nation*' ('Addresses to the German Nation'), a bombastic speech packed with advice about how to strengthen national identity. Germany, Fichte said, was not merely a collection of disparate entities, but a distinctive culture with roots going back to the time of the victory over the Romans at Teutoburg. The Germans, he said, were a people who were 'joined to each other by a multitude of invisible bonds . . . by nature one and an inseparable whole'. Later, this would all come to be seen as having laid some of the foundations for Nazism, but at the time, it was stirring stuff. Searching for new symbols of national culture, Fichte's followers turned for inspiration to the past. Germany, they argued, was not an artificial construct, but something timeless and majestic; the wellspring of a culture which had shaped European history and defied the Romans.

Nature, in particular, played a central role in the emerging national identity. This principle wasn't unique to Germany, of course: Americans often saw their country as embodied in the cowboy-filled open plains of the west, while the Dutch identity was deeply intertwined with the acres of flat land reclaimed from the water. For many Germans, meanwhile, their emerging national identity was epitomised by the wilderness: forests, lakes, mountains and rivers. The idealised German citizen would not be a sophisticated urban dandy, but a rugged woodsman, huntsman or boatman.

Forests were seen as particularly important. Early Germanic tribes had seen the wild woodland as an object of worship, and when they defeated the urbane Romans at Teutoburg Forest, woodland's status as a symbol of Germanic invincibility was assured. Later still, woodland would be a recurring motif in German literature. Goethe's *Faust* tells of how 'A longing pure and not to be described / drove me to wander over woods and fields', while Rainer Maria Rilke said true beauty was to be found not in fine art but in the forest, with 'colour made of apple bark'. For many Germans, the forest was (and is) as closely linked with their identity as any flag or song.

As nationalist rhetoric bloomed, the river Rhine also loomed large in German nationalists' minds. Rivers have long been seen as gushing with symbolism: fertility, creative power, the unstoppable passage of time; the rosebud at the crux of everything from *Heart of Darkness* to *Huckleberry Finn*. For early German nationalists, the Rhine was an intoxicating brew: something which served simultaneously as pure and cleansing in an era of rapid industrialisation; as a unifying belt which tied together disparate states and cities; and as a symbol of an idealised past where heroism, honour and loyalty prevailed. 'Memories of what the Germans once were and could be in the future are evoked nowhere so clearly as on the Rhine,' wrote Friedrich Schlegel in 1803. The Rhine also made for a powerful symbol because of its geographical position, close to the border between Germany and its great rival France. Ernst Moritz Arndt, one of the most strident early patriots, called his influential polemic, inspired by the sight of ruined castles along the river, 'The Rhine – Germany's River, but not Germany's Border'.

In 1840, German nationalists were given a significant boost by the Rhine Crisis, a diplomatic tiff triggered by the French prime minister's insistence that France should own the left bank of the river. Responding to this outrageous claim, a German lawyer called Nikolaus Becker wrote a poem called '*Rheinlied*', in which he directly rebuffed the idea that the French might try to stake a claim to the river:

> They shall not have him,
> The free German Rhine,
> As long as hearts refresh themselves
> With his fiery wine

The poem was set to music dozens of times, and inspired numerous imitators and adaptations. By far the most famous of these was Max Schneckenburger's '*Die Wacht am Rhein*' ('The Watch on the Rhine'), a rousing call to arms which was printed on postcards given to soldiers and nearly became the German national anthem:

> The Rhine, the Rhine, the German Rhine,
> We all shall stand to hold the line!

By the mid 1800s, then, the river had become an important source of not only prosperity, but also of identity. In the minds of those striving to construct a unified national identity, the Rhine was conveniently both wild and cleansing, modern and historic, mythical and industrial. Like a lover's eyes, people could see in it whatever they wanted to see.

Leaving the fortress, I returned to the cable car and rocketed back down to the Deutsches Eck. The dog, having been cruelly thwarted in her quest to steal sausages, was getting restless, so we took a short walk along the Moselle, pausing to take photos of the bridges (me) and bark at mud-coloured geese (her). I'd noticed Dutch people often didn't much like dogs: they were too messy for such a tidy country, and too difficult to keep in small apartments. The Germans, though, appeared to be more like the Brits in their enthusiasm for all things canine. Our short walk was constantly interrupted by people who completely ignored me and dropped into a crouch to lavish attention on my hound, fondling her ears and telling her how '*schön*' she was. Eventually I dragged her away, and behind the Kaiser's statue we found another great symbol of German unity: three big slabs of the dismantled Berlin wall, propped up on the grass like tombstones. The dog was once again unimpressed, and became perhaps the first African stray in history to urinate on a piece of Cold War history.

I'd made a plan to travel as most visitors to the region always had done, and many still did: by boat along the river. Like the ferries I'd taken in Bonn, the one I boarded heading south wasn't exactly peaceful. The open-top deck was packed with wicker armchairs, a waiter rushed back and forward with trays of drinks, and a loud tannoy provided snippets of European history in three languages. To my amazement, there was even a Subway sandwich shop on board, selling traditional German delicacies including foot-long 'Tuna Ahoi' baguettes.

Despite these gripes, however, the whole experience turned out to be lovely. The weather was mild and breezy, and as we headed south the scenery became increasingly marvellous. A procession of chocolate-box towns lined up to greet us on the shore, each with beautiful whitewashed houses, grey church steeples, hills rising sharply behind, and a castle standing sentry high above. The riverbanks were so thickly forested that they looked as if they could have been knitted from bright green wool. Forests, castles, churches and mountains; it looked like a tourist's fantasy of what Europe should be.

I'd enjoyed walking and cycling along this stretch of the river several times in the past, but was surprised to find that the way in which most towns backed onto the surrounding hills meant they looked far prettier from the water than they did from the roads behind. The boat ploughed into a stiff breeze, but the water was completely smooth and our speed – about that of a brisk cyclist – proved just slow enough to be relaxing, but just fast enough to be interesting. I bought my dog a Tuna Ahoi and she happily ripped it apart all over the deck before falling asleep again.

Just south of Koblenz, we passed another small confluence on the east bank where another small river flowed into the Rhine from the east. Consulting my map, I realised it was something I'd been planning to look out for: the end of the river Lahn. Along it, a few miles to the east, lay the town of Nassau. This was, as I'd seen on a previous visit, a fairly unremarkable place, but for a person who lived in the Netherlands it had a certain significance: it was here, in the twelfth century, that a local count called Walram awarded himself title of Count of Nassau. His descendants later took control of extensive Dutch territories around the Rhine to the north, and these eventually passed to a young nobleman who would become William the Silent, who also controlled a patch of land in France known as Orange. For centuries to come, the Dutch royal family would be known by the name of two obscure towns which lay hundreds of miles from Amsterdam or The Hague: the House of Orange-Nassau.

The boat continued southwards, passing neat rows of vines which rose up from the riverbank like staircases. Along the railing at the bow of the boat, French passengers peered carefully at the vineyards, Germans talked about the schedule, and Brits complained about the limited supplies of bacon at the hotel breakfast. 'Why are we going so slow?' a cheerful Mancunian hollered. 'I just wanna get out and push!' 'I feel a bit seasick,' said another. Besides the scenery, the main attraction was my dog, who stretched out on her back and revelled in the attention of dozens of German tourists. I put my notebook down and fielded numerous questions about her birthplace, her diet and her favourite toys, while she wriggled happily on the deck.

After two hours of cruising, the boat arrived at my next destination, Boppard. Dragging the reluctant dog behind me, I walked down the gangplank and into an utterly charming town, with a row of nice little restaurants by the river, maps showing walking trails through the surrounding hills, and a flotilla of small boats coming and going on the water. Stopping at an estate agent's window, I saw it would be easy to buy a nice little terraced house here for 59,000 euros. I fiddled with the credit card in my pocket and thought: one day . . .

I'd stopped here partly because I'd seen on the map that there was supposed to be another cable car here, and I thought it might offer a good way to see the Rhine from above again. After a few confused circles, I found it: not the sleek modern cabins of Koblenz, but a rattly old thing which consisted of little more than wooden park benches slung beneath a long cable. It was hard not to feel nervous as we lurched high over the treetops, the dog sitting on my lap and peering nervously over my shoulder at the river. The bench swayed wildly in the wind and the thin wooden slats creaked beneath me. I wished I'd packed a parachute. Finally, to the dog's immense relief, we arrived at the top, and both rushed to the panoramic terrace to give thanks that we were still alive. The view was predictably spectacular, looking down across crumpled emerald hills, Swiss-looking towns, castles crumbling gracefully on top of almost every hill, and curving through it all, the river; grey-green and timeless. In the distance, a helicopter buzzed low over one of the vineyards, performing balletic gravity-defying twists and turns, spraying white clouds of pesticide on the vines below.

I was eager to give the dog some exercise after a morning stuck in boats and cable cars, and set out to walk back down the hill to the riverside town of Rhens, about two hours away. We descended gently at first, following a gravel fire-road through a dense pine forest. Through the trees, I caught glimpses of both the river and car-sized humps of brown earth – the remnants, I read later, of Iron Age burial mounds dating back more than two thousand years. Further down, the hills steepened and we emerged from the trees into a vineyard, the dog galloping gleefully up and down the rows as I picked sour grapes to suck on. In the distance, the river glinted like a jewelled highway. Not for the first time, I wondered how it was that north

Europeans had become so obsessed with flying to far-flung corners of Asia and the Americas in search of forests and ruins and waterfalls, when they had scenery like this in their own backyards.

I wasn't the only one beguiled by the region's landscapes. In the nineteenth century, as the Rhine began to take shape as a symbol of German strength and unity, people flocked to immortalise it: poets, writers, artists and musicians. In particular, the movement known as Romanticism took the Rhine as one of its major recurring themes. Like being in love or enjoying football, Romanticism is notoriously difficult to explain, but was essentially a nineteenth-century cultural movement which exalted the imaginative, spontaneous and emotional. The Rhine, timeless and dramatic, made a perfect subject.

The first romantic work about the Rhine to win a wide audience came in the early 1800s, when *Des Knaben Wunderhorn* (*The Boy's Magic Horn*) was published by Achim von Arnim and Clemens Brentano, a lyric poet who was born next to the Rhine at Ehrenbreitstein. The book – a finely illustrated collection of old German love songs and folk poems – presented Germany as the possessor of a unique national culture, and was wildly popular. Where Brentano had gone, others followed. Johann Wolfgang von Goethe studied for a doctorate near the Rhine at Strasbourg, travelled on the river several times, and spent part of the 1770s living on a farm where he fell for a local girl and enjoyed a rustic lifestyle. Goethe later described the Rhine as 'that beautiful river, so lovely in its windings, so various in its shores'. Samuel Taylor Coleridge visited Cologne, while John Ruskin took several tours and wrote: 'I see the Rhine in his native wild / Is still a mighty mountain child'. William Wordsworth travelled extensively in Germany, writing of 'the venerable pageantry of time' to be seen at 'the bright river's edge'. 'Beneath me flows the Rhine,' wrote Henry Wadsworth Longfellow in 1839, 'and like the stream of Time, it flows amid the ruins of the Past.' Many others trafficked in similar clichés – soaring eagles, roaring cannons, twinkling streams – and were enthusiastic to the point of being (to modern ears at least) foolishly giddy: 'Oh! This, to me, were earthly bliss,' wrote James Blake in 1840. 'My nature sure was made for this!'

Of course, the Rhine wasn't just celebrated in literature, but also in other forms of artistic expression, including music. The most famous composers to take inspiration from the river were Beethoven and Wagner (of whom more later). But there were also many others. Robert Schumann, for example, was inspired by a journey downstream to compose what became known as the Rhenish Symphony, a striding, surging work which painted a grand musical portrait of the river.

Painters, too, flocked to the middle Rhine. Further north, Dutch artists had long used the Maas, Rhine and other rivers as subjects. Johannes Vermeer's riverside *View of Delft*, Jacob van Ruisdael's watery Dutch landscapes, Aelbert Cuyp's paintings of barges around Dordrecht, Salomon van Ruysdael's mirror-like river scenes and Hendrick Avercamp's colourful pictures of lowlanders frolicking on frozen rivers all became hugely famous, helping satisfy urban Dutch merchants' longing for clean air and wide open spaces. Further south, the English painter J. M. W. Turner made several long journeys along the river, and sketched hundreds of bucolic rural scenes. Like many other artists, Turner had a habit of presenting the Rhine in idealised form – sunlight glinting through patchy clouds, craggy castles and happy peasants, with not a beggar or steelworks in sight. Some might say this habit never really died – in 2011, Andreas Gursky's *Rhine II* photograph of the Rhine, digitally edited to remove an ugly factory building, sold for $4.3 million at auction in New York, making it the most expensive photograph ever sold.

After a couple of hours walking downhill through the forest and vineyards, I arrived back at the riverbank. The dog drank heartily from the green current, and then we boarded another boat packed with sightseers, continuing southwards towards Bingen and Rüdesheim. This was reputed to be one of the most scenic stretches of the whole Rhine, and it didn't disappoint: within half an hour or so, we'd passed too many castles to count. One of the best was at Sankt Goar, where the Rheinfels castle stood proudly above the little town, looking across the water at two smaller rivals. I remembered I'd stayed just below the walls of one of them for a few days a year or two before, and had emerged one morning to find a fellow hotel guest telling me the result of the 2016 US presidential elections. '*Alles wird jetzt anders sein*,' he'd said with a worried frown, 'Everything will be different now.'

Just past Sankt Goar, the river bent quite sharply to the right and narrowed, the water suddenly foaming with white tails flung up by hidden rocks. The boat slowed. An automated recording announced, in English, Dutch and German: 'On your left is the famous Lorelei Rock.' Many of my fellow passengers had come specifically to see it, and there was another brief flurry of activity as dozens of beers were set down on tables, cameras drawn from bags, and people rushed to stand eagerly at the portside railings. The rock itself was hard to miss: a steep grey cliff, rising vertically from the water into the forested hillsides like a stretched pyramid. Near the base, a long artificial arm of rocks stretched out into the channel, with a buxom statue at the end – lady Lorelei, I presumed.

Like any good myth, the Lorelei story had countless versions and variations, but the most popular had it that Lorelei* was a beautiful maiden who, despairing over her cheating lover, threw herself from the clifftop into the river. Not content with her watery grave, she returned to the rock as a ghostly siren, luring countless fishermen to destruction on the rocky shore below. The story inspired countless songs, plays, operas and poems, including music by Shostakovich and Mendelssohn, a poem by Sylvia Plath and a song by Roxy Music.

The undoubted high prince of Lorelei Romanticism was Heinrich Heine, born a stone's throw from the Rhine in Düsseldorf in 1797. As a writer, Heine found himself living very much in the shadow of giants like Goethe, but managed to find a niche writing poems which were Romantic in their whimsy, yet also teased other Romantics for obsessing over the glories of the past. He also made a habit of criticising Germany's repressive political climate, calling it a 'country of oaks and apathy', mocking the glorification of the tribal victory over the Romans and praising the ideals of the French Revolution. 'Paris is the new Jerusalem,' he wrote, 'and the Rhine is the Jordan that separates the consecrated land of freedom from

---

* Again, the spelling varies according to taste and nationality, but is usually Lorelei in English and Loreley in German. The name is said to come from the Old High German *lauern* – 'to lurk' – and *lai* – 'rock'.

the land of the Philistines.' Unsurprisingly, such talk didn't win Heine many friends in Germany. The nationalist Heinrich von Treitschke complained: 'of all our lyric poets, he was the only one who never wrote a drinking song'. Many of Heine's works were censored or banned, partly because of his Jewish ancestry. Later, though, one of his works became known as an exemplar of Rhine Romanticism, popularising the Lorelei legend for centuries to come:

> And yonder sits a maiden,
> The fairest of the fair,
> With gold is her garment glittering,
> And she combs her golden hair.

I'd walked over the hills near Lorelei before, seen the rock from above, and found it hard to see what the fuss was about. Viewed from above, the muddy off-white crags looked more like a builder's rubble pile than the White Cliffs of Dover. Viewed from below, from the boat, I found it rather more impressive. The steep facade rose suddenly from the water like a tidal wave, and the nearby statue was pleasing in a vaguely discomfiting soft-porn sort of way. Yet on a stretch of the river which was crowded with spectacular castles and peaks, I still found it hard to see what made this particular rock so special. Around me, cameras clicked and people gasped, but I couldn't help feeling that – like the city of Havana and *The Godfather* – most people found Lorelei amazing mainly because they'd been told in advance that they would find it amazing. It was – as I grouchily scribbled in my notebook – 'nice enough, but perhaps the twelfth nicest big rock of the day'.

The boat continued its stately progress southwards. With the Lorelei receding over the stern, everyone's cameras were once again stowed, but the scenery was no less spectacular. Green forested hills were interrupted by rocky cliffs and pretty little towns, each with a castle peering down on it from above. My dog dozed in the sun and I succumbed to the inevitable, ordering a globe-like glass of wine from the overworked waiter rushing between the deck-top tables. It arrived almost immediately; a sweet, syrupy red which, according to the waiter, came 'not from here, but from another region'. He rushed off before I could ask for further details, but judging by the taste, the 'other region' may have been Lidl.

The river itself was much quieter here than it had been to the north, but there was still a steady flow of traffic, with a barge or container ship passing by every minute or so. A few minutes later we arrived at the next picturesque attraction: Kaub, the site of a tiny island in the middle of the Rhine which was barely bigger than our boat but adorned with a picture-perfect white-painted castle. Chains were once strung across the river here, forcing passing boats to stop and pay a fee, with any who refused confined to the dungeon. Today, it looked like a fairy-tale castle cut adrift. The boat passengers rose to their feet as one, rushing to once again unholster their phones and unpack their cameras and tripods. 'It looks even prettier than it did last year!' a happy Englishwoman said to her husband.

Excitable foreigners were nothing new around here. Tourists first began journeying along the Rhine in significant numbers in the late eighteenth century. Among the early visitors was Thomas Jefferson, who in 1788 took a break from his job as American minister in Paris, bought ten maps of the Rhine, and set out on a two-week trip along the river by horse and carriage. The future president grumbled about the region's 'ruinous' Gothic architecture, but enjoyed seeing first-hand the land from which many of his countrymen had emigrated: 'It is from . . . this part of the Rhine that those swarms of Germans have gone who . . . form the greatest body of our people,' he wrote to a friend. To a proud American, the Rhineland, Jefferson wrote, was 'a second mother country'.

The many nineteenth-century Brits who visited were equally besotted. Sensitive souls felt nature at home had been ruined by the arrival of the steam engine and spinning jenny, and (like many Germans) thought the middle Rhine landscape harked back to a more innocent age. William Beckford, for example, travelled upstream in 1783 and went home filled with stories of the river as a 'landscape of the soul's dreams'.

One of the most significant early visitors was a seventeen-year-old girl, who ran away with her older lover in the summer of 1814. The girl was Mary Godwin, the daughter of the English novelist

Mary Wollstonecraft, and the lover was Percy Bysshe Shelley, then the *enfant terrible* of the London literary scene. Together they roamed far across Europe, visiting the Alps and then returning along the Rhine from Switzerland towards the Netherlands. Their trip coincided with an infamous spell of bleak wintry weather in the Rhineland, triggered by a volcano in Indonesia, and the journey wasn't exactly a luxury cruise.* Mary, in particular, loved the dramatic scenery, but was appalled by the vulgarity of her fellow boat passengers, who boozed all day: 'Such monsters,' she wrote in her diary. In September the boat stopped in a town called Gernsheim, about seventy miles south-east of Koblenz, where Mary and Percy enjoyed a walk along the Rhine's banks and up through the town's pretty cobbled streets. In the distance they could see the towers of a castle called Frankenstein, peeking over the pine trees. Talking to a local man, Mary learned the legend associated with the castle: an alchemist called Konrad Dippel had been born there in the 1670s, and later became notorious for allegedly conducting experiments in which he tried to find a cure for death, digging up body parts from local cemeteries, grinding bones and blood together, and injecting the gruesome mixture into other corpses in the hopes of bringing them back to life. The technique didn't work, of course, but Mary enjoyed the story, and it gave her an idea for a tall tale of her own.

A few years later (back in England, married to Percy, and known as Mary Shelley), she published first a travel diary recounting her trip down the Rhine, and then a horror novel inspired by the story of the mad scientist in the castle; *Frankenstein, or, The Modern Prometheus.* The novel was initially dismissed by reviewers ('a tissue of horrible and disgusting absurdity', the *Quarterly Review* called it), and many misogynists assumed that Mary's more famous husband must have ghostwritten it. Today, the book is remembered mostly for its clunky movie adaptations and lurching monster with a bolt through his neck. In reality, though, it was a richly layered and structurally complex work, including the then unthinkable plot twist whereby the doctor was not proud of the creature he'd created it, but horrified by it. In parts of the novel, the scenery Mary described reflected the apocalyptic weather she'd seen in the

---

* For more on the volcano and its impact on the Rhine, see Chapter 9.

Rhineland: 'never was a scene more awfully desolate . . .' More happily, the book was also notable for a long section in which Frankenstein (the doctor, not the monster) travelled down the Rhine. In a novel filled with horrors and haunting encounters, the protagonist's Rhine trip stood out as a rare oasis of peace; one of the few places where he could get some relief. 'I lay at the bottom of the boat, and, as I gazed on the cloudless blue sky, I seemed to drink in a tranquillity to which I had long been a stranger,' the doctor said.

Thanks to writers like Shelley, travel on German rivers quickly became something of a cliché of Victorian literature. Henry Bulwer-Lytton, a British MP who voyaged along the middle Rhine in the early 1830s, wrote in the bestselling *The Pilgrims of the Rhine* that 'the best commentary to the German genius is a visit to the German scenery'. * William Makepeace Thackeray's novel *Vanity Fair* told the tale of George Osborne – an 'imperious young gentleman who gobbled the biscuits' – travelling along the river through 'fair scenes of peace and sunshine [past] noble purple mountains, whose crests are reflected in the magnificent stream'. Eventually, the Rhine became so famous that it was even rhapsodised by writers who'd never been there. Felicia Hemans, for example, was a Liverpudlian who wrote gushing poetry about kings and knights and the scenic beauty of the ivy leaves on the ruins of Rheinfels, despite never having seen them.

The most influential traveller, however, did indeed visit. George Gordon, Lord Byron, was the archetype of a foppish, footloose Romantic poet – a club-footed over-eater famously described by Lady Lamb as 'mad, bad and dangerous to know'. Byron spent much of 1809–10 touring Europe in grand style, visiting Troy and Constantinople and swimming the Hellespont. At times, he seemed more like a rampant sex tourist than a thoughtful poet – 'none female nor under ten nor Turk' was his main rule. However, he did use his European experiences as the inspiration for a long poem called *Childe Harold's Pilgrimage.*† Byron's text, published by the

---

* Bulwer-Lytton, who later became known for his florid turns of phrase, is generally considered the first writer to ever use the much parodied phrases 'It was a dark and stormy night' and 'The pen is mightier than the sword'.

† *Childe* was a medieval term referring to a young nobleman who hadn't yet been knighted.

Rhine-loving publisher John Murray, was intensely autobiographical. It described the dreamy adventures of a young man who sought distraction and adventure in foreign lands. In well-heeled London, *Childe Harold* caused a sensation. Byron 'woke to find himself famous', lionised in London society and swept into a series of passionate affairs with upper-class women, including (according to several biographers) his own half-sister. Seeking to escape this disastrous personal life, he fled England in 1816 and sailed up the Rhine all the way to Geneva, where he wrote the third canto (section) of *Childe Harold*, following the hero Harold from Belgium up the Rhine River to Switzerland. This was another publishing sensation. Like modern-day celebrity spotters carrying maps to 'Homes of the Stars', tourists began carrying copies of Byron's *Childe Harold* as they went up and down the river.

For the English in particular, the middle Rhine was, if not quite the Costa del Sol of its day, then at least the Luxor or Marrakesh – a place where mildly adventurous, well-off travellers could go in search of their own tall tales to share. Some were inevitably disappointed to find the 'unspoilt' river almost as busy as home towns they'd left behind. Others, though, were utterly entranced. 'Are we on earth?' wondered one English female traveller in 1880s. 'It was as though I had awakened in fairyland.' To Germans and foreigners alike, the Rhine had become not just a river, but a myth.

The boat arrived in Bacharach, yet another little town squeezed between the river and the hills. The sleepy dog and I disembarked and walked into a roll-call of touristic German clichés: cobbled streets, half-timbered restaurants, beer gardens, creeper-covered walks, churches and fountains, a turreted castle above and vineyards stretching across the hills in the distance. In years of wandering Europe's scenic hotspots, I'd rarely seen anywhere prettier.

I took a room at a drab little hotel which looked like it hadn't been cleaned since Byron's time, and collapsed into a chair at the first riverside café and ordered a cold drink. The Romanian waitress, blue-eyed and black-haired, stopped to pet the dog and we talked for a while. 'Life here is better,' she said. 'The money is good, but the language is difficult, and we're always working. It's much better for me here, but when I see people like you travelling around, having fun, I think: my god! I'm so jealous. I miss my dog.' I ordered dinner, splitting my meagre budget between one of the cheapest meals on the menu and one of the most expensive, and then sat unhappily munching a dry cheese sandwich while the dog guzzled her rib-eye steak.

The next day, I awoke early and continued my journey south-wards, taking another boat for what would be my last on the Romantic Rhine. Early one grey weekday morning, the boat was half empty, but it was another lovely journey, cruising under a bruised and brooding sky which gave a faint air of menace to the castles and forests looming overhead. My dog, deeply unimpressed at the prospect of another day on boats, stared mournfully at the water.

We alighted in Bingen, and took a small ferry quickly across the river to Rüdesheim. Another glassy cable car ferried people up from the riverbank to the hilltop, but I opted to walk again, following a curving track upwards through the vines. The dog ran happily ahead, sniffing at unripe grapes and occasionally turning to bark at me when I failed to keep up. A friend was due to pick her up that evening and give her a ride back home to Rotterdam, so this would be our last day on the river together, for a while at least.

Arriving at the top of the hill, I emerged from a small patch of forest to another breathtaking panorama: sloping emerald vineyards, the wide river studded with splintery islands, barges leaving long white plumes down the centre of the channel. The real attraction, though, lay not down in the valley but behind me, sprouting from the treetops atop the hill. The Niederwalddenkmal, or Niederwald Memorial, was perhaps the ultimate expression of German Rhine patriotism. Constructed in the 1870s–80s to celebrate the union of the peoples of Germany, it consisted of a forty-metre-high series of stone plinths adorned with an explosion of greenish bronze plaques and statuary, including a life-sized winged angel blowing a mighty trumpet, and a bare-breasted woman accepting a drink from a bearded Neptune. Thick metal letters spelled out several verses of the song 'Die Wacht am Rhein' ('The Watch on the Rhine'). Atop it all stood a twelve-metre statue of Germania – a sturdy woman with robes, sword and shield, who in the late nineteenth century was increasingly adopted as the personification of the German nation. The overall effect of the monument was terrific; as if excitable children had been given a break from decorating a Christmas tree and allowed instead to choose as many statues and plaques as they liked, and then compress them into a single monument.

Long before he became a two-bit politician, Adolf Hitler passed by here with a group of fellow soldiers, and later wrote: 'As the first soft rays of the morning sun broke through the light mist and disclosed to us the Niederwald statue, with one accord the whole troop train broke into the strains of *Die Wacht am Rhein*. I felt then as if my heart could not contain its spirit.' Today, any such public display of nationalism in Germany would be considered deeply taboo. While the Dutch looked for any excuse to celebrate together in orange clothes, and the Brits loved nothing more than the nostalgic pageantry of a royal wedding or the London Olympics, most modern Germans left their love of country unstated. Things which were common in other countries (military parades, fighter jet display teams) were unthinkable. Leaders like Merkel would never use the kind of proud patriotic language ('global power', 'force for good', 'born to lead') which came easily to their American, British or French counterparts. Yet as the crowds of German visitors posing for photographs in front of the memorial testified, both the monument and the river still exercised a powerful hold. The Rhine might flow through half a dozen countries, and have its source in Switzerland and its mouth in Holland, but to most Germans it would always be quintessentially German.

I bought two ice creams – one for me and one for the dog – and we sat side by side in front of the monument, happily slurping away and looking down at the river. I started to take a picture and was interrupted by cheerful young American women who asked me, in Dolly Parton tones, 'Is this the All-saze Lorraine?' No, I replied, as politely as I could, we are not in France.

9

Gamblers and Creators

Wiesbaden to Mainz and Mannheim

I USUALLY MADE it a rule not to go naked in public before break-fast, but in Wiesbaden I made an exception. I'd arrived late at night after several long days hiking, cycling and jogging around the middle Rhine, and by morning my muscles were aching so much that I could hardly lift my sixth croissant at breakfast. I was nearing the end of my time in Germany, and Wiesbaden seemed a perfect place to catch my breath for a few days: a spa town nestled close to a big bend in the Rhine, in the foothills of the Taunus moun-tains, famed for its curative properties and escapist atmosphere. It also made a good staging post for the final German phase of my Rhine journey, which would take me through a region which blended idle indulgence with industry and invention. In particular, I was looking forward to learning more about a few of the other Germans who'd helped shape the region's history and imprint it on the global consciousness, including those who'd come up with world-changing inventions on the river's banks.

The Wiesbaden spa looked more like a Greek temple than a municipal swimming pool. The main feature was an ice-cold blue pool about the size of a tennis court, surrounded by mosaics and statues of cherubs. Off to the sides, smaller chambers offered various low-level torture options: unbearably hot tubs, sweltering steam rooms and saunas of varying intensity. The water which spouted from the ground around Wiesbaden was reportedly rich in salt and other chemicals, and naturally heated to over 100 degrees Fahrenheit, but cooled slightly for bathing. Back in the library in Rotterdam, I'd read old travellers' accounts which complained it was like 'weak chicken broth', but to me it looked glassily clean, albeit with the slight sulphurous scent of a teenage boy's bedroom.

Several years living in the Netherlands had reduced my innate

English prudishness somewhat, but I still suffered from a typical Englishman's angst at public nudity. Cowering between the changing rooms and the pool, I spent ten anguished minutes trying to decide whether to keep my swimming trunks on or risk taking them off. Would the other patrons run screaming if I stripped off? Or would they run screaming if I didn't? I eventually decided to assimilate as best as I could, and marched to the poolside dressed as God made me, flinging my towel aside with carefree abandon. No one ran screaming, although I did get a big smile and a wink from a bearish, Russian-looking man twice my age, and wondered briefly if I'd strayed into the wrong kind of bathhouse.

The biggest surprise was that men and women were mixing freely not just in the pools but in the showers and changing rooms too, all as happily naked as the day they first drew breath. A group of older men sat talking about football in the hot tub, and a pair of middle-aged women were busily planning someone else's wedding while swimming lengths in the icy main pool. Yet despite the mixing of the sexes, the atmosphere was reassuringly chaste. I was almost certainly the only person who wasn't retired, and there were (to put it politely) more raisins on display than grapes. I didn't quite know where to look, and spent a lot of time feigning great interest in the ceiling.

In contrast with the more industrial cities to the north, Wiesbaden had a long history as a place of leisure dominated by two pursuits – gambling and lying in the bath – which were, coincidentally, two of my favourite hobbies. Like so much else in the Rhine region, the bathing habit was pioneered by the Romans. Pliny wrote of enjoying himself at 'hot springs . . . across the Rhine'. The famous Limes frontier passed close to Wiesbaden and it soon became a popular retreat where soldiers bloodied by tribal skirmishes could go to heal and relax.

After the Romans left, the spas fell into disrepair, but as Rhine trade increased, Wiesbaden was gradually resurrected as a place where weary merchants and statesmen could unwind. Between 1800 and 1820 alone, the number of visitors to Wiesbaden doubled. Under Germany's fragmented political system, spas became a popular source of revenue for local rulers who, like modern-day mayors building theme parks or shopping malls, invested in water attractions to boost their earnings. The dukes of Nassau built a residence on the edge of Wiesbaden, right on the riverbank. Like all tourism promoters, they were careful to promote a sense of tranquillity, presenting Wiesbaden as a safe haven where the wealthy could wander freely. In time, the Germans developed a name for the feeling which a visit invoked: *badefreiheit*, or 'spa freedom'. At first, the focus was on attracting blue bloods, but as German incomes rose and transport links improved, the spas became more shamelessly commercial. By the 1860s, there were dozens of baths in Wiesbaden, marketing their services aggressively and publishing daily registers bragging about which celebrities had visited: duke such-and-such came with a relative of Napoleon's yesterday!

The spas also made a pleasant pit-stop for many Grand Tourists travelling up and down the Romantic Rhine. Thanks to steamships and railways, Wiesbaden was (by the later 1800s) a mere twenty-four hours travel from London. 'Every soul must have his . . . autumn tour,' *The Gentleman's Magazine* reported in 1843. 'He must visit the watering-places, drink and bathe – he must traverse the Rhine . . . Baden, Baden-Baden, Wiesbaden, all the Badens.' Others were attracted by the health benefits of the spa. Decades before cigarette companies paid for 'scientific' studies 'proving' the health benefits of smoking, the people who ran Rhineland baths were paying doctors to write that bathing could cure everything from gout to kidney disease, rheumatism, syphilis, arthritis, constipation and 'old gunshot wounds'. One German doctor's report even claimed bathing in the waters could cure hypochondria.

After three hours circulating between various hot tubs and icy pools, I was starting to feel like a chicken which had been repeatedly boiled, broiled and returned to the freezer. Leaving the pools, I made a final trip to the sauna, where I sat sweating and chatting in stop-start German with an obese man as he ladled water onto a sizzling tray of rocks. 'I come here every day,' he told me. 'My wife refuses, but it makes me strong.'

I didn't feel strong, just hot, and after a few minutes more I bid my naked companion *'guten Tag'*, paid the bone-chilling bill and left the spa. Outside, the weather had brightened and the air felt unbelievably fresh on my skin. In future, I thought, I'd have to break my no-nudity-before-breakfast rule more often.

Beyond the spa, Wiesbaden was a compact, prosperous place dominated by a red neo-Gothic church and shops selling cashmere sweaters, grand pianos and Bang and Olufsen speakers. The German banking city of Frankfurt was only about twenty miles away, and you could smell the money from here. The atmosphere was different from most of the other German cities I'd visited so far: sleeker and calmer, with fewer tourists. The whole place felt grandly bland, like a bank.

As well as the spas, Wiesbaden had long been famous as a place where it was easy to waste money. The first casino opened in the 1770s, with the idea that its revenues might help cover the costs of maintaining the baths. Later, steamships travelling down the Rhine provided many customers. 'The student, the poet, the steady-going lover of nature and art, will not care for Wiesbaden,' an early guidebook said, 'but the pleasure-seeker will.'

For the most part, the casinos helped enhance Wiesbaden's reputation as a place of leisure and luxury. But for individuals, the consequences of a trip along the Rhine could be devastating. In the late 1800s, for example, locals told of a young woman who'd arrived in their city from Paris carrying all the money she had in the world; a total of 100 francs. After a few days of tremendous luck, she'd won no less than 200,000 francs, and set out for home thrilled to be free from the shackles of poverty. At the train station, however, she found her train was delayed and popped back out to a casino, where she promptly lost the lot. A kindly casino owner paid for a train ticket back to Paris, but that wasn't enough to lift her spirits, and her body was found floating in the Seine the next day.

Another hapless high-roller was the Russian novelist Fyodor Dostoyevsky, the author of *Crime and Punishment*. Dostoyevsky spent much of his forties roaming around Europe, and by the time he arrived in Wiesbaden in 1865 he was ruinously addicted to gambling. In Wiesbaden, he bucked his usual bad luck by winning 10,400 francs in a casino, but the inevitable soon followed. 'I then came home,' he later wrote to his sister-in-law, 'and shut them up in a bag and intended to leave Wiesbaden the next day . . . but I got carried away.' Within a few more days, he'd gambled away all he had, including an extra emergency loan he'd begged from Ivan Turgenev, and was reduced to wandering the city's pawnshops in search of few extra coins. 'All the servants treat me with unspeakable, quite typically German contempt,' he complained. 'The German knows no greater crime than to be without money and not to pay one's bills promptly.'

On the plus side, the stay did inspire Dostoyevsky's creativity. Too broke to afford food or even a candle, he retired to his hotel room and began to write – 'burning with some kind of inner fever'. The words tumbled out, including many which would later be published as *Crime and Punishment*. He also dictated another novel – *The Gambler* – set in a thinly disguised version of Wiesbaden; Roulettenburg – a 'dismal little town' dominated by the addictive appeal of 'roulette, a game pre-eminently for the Russians'. 'With what trembling, with what faintness of heart I hear the croupier's cry!' the novel's protagonist exclaims. 'As soon as I begin to hear the clinking of money being poured out, I almost go into convulsions.' Inevitably, the money Dostoyevsky earned from *The Gambler* was mostly gambled away.

The morning in the spa had left me feeling unusually refreshed, and I decided to explore the area further by going for a run. After changing in my hotel, I jogged west from the city down towards the river. At first, the scenery was bleakly suburban – all out-of-town shopping centres and drive-through 'restaurants' selling heart attacks packaged in polystyrene. Further from the city centre, though, it became quietly wonderful: narrow, curving streets lined with stately old brownstone buildings and pretty patches of parkland. Unlike many Rhine cities, Wiesbaden had survived the Second World War relatively unscathed – 'Wiesbaden [the Allies] want to save', an observer wrote, 'because they want to live there'. Nearing the river, I passed through a lovely green park dominated by the enormous Schloss Biebrich, the former residence of the dukes of Nassau. Wide and low-rise, the building was strikingly attractive in the sunlight, its white walls fringed with orange-pink crenellations and statues. It looked like an English country house crossed with a striped candy cane.

Immediately behind the park was the Rhine, tree-lined and breezy. Looking south, I could just see the port of Mainz, with a great stack of shipping containers on the bank nearly obscuring the spires of the cathedral. Outside the Schloss, the riverbank was lined with rows of neatly manicured trees and big potted palm trees. A café near the front steps was filled with people having ice cream for brunch. The water glinted in the sunlight. I stopped and rested for a minute on the riverbank, near a sign explaining this spot was beloved by Goethe, Germany's Shakespeare, who visited in 1814 and pronounced it '*sehr schön*', 'very beautiful'. He was right.

The next day I headed to Mainz, cycling a few miles south along the river and then over a high bridge towards the city spires. Mainz was yet another city which had benefited from a position at the confluence of major rivers, lying close to the point where the river Main flowed into the Rhine from the east. Mogontiacum was another important Roman military base, home to a fleet of little wooden battleships which were dispatched up or down the river to fight rebellious locals. As the Romans retreated, the city was abruptly abandoned, but rose again as an important ecclesiastical centre and Rhine trading hub. Since 1992, it had also been connected to the river Danube by the Main–Danube canal – a grand piece of engineering first dreamt up by Charlemagne – which made it possible for mid-sized vessels to float some two thousand miles from Hoek van Holland to the Black Sea. Mainz's harbour was small but appeared to be thriving; another clear riposte to those who thought riverine trade had gone the way of the fax and the dodo.

In 1944 and 1945 Mainz had been hit by over twenty thousand British and American bombs and over a million incendiary sticks, which destroyed most of the city centre. It looked well preserved, however, packed as it was with grand old buildings, gently sloping brick-floored streets and leafy squares where people were eating yet more ice cream. At the centre was the cathedral, a stunning pinkish structure which looked as if it were made from bricks of salmon. 'It looks just like my office back home,' a passing Canadian tourist said.

The weather was too nice for going to church, but I walked around the outside of the building, skirting the edge of the main

square. Close to the cathedral wall was an impressive statue of St
Boniface, looking wizardly in a great flowing robe and beard.
Boniface, I remembered, was another English traveller up the Rhine
– a Benedictine monk, born in about AD 675, who set out on a
long-distance mission to convert the heathens of the Rhineland to
Christianity. He apparently did this well enough to catch the eye
of the Pope, and got himself appointed archbishop of Mainz.
Ultimately, though, Boniface's evangelistic efforts were not entirely
successful. When he set out to convert the Frisians in the present-day
Netherlands, he was stabbed or beaten to death while reading the
Scriptures on Pentecost Sunday – proof, perhaps, that the Dutch
weren't always as welcoming as they seemed. Studying the statue
closely, I was pleased to note that Boniface did indeed have a bony
face. I looked around for someone to tell this hilarious joke to, but
sadly there was no one.

Today, Boniface may have been largely forgotten by the people
of Mainz, but another ancient figure loomed large, hogging the
limelight as greedily as a talent-show crooner. More than five
hundred years after his death, Gutenberg had been embraced by
the people of Mainz with an enthusiasm which made the people
of Stratford look rather ashamed of Shakespeare, and residents of
Amsterdam embarrassed to be associated with Rembrandt. 'Welcome
to the city of Gutenberg, the father of the printing press!' a tourist
guide hollered as I walked into the Gutenberg square, past the
Gutenberg statue and into a shop filled with Gutenberg souvenirs.★

Johannes Gutenberg was born in Mainz sometime in the late
fourteenth century. An early clue to the boy's fate perhaps lay in
his full name: with a moniker like 'Johann Gensfleisch zur Laden
zum Gutenberg', it was inevitable he'd get tired of writing things
out by hand. To a modern reader, well schooled in Eureka moments
and world-changing innovations, it's perhaps difficult to appreciate
just how much of a breakthrough Gutenberg's press represented.
Before Gutenberg, the vast majority of books were essentially religious. Books were usually written in Latin, and had to be

---

★ For many years, the Dutch city of Haarlem lay rival claim, arguing Gutenberg
had stolen his idea from a Dutch printer called Laurens Coster, and commemorated
the latter with a statue in the town's main square. The theory has now been
thoroughly discredited by most scholars, even Dutch ones.

painstakingly copied out by hand. Errors were common, and a scribe would find it tough going to copy more than two high-quality pages per week. Some printers used carved wooden blocks to print whole pages of text, but they were still forced to carve a whole new block for every page. To a fifteenth-century German, the idea that a normal working person might own a whole shelf of books would have been almost as fanciful as the idea of having a laptop.

Gutenberg's breakthrough, which he made sometime around 1450, was to make metal stamps representing individual letters. These letters could be lined up in a wooden frame like bricks in a wall, coated with ink and then stamped on paper using a press similar to those found in the nearby vineyards. Using this 'movable type', it was possible to print whole pages at once, without having to make a whole new stamp for every page. At a stroke, bookmaking was transformed from a painstaking business into something relatively quick and easy. A text which would have taken a month to produce could now be printed hundreds of times in a week.

Gutenberg was quick to capitalise on his breakthrough, printing everything from Bibles to a calendar decorated with a 'warning to Christendom against the Turk', exhorting the 'noble German nation' to unite against the threat posed by Islam. The early books usually were sold without colours or illustrations – most customers would hire a private artist to fill in the gaps, meaning no two books were exactly the same. A rich man's Bible might end up decorated with gold leaf and colourful hand-painted flowers, while his poorer neighbour's might have simpler pictures quickly scribbled in cheap Indian ink.

The Rhineland, with its good transport networks, metal mines, skilled workers and prosperous investors, proved a particularly fertile ground for the new technology, and print works soon opened in Mainz, Strasbourg and Cologne. The printing of maps, charts and travellers' tales helped spread trade and build empires, while the printing of religious texts famously helped catalyse the Reformation. Gutenberg had hoped his invention would help reunite Christendom, and that it would generate income for the Catholic Church, but ironically it did the opposite. In due course, Martin Luther's writings, which protest against the excesses of the Church, were printed so often that a third of all the books published between 1518 and 1525 were said to bear his name. 'Luther is the man who can keep two printers busy, each working two presses,' said one of his friends.

Less controversially, other Gutenberg volumes included classics by Aristotle and Ovid, German adventure stories and even – bewilderingly – books which explained how to read. Errors still occurred: the philosopher Erasmus of Rotterdam complained that 'in earlier times, a single writing mistake would only affect one copy, but now it appears in an edition of thousands'. But the new methods meant students and worshippers were no longer dependent on others to curate knowledge for them; they could learn for themselves. After centuries in which most information had been local, it was also easier for people in different places to share it. When, in the winter of 1492, a meteorite crashed into a wheat field near Ensishem, a local professor printed a one-page account explaining how the impact had been heard dozens of miles away. It was one of the world's first recorded newspapers.

Like Heinrich Heine and Bruce Lee, Gutenberg wasn't much appreciated in his own lifetime, but a second chance at fame came with the French Revolution, when he was hailed as the inventor of 'the tool with which we will rework the future!' The French – who seized control of Mainz in 1792 – spent millions of francs tearing down old Germanic buildings and building a shiny new Gutenberg square at the heart of the city. Later, as the Germans tried to build the trappings of a unified country, they saw in Gutenberg yet another perfect symbol of German innovation and industry. His celebrity was assured. In 2000 a panel of world leaders voted him Man of the Millennium, narrowly beating Shakespeare, da Vinci, Stalin and Chuck Berry.

The Gutenberg Museum had been recommended to me several times as a must-see attraction, and I went there almost as soon as I arrived in Mainz. The museum was nearly empty of visitors, but for a bibliophile its contents were beguiling: codices kept chained to tables, great vicelike printing presses, and books filled with slabs of wax in which people once scratched notes in medieval version of Etch-a-Sketch. The most valuable texts were stored in a great vault which had thick doors like those of a submarine. I spent a hour or so browsing some early texts which shared the kinds of things medieval readers were desperate to know: how to best grow grapes; how to make wine; how to navigate the North Sea; how to fix a broken leg which had healed crookedly. The answer to the latter question, according to the 1497 *Manual of Surgical Medicine*, was to lie across a couple of rollers and have two friends stamp on the offending bone.

Leaving Mainz, I continued southwards towards Worms, where I hoped to spend time learning about another great German who'd helped transform the fortunes of the Rhine region; the composer Richard Wagner. The scenery between the cities wasn't quite as impressive as it had been along the Romantic Rhine, but was still beautiful – the river wide and winding; the thick forests spreading upwards from its banks like a great green rug.

About thirty miles or so south of Mainz, I stopped for a couple of hours in a small village called Ibersheim. There wasn't much to see, but the surrounding countryside was bucolic; an agricultural area which looked as if it hadn't changed in a hundred years or more. Between the village and the river, vast, flat fields of beets and onions were separated by hedgerows studded with pear trees. The weather was wonderful – bright, warm and blue – and the river tranquil but wild-looking. A sign warned passers-by not to disturb the wild deer. I climbed a tree and ate a pear, and immediately decided it was one of the prettiest places I'd been so far. Only one thing slightly spoiled the illusion: the steady hum of the nuclear reactor.

Directly across the water from Ibersheim, right next to the riverbank, was Biblis, comprising a set of four enormous drum-shaped grey cooling towers and two bulbous reactors. Along the grassy overgrown track by the riverbank, Beatrix Potter scenery was marred by a sign noting it was a muster point for emergency services in the event of some apocalyptic catastrophe. A massive chemical tanker slid past, moving at running speed, and I couldn't help but wonder what would happen if it crashed into a reactor, and half of western Europe became uninhabitable.

Although there was once plenty of oil and gas under the North Sea, and coal in some parts of the north, the Rhine region had long lacked easy energy sources. During the turbulent 1970s, when oil prices sky-rocketed, many nuclear power stations were built. By 2015, Germany was generating about a sixth of its electricity from nuclear power, Switzerland a third, and France a whopping three-quarters. The need for massive amounts of cooling water meant several major nuclear power plants sat right by the Rhine, including the one at Biblis and others at Fessenheim in France and in Switzerland. The Netherlands also had a reactor at Borssele, on the southern edge of the Rhine–Scheldt delta.

Many Rhinelanders initially viewed nuclear plants as clean and green; vastly preferable to smoking chimneys or enormous dams. Others, though, were appalled at the prospect of a French or German Chernobyl, and as the green movement grew increasingly influential, uneasiness about plants like the one at Biblis increased. A more abrupt shift came with the 2011 Fukushima disaster in Japan, which resurrected old fears about the safety of nuclear power in heavily populated regions. The French announced plans to radically reduce their reliance on the energy form, even proposing to convert Fessenheim to a Tesla factory. The boldest reaction, though, was in Germany, where in 2011 Angela Merkel (in a foreshadowing of her subsequent U-turn on gay marriage) abruptly decided to close all nuclear power plants by 2022, including several facilities along or close to the Rhine. Merkel's decision was popular with the public, but in practice, implementation of the shutdown was decidedly bumpy. By the time of my trip, power companies up and down the Rhine were struggling to meet shutdown bills and had filed huge lawsuits to recoup their costs. As plants went offline, authorities were also grappling with an obvious question: if a quarter of Germany's electricity generating capacity was closed, how would they make up the shortfall? Hydro-power plants couldn't help much – the need to keep shipping channels open made it hard to build more on the Rhine, and a single nuclear plant like Biblis could produce roughly the same amount of power as every Rhine hydro-power plant combined. Along the forested middle Rhine, many people were also hostile towards the idea of building new wind turbines, dams or transmission cables. For now, the plant at Biblis remained in a strange state of suspended animation; in the process of being shut down but still producing power. From the riverbank it looked deserted, but the fences were high and the gates stoutly padlocked, and I had to make do with sitting on a bench on the riverbank for a while, looking for three-eyed fish.

Ten miles south of Biblis came Worms. The city's name could have been chosen to make English speakers think of it as a mucky, grubby place where there were more frogs than princes, but in reality it was another typically pleasant little German cathedral city. Its geography followed the now familiar format: a wide river spanned by a couple of leapfrogging bridges; a labyrinthine old town spreading from the west bank; a spectacular cathedral bristling at the centre. By now, I could even recite the city's history without checking: a small farming and fishing settlement which evolved into a sturdy Roman staging post, then a religious and trading hub; bombed badly in the Second World War, and then resurrected as a modest inland port and a place where tourists could punctuate their river cruises with a quick cathedral tour.

I left the river and headed into the city centre on foot, making my way towards the grand cathedral of St Peter. More than a thousand years old, this was said to be the finest Romanesque cathedral on the whole Rhine, but sadly it was – like almost every cathedral in Europe – clad in scaffolding and green mesh, leaving it looking like a wedding cake caught in a fishing net. Eventually, after ten minutes walking in circles, I found what I'd been looking for: the Nibelungen Museum. This was dedicated to another of the Rhine's great cultural exports: the *Nibelungenlied*, or 'Song of the Nibelungs', an epic poem in which the river was a major supporting character. Reading up in libraries in London and Amsterdam, I'd learned a bit about the *Nibelungenlied* already, and read some big chunks of the text. The story was complex enough to make even Dutch politics seem straightforward, but as far as I could tell it was essentially standard *Game of Thrones* fare. It told the tale of a heroic Rhine prince called Siegfried who, determined to win the heart of a Burgundian princess called Kriemhild, embarks on an epic quest involving long boat voyages, invisibility cloaks and trips to Iceland. At the end, most of the main characters fall in love with one another, and then most of them die.

The saga's authorship remains hotly disputed, but in the eighteenth and nineteenth century, it became hugely popular. At a time when most German literature was refined and romantic, the *Nibelungenlied*'s focus on bloody treachery and vengeance was a revelation; a Mel Gibson movie unleashed on a Jane Austen audience. Later, it was even said to have influenced the author of another great tale of an unobtainable, all-powerful ring; J. R. R. Tolkien.*

Unfortunately, the museum in Worms turned out to be (to put it diplomatically) not the best museum I'd ever been to. When I checked my notebook later to see what interesting observations I'd recorded there, I found only four words: 'Like watching paint dry'. This was unfortunate, not just because the *Nibelungenlied* was so colourful and dramatic, but because the story of how it came to play a central role in Rhenish culture was actually quite an interesting one. The modern significance of the *Nibelungenlied* rested largely on the shoulders of one man. Unlike Heine, Beethoven or Gutenberg, Richard Wagner wasn't a natural-born Rhinelander. Born in Leipzig in 1813, he decided at a young age to be composer. Like any young person of good sense, in his early twenties Wagner behaved as if there was no tomorrow; drinking heavily, dancing all night, skipping classes and joining in student riots. At one point, he terrified his friends and family when he tried to tame a wolf as a pet. Wagner effectively dropped out of university, and his first attempts at composition weren't wildly successful. Neither does he seem to have been a particularly charming individual. Franz Liszt described him as 'a sort of Vesuvius', and the painter Friedrich Pecht agreed that despite Wagner's 'long body and short legs', he 'resembled a volcano spewing out fire'. Wagner himself unsurprisingly took a milder view. 'I am,' he once said, 'energy personified.'

Like many of his generation, as the nineteenth century progressed Wagner became intoxicated by the idea that Germany had a mythical history and a glorious future. In practice, he often loved the idea of Germany more than the reality. 'I feel terrified when I think of Germany and my future enterprises there,' he wrote to Liszt. 'I can see nothing there but miserable pettiness, a mere show and boast of sterling worth, without any real foundation.' Determined

---

* It's proven Tolkien took a close interest in Wagner's Ring Cycle before writing his fantasy novels, but Tolkien himself firmly rejected any suggestion that he'd been inspired by the music. 'Both rings were round, and there the resemblance ceased,' he said.

to help right those wrongs, he gradually developed what was effectively a new style of music; grand epic dramas set to music, which would be a purifying and unifying force.

The most famous of these was, of course, based on a boiled-down blend of old Scandinavian sagas and old German folk tales known as the *Nibelungenlied*. After a quick start, the project took Wagner years to finish, interrupted as it was by other works, money troubles and a bout of stomach trouble caused by 'eating too many ice creams'. Eventually, though, some twenty-six years after Wagner began the project, he finished it, producing a vast work called '*Der Ring des Nibelungen*', better known as the 'Ring Cycle', consisting of four grand operas. The story – like the original sagas – was a fiendishly complex tale of dragons and dwarves, heroes and villains, maidens and gods. The themes, though, were timelessly simple: power corrupts, bravery is glorious, and love saves. The epic first performance of the Ring Cycle took place in 1876, in a specially built theatre in Bayreuth packed with gigantic sets and special effects; woven rainbows, flying dragons and Rhine maidens. The reception wasn't universally positive. Some thought Wagner's music was unhealthy; others, just bad. 'The more we see and hear of Herr Richard Wagner,' the London *Times* once said, 'the more we are convinced that . . . music is not his special birth right.' Overall, though, the work was a triumph. King Ludwig II of Bavaria – one of the few people who liked Wagner's music almost as much as Wagner did – attended a performance and gave it a royal standing ovation. 'You are a god-man,' Ludwig later wrote to Wagner, 'The god-man who truly cannot fail and cannot err!'

Unfortunately, Wagner's reputation didn't survive unblemished. The composer was a notorious anti-Semite, and the Nazis inevitably appropriated his works as symbols of a romanticised 'Old Germania' swelling with purity and pride. Wagnerian imagery became a recurring motif in German wartime history – during the siege of Stalingrad, for example, Hermann Göring deliberately evoked the *Nibelungenlied* with his call to remember how mythical warriors had 'fought and fought to the end'. The defensive line along Germany's western frontier was named after Siegfried, and when a group of renegade Nazi officers attempted to assassinate Hitler with a briefcase bomb, they named the assassination plot '*Die Walküre*',

('Valkyrie'), in a nod to the theme of redemptive sacrifice. Parts of the Ring Cycle were played at Nazi state occasions and featured in newsreels, as well as in Leni Riefenstahl's famous film *Triumph of the Will*. When Hitler killed himself in his bunker, the announcement of his death was accompanied by Siegfried's Funeral Music from the Ring. More than seventy years later, the stain had not faded. This isn't to say Wagner was unpopular: his music was beloved by many, and performances of the Ring Cycle sold out months or years in advance, despite typically lasting longer than the average flight from Bonn to Bangkok. Many defended his record: 'Wagner died before Hitler was even born!' one German music lover told me. Others pointed out that many Nazis were not big fans – when Hitler made a block booking for one of Wagner's operas, most of the party members who were ordered to attend fell asleep. Yet in many people's eyes, Wagner's works were still deeply tainted. When, in 1981, the Israel Philharmonic played a small piece of his music as an encore, a Holocaust survivor walked to the front of the stage, bared his scarred stomach and shouted that the orchestra should 'Play Wagner over my body!' In Germany, choosing what to remember and what to forget remained a tricky business.

Continuing south along the river from Worms, the dominant colour scheme quickly reverted to green. The border with France was approaching fast, and the scenery looked (to my English eyes) vaguely French already; a little rougher and dustier than the sleek agro-industrial plains of north Germany and the Netherlands. Rolling grass-coloured fields stretched into the distance, backing onto rumpled hills studded with dozens of modern windmills. Nearer the river, the terrain was flattish, but still crowded with vineyards; long rows of vines stretching furrow-like into the distance. In several places, young workers (migrants, probably) stood bent over in long rows, picking beets, cabbage and onions.

The scenery along this stretch of the river wouldn't always have been so gentle and fertile. Before the mid nineteenth century, the channel around here was wild and fractured, studded with nearly 1,600 islands in the seventy miles north of Strasbourg alone. As in the Netherlands, terrible flooding was routine, and numerous fishing villages were completely submerged in the seventeenth and eighteenth centuries. The riverbanks were also rife with typhus, dysentery and malaria. According to the environmental scholar David Blackbourn, in the eighteenth-century Rhineland, malaria killed more people than war did. In the early 1800s, though, the great engineer Johann Gottfried Tulla began his series of grand projects to 'correct' the Rhine between Basle and Mainz, removing islands and cutting the river channel straighter so that water could flow along it much faster, not only accelerating shipping but reducing the risk of flooding. 'No river or stream, including the Rhine, needs more than one bed,' Tulla said. Hundreds of miles of dikes were built, and thousands of tons of rock and mud removed by men using little more than picks and shovels. Numerous meandering riverbeds were consolidated into a single, more canal-like channel. Tulla's project took decades to complete, but was a triumph. A grateful resident of one previously flood-plagued town wrote to him: 'Praise and thanks are due to this man, who through the wisdom of his plan . . . has liberated us from the Rhine'. With his vision and audacity, Tulla had turned the wild river plain 'into a blooming garden'.

A little further on, though, the river underwent another sudden personality change. Approaching Ludwigshafen, the bucolic onion fields and small villages gave way to a Rotterdam-style sprawl of tangled pipes and smokestacks, giant chemical crackers and lunglike silos. Three big tankers manoeuvred past each other on the water like synchronised swimmers, and a crowd of boilersuited workers poured out of a factory at closing time. The contrast with the landscapes further north was stark: more L. S. Lowry than J. M. W. Turner. Numerous signs indicated that the biggest game in town was BASF, one of the world's largest chemical companies, which depended on the Rhine both as a source of water for its refineries and as a highway for shipping. The local tourist board called Ludwigshafen 'a compelling destination, with an urban face and green lungs', a piece of PR-speak so brazen in its untruthfulness that one had to admire its bravado.

Across the river, and rather more interesting, was Mannheim, a mid-size city lying at the confluence of the Rhine and Neckar rivers. Mannheim was one of the relatively few Rhine cities which

I'd never visited before, and my first impression was that I hadn't been missing much: it seemed a centreless and essentially charmless place; visibly less prosperous than the likes of Wiesbaden. Even my modern guidebook, which was determined to make everywhere sound fantastic, admitted Mannheim 'isn't Germany at its prettiest'. However, as I walked away from the river through the city centre, I thought my initial assessment might have been too harsh. Mannheim wasn't Venice, but it was attractive, with a big red *Schloss*, some nice old churches and an unusual chessboard layout, with perpendicular streets named with letters and numbers: Q6, D2, G7. The main tourist attraction was a beautiful stone water tower which looked like a giant chess piece.

In many ways, Mannheim struck me as emblematic of a certain type of mid-sized German city; almost unheard of abroad, but possessed of a wealth, confidence and status which would have made it a major metropolis in any other country. This was largely a consequence of the way in which political power was decentral-ised in Germany. National institutions like the central bank and constitutional court were not clustered in Berlin, but scattered across the country. *Länder*, or states, had (via the *Bundesrat* council) a significant say over new legislation introduced by the government in Berlin, and most chancellors before Merkel had built their careers and reputations in local rather than national politics.* As recently as 1934, there was still no such thing as a 'German' passport – bearers were still identified as being Bavarian or Prussian and so on. As a result of all this, Germany – and the Rhine region in particular – seemed packed with cities which were modest in scale but had the trappings of much larger places. With their banks and thriving industries, newspapers and television stations, Rhine cities like Mannheim, Koblenz and Cologne had more in common with the old Hanseatic city-states than they did with docile suburban towns like Gloucester, Reims or Tilburg.

I also quickly noticed that compared with the other cities I'd been visiting recently, Mannheim had a large immigrant population

---

* Most of the big cities of the German Rhine lie within two states, both named for the river: North-Rhine Westphalia and Rhineland-Pfalz (also known as Rhineland-Palatinate). The river also borders or passes through the states of Hesse and Baden-Württemberg.

– attracted, presumably, by the jobs available in the chemical works and ports. As lunchtime approached, it took me a full fifteen minutes of walking in circles to find a German restaurant, hidden away amid countless Turkish restaurants and kebab shops. Many of the shops were Turkish, the newsagents sold Turkish newspapers, and there were a lot of women in headscarves. I found it all rather charming, but it also wasn't hard to imagine how Germans of a certain age and background could feel their culture was threatened if many of their neighbours spoke a language they did not, and if it was easier to find a piece of *baklava* than a *streusel*. On the whole, though, the rough cosmopolitanism of the industrial areas had added colour to a place which might otherwise have been a boring backwater. When I stopped for coffee, the man in front of me in the queue was a Liverpudlian engineer in greasy overalls, and the woman behind me was a Norwegian lawyer in an expensive suit. A little later, I stumbled upon an amazingly shiny modern shopping centre tucked away on a quiet street, full of designer shops and gourmet cafés. It was the kind of place I probably should have hated for its characterless conformity and commercialism, but to a tired traveller it seemed very pleasant indeed. I sat outside drinking iced tea for a while, eavesdropping on the young Swiss-American couple having lunch at the next table. 'I liked Berlin before it was famous,' the woman said.

With the French frontier looming just over the horizon, I decided to go for a final run along the river in Germany, keeping an eye out for traces of two final German Rhine heroes, Bertha Benz and Karl Drais, as I went. Leaving the chessboard city centre along L12 and L15, I loped east along the bank of the river, through a pretty park. This began as a narrow strip of grass tracking the river, but soon widened into a big pearl of a forest, surprisingly lush and wild-feeling, littered with toadstools and shady glens. At one point I saw an elderly man who looked like a huntsman from a Grimm story book, cutting up a tree with an axe. It was hard to believe one of Europe's biggest chemical works lay just a few hundred metres away across the water. A little further on, a sign pointed to the wine-producing village of Kallstadt, from where a young man called Frederick Trump had set off for America in 1885; a refugee in search of a better life. His grandson Donald apparently went on to do great things.

After a rest on a pretty little riverside beach, I turned and ran back the way I'd come. Approaching the city, I noticed an odd piece of public art on the grass: a sort of fence of round metal tubes, decorated with coloured stripes which from a distance made up a picture of a cyclist. I checked my map, and realised this was somewhere I'd been reading about a few days previously, and had hoped to visit: the world's first bike path, as used by the world's first bike.

In the early 1800s, people in Mannheim (like those almost everywhere else in Europe) were essentially limited to three different ways of getting around: on foot, by boat or by horse. For longer journeys, horses were especially important: they could not only carry individual riders long distances over rough terrain, but also drag carts and carriages filled with passengers or cargo, or tow boats upstream along the Rhine against the current. Around 1815, however, the business of horsing around began to run into serious problems, thanks to a sudden shortage of horse food. These shortages were partly due to geopolitical factors, including Franco-British blockades and the antics of Napoleon's armies, which destroyed or consumed acres of crops on their way through the Rhineland. Regular floods along the river around Mannheim had also affected farming. The main problem, though, was rather more exotic: an Indonesian volcano.

In August 1815, Tambora – a volcano on the island of Sumbawa, in present-day Indonesia – suddenly erupted, producing a plume of volcanic ash twenty-seven miles high. Around Tambora itself, tens of thousands of people were killed, burned by rivers of lava or choked under great snowdrifts of ash. Outside Asia, the main impact was climatic. Tambora's enormous ash cloud so disrupted global weather patterns that global temperatures plummeted. Food production slumped, and people went hungry from Boston to Moscow. Volcanic ash fell as brown snow in Hungary, and New England saw snow in July. In the Netherlands, one British newspaper reported that 'in several provinces . . . the rich grass lands are all under water'. Parts of the lower Rhine were flooded for five full months, and Mary Shelley's boat holiday was overshadowed by gloomy weather, inspiring her (as mentioned above) to write a gloomy novel. In Germany, the Rhineland was plunged into a prolonged period of cold and darkness, marked by heavy rains, summer snowfall and devastated crops. Thousands of Rhinelanders emigrated to the United States, many of them travelling downriver by boat and then out to sea via Rotterdam. For the people who lived near the river, ignorant of what had caused the sudden change, the effects were as confusing as they were devastating. In his book *On War*, the military strategist Carl von Clausewitz described south-western Germany as suffering 'a complete harvest failure' and being filled with 'ruined figures, scarcely resembling men, prowling around the fields searching for food among the unharvested and already half-rotten potatoes that never grew to maturity'. In Munich, one observer noted that 'beggars appeared from all directions, as if they had crawled out of the ground'. 'The Rhine rots with corpses,' Baroness von Krüdener wrote.

More relevantly to this story, the terrible weather also meant that around Mannheim, farmers' yields plummeted, and the price of oats soared further. Thousands of horses starved to death, and many others were hacked up and eaten by starving families. Even for those who did have food, travel by horse and carriage began to seem less like a daily necessity and more like an unaffordable luxury. And so it was that a Mannheim man called Karl Drais – an inventive soul who'd been born up the river in Karslruhe – literally went back to the drawing board, and began designing a new invention to replace the hungry horse altogether: the *Laufsmachine*, or 'running machine' (its other names included '*draisienne*', '*velocipide*' and 'dandy-horse').

Drais's contraption, which he unveiled in 1817, was made of wood but looked not completely dissimilar to a modern bicycle, with two spoked wheels and a soft leather seat behind curved handlebars. In other ways, though, the resemblance was limited: the vehicle lacked a chain or pedals, and riders were expected to propel themselves forward by paddling their feet against the ground, like a dog swimming across a river. The wheels were like wagon wheels, made of wood covered with metal plates, and the wardrobe-like dimensions of the wooden frame meant the whole thing weighed about 22 kilos – almost three times as much as a modern road bike.

On the bumpy, rutted roads around Mannheim, it did not offer a smooth ride, and the gentle hills which rose up from the riverbanks were insurmountable.

Given these limitiations, it was inevitable that Drais's contraption would be mocked and mistrusted at first. Almost everyone who saw the *Laufsmachine* refused to believe it offered any benefits over a pair of legs or a horse. Drais, however, believed firmly in its potential, noting that on the flat it could travel at twice walking speed 'even directly after a strong rain', and that going downhill it went 'faster than a galloping horse'. Early in the summer of 1817, he perfected his prototype and set out on an epic test drive, following the Rhine south from Mannheim roughly along the route I'd been jogging on. After perhaps an hour of scooting along, he reached a coaching inn in Rheinau, where he rested awhile before turning around and headed home again, covering a total of about nine sweaty miles. It wasn't much, but it proved the bicycle might not be such a bad idea after all. News of Drais's invention spread, and thousands were bought by gadget-savvy commuters in London. Within a few decades, other inventors had adapted the design, replacing hefty wooden planks with lighter steel tubes, developing shock-absorbing rubber tyres and adding pedals, which meant riders could travel much further and faster without wearing out their shoes. However, Drais's place in the history books was assured, as inventor of the world's first 'two-wheeled, rider-propelled vehicle', or, as it later became better known, 'bicycle'.

Curiously, Karl Drais's bike ride wasn't the only groundbreaking journey to take place around the river in Mannheim. Another Karl – Karl Benz – was also born just up the river in Karlsruhe, and moved to Mannheim in his twenties to work as an engineer. In 1883 he set up a new company to develop one of his own inventions: the world's first practical automobile powered by an internal-combustion engine – or, as a lover of modern slang might call it, 'car'. At first, Karl's Benz Patent-Motorwagen didn't seem terribly impressive: it was a flimsy machine which looked like a three-wheeled bicycle with a lawnmower engine tucked behind an armchair-style seat. Equipped with a two-stroke engine, it could just about putter along at jogging speed, and many were sceptical about its safety and reliability. Even Benz's early business partner,

Emil Bühler, was unconvinced and pulled out of the project, adamant that the automobile was going nowhere fast. At first the vehicle broke down almost every time he took it out. Another problem was that test drives usually had to take place at night, because of the enormous crowds of spectators which the contraption drew. Benz pesisted, though, and slowly the technology improved. The turning point came in 1888, when Karl Benz's redoubtable wife Bertha Benz went out for a joyride.

Bertha was perhaps an unlikely innovator. Born in 1849 in Pforzheim, about fifty miles south of Mannheim, she grew up in an age when it was generally accepted, in Germany and elsewhere, that women were naturally less intelligent than men, and hence barely worth educating at all. According to a history later produced by the Mercedes-Benz company, Bertha's father marked the occasion of her birth by writing: 'Unfortunately only a girl again'. Despite these attitudes, however, young Bertha was fascinated by all things technical, and as she grew older regularly pestered her father – a wealthy carpenter – to explain how newfangled technologies such as steam trains worked. By her late teens, Bertha had by all accounts grown into an attractive and intelligent woman, and could probably have had her pick of successful young bachelors to marry. She had other ideas, however, and during a coach trip in 1869 she met a penniless young engineer, Karl Benz. He was scruffy and disorganised, and Bertha's father warned that he was unlikely to be able to support her in the style to which she was accustomed. However, as Karl explained the various technical projects he was tinkering with, including the horseless carriage, the technophile Bertha was smitten. She ended up not only marrying Karl, but agreeing to support him financially while he developed his designs.

By 1888, Karl's design was quite well advanced, but still suffered serious problems with reliabilty. The brakes were terrible, and without gears it couldn't drive up hills. Furthermore, Karl personally didn't seem to have the skills needed to take things further: the technology he'd developed was very promising, but he lacked the marketing nous to drum up investment or attract customers. And that was when Bertha stepped in. Early one summer's day, she woke two of her sons and sneaked out of the house while Karl was still sleeping. She started one of his prototype cars and began

driving south towards the village where she'd been born. The drive
was not an easy one. Roads then were used only by horses and
carriages, and so were bumpy and deeply rutted. In some of the
villages she drove through spectators were enthralled, but in others,
people were horrified by the clanking, rattling monster which
appeared in their midst. According to Mercedes-Benz: 'Some of
the onlookers would prostrate themselves on the road in prayer,
fearing this "smoking monster" as a harbinger of the Last Judgement'.
The car broke down repeatedly, but Bertha was undeterred, hiring
a blacksmith to repair a broken chain and fixing the flimsy engine
with her own hat-pins and bits of clothing. When the car ran out
of fuel near the town of Wiesloch, she recruited some passers-by
to help her push it to a nearby chemist and bought a litre of cleaning
fluid to use as fuel – making a surprised local pharmacist the owner
of the world's first filling station. Arriving intact in her southern
home town of Pforzheim that evening, Bertha sent a message
to a very surprised Karl before turning around and driving back to
Mannheim again. The round trip of over a hundred miles was a
sensation, making Bertha a minor celebrity and – more importantly
– proving that, with a little added ingenuity, the motor car could
be reliable even on longer journeys. The rest, as the saying goes,
is history.

Back in Mannheim's city centre, I changed quickly out of my
running clothes and went out for a last serving of German food
– not the traditional kind (meat and potatoes), but the modern
kind (lamb kofta). The French border was almost in sight, and I
was sorry to be leaving Germany, a country which I'd long loved
and enjoyed getting to know better.

I was particularly sorry to be leaving the German upper Rhine.
As a foreigner, I sometimes found it hard to track all the differences
between cities and regions within Germany, but it was clear that
local identities and cultures were as strong as they were varied.
Bonn, Cologne and Mannheim were, in subtle ways, almost as
different from one another as London, Edinburgh and Cardiff.
As I followed the river towards the Alps, it generally seemed to me
that people further south, between Koblenz and Karlsruhe, were
perhaps a fraction more Mediterranean in their outlook than their

neighbours to the north. 'We have a little bit more taste for beauty here, for the good things in life,' a Wiesbaden man on one of the boats had told me. 'Up there around Bonn they take things too seriously.' In other ways, however, all the Rhine towns and villages I passed through seemed broadly similar in character: worldy and outward-looking; prosperous and hard-working.

Like most places, the region's culture was riven with contradictions. In some ways, the places I'd travelled through were quite conservative: often predominantly Catholic, and often slightly stern in their industriousness. On the other hand, though, the Rhineland was a strikingly international place. As I'd seen in Mannheim, the river had brought investors, guest workers and tourists who'd transformed otherwise quiet corners of the country. The Romans and the neighbouring French had infused the region with a Latin love of good food, wine, public baths and socialising. For all their sensibleness, Rhinelanders loved nothing more than a table-thumping singalong in a *Brauhaus* or at a parade, thought nothing of taking their clothes off in a public bath, and thought driving at 160 kilometres per hour was rather slow. '*Et kütt wie et kütt*', more than one person said to me as I fretted over something or other – don't worry about the future; what will be will be.

With that thought in mind, I wheeled my bike through the town towards the river, ready to continue my journey southwards. To the right was a forest of chimneys, collectively doing their best to turn the skies of western Germany even greyer than they were already. To the left, less than fifty miles upstream, was France.

PART THREE

France

10

Borderlines

Strasbourg and Alsace

I N THE CENTRE of Strasbourg, the French soldiers were kissing one another while the German soldiers looked on. One of the regular memorial services to commemorate the fallen was underway, and the grand Place de la Republique was filled with people, standing silently in rows as the soldiers embraced. I arrived late, sweating from a speedy cycle over the river, and squeezed in behind a few elderly French soldiers in red berets and neatly pressed suits, richly moustachioed and holding their walking sticks with undiminished military vigour. Behind us, dozens of French flags flew from the balconies of the sand-coloured Palais du Rhin (Rhine Palace), its dome pointing skywards like a stone rocket ready for take-off.

Shuffling forward through the crowd, I saw the commemoration was focused on a big statue of an anguished woman clutching two wounded soldiers to her bosom. Engraved on the plinth below were the words Á NOS MORTS, *1914–1918, 1939–1945, 1945–1954, 1952–1962*. An old soldier noticed me copying the phrases into my notebook and whispered a few words of explanation. 'The statue, the woman, she represents Strasbourg. The dying people she is holding are her children – one from Germany and one from France; brothers. Today we're all together.'

Looking around, I saw he was right. There were many French soldiers present, but also many German ones, and lots of German flags as well as French ones. To my amazement, when a French bugler played the French '*Marseillaise*', he followed with a swift rendition of '*Deutschland Über Alles*'; the German national anthem wafting over the French soldiers gathered in France to commemorate Frenchmen killed by Germans. The old enemies were mourning their dead together.

I was excited to be in France, but reading history books and chatting with jovial boatmen and fishermen, I'd quickly realised it would be unwise to overstate the Rhine's influence on the French. France's land borders in Europe total roughly 1,500 miles, of which only about 120 are made up of the Rhine. Perhaps as a result, the river had far less symbolic value than it did for the Germans or the Dutch. The French people I knew weren't in the habit of taking romantic holiday cruises through the eastern border region of Alsace, and the hearts of great French artists and poets were more likely to be set aflutter by the Seine than the Rhine. Economically, the French looked reflexively towards great Atlantic, Channel and Mediterranean ports rather than downriver to Duisburg or Rotterdam. Overall, the French people I knew seemed barely more enthusiastic about the river than they were about German wine or Dutch cuisine.

Yet despite all this, the river was still deeply important to France. From a French perspective, it had long provided a natural bulwark against German expansion; one of the sturdy sides of what they called *L'Hexagon*, the six-sided mainland of France roughly defined by the natural boundaries of the Channel, Atlantic, Pyrenees, Mediterranean, Ardennes and Rhine. The Germans, however, disagreed. From their perspective the Vosges – a low ridge of mountains lying parallel to the river on the French side – often seemed a far more sensible boundary, ensuring the river itself lay firmly in German hands. Time and again, the two great powers had found themselves disagreeing over a simple question: were the river and the surrounding region of Alsace German or French, or both, or neither? Between 1870 and 1945, control over Alsace switched hands more times than an ambidextrous octopus.

Today, custody of the Rhine was shared. From Mannheim and Ludwigshafen, the river went almost due south before abruptly hitting France about fifteen miles south-east of Karlsruhe. From there, the river itself formed the border between France and Germany for an uninterrupted 120 miles to Basle, where it passed into Switzerland. Travelling south from Mannheim towards Strasbourg, I'd passed into a proverbial melting pot of cultures. Signs and newspapers were in two languages, and menus in the riverside taverns offered a heady mix of French and German staples as well as local specialities like *choucroute* sauerkraut and *baeckeoffe* three-meat hotpot. Some people spoke French, some German, and some the Alemannic dialect of Alsace, which was similar to German, but different enough to be confusing. Criss-crossing the river, I often was unable to remember which country I was in without looking to the waterway itself for orientation. Yet despite this, the Franco-German relationship was still clearly a slightly uneasy one, and the Alsace region still schizophrenic in character. In Rheinmünster, a German man told me *der Rhein* was 'the greatest river of Germany'. Twenty minutes later, across the river in French Drusenheim, a woman was confidently asserting exactly the opposite: *le Rhin* was 'part of the soul of our country'. For all the talk of unity, the Rhine, as in Roman times, still served as a border between the Gallic and Germanic worlds; a Limes-style frontier between France and the uncivilised land of the currywurst.

Back at Strasbourg's Rhine Palace, the memorial ceremony drew to a close. A French officer pinned medals to the chests of a few younger soldiers as an announcer named where they'd served with distinction: Kosovo, Chad and Afghanistan. After each medal was pinned, a trumpeter played a jolly little riff and the commanding officer gripped his men by the shoulders, kissing them firmly on both cheeks in time with the music. A young woman with chocolate-brown hair – the daughter of a fallen soldier, I think – then stepped up and paid tribute to both French and German forces. Their 'courage and sacrifice' had, she said, helped build 'a European community'.

I joined a small crowd shuffling across the gravel back towards the city centre. I hadn't been to Strasbourg for a couple of years but was pleased to find it just as I remembered; a maze of ancient half-timbered houses and cobbled streets. Technically the city didn't lie directly on the banks of the Rhine, but was literally surrounded by its waters, with almost as many canals and hump-backed bridges as Amsterdam. A sizeable Rhine port lay on the edge of the city, and almost everywhere in Strasbourg was within splashing distance of the River Ill, a tributary of the Rhine which sounded like it had been named by the Beastie Boys, and looped around the city centre like a dropped stitch.

I stopped for lunch at a café in a sandy-floored little square hemmed in by tall townhouses and leafy vines, ordered a *planchette charcuterie* and sat reading *Le Monde*. After several weeks in sleepy southern Germany, I was amazed by how many tourists there were. Strasbourg's narrow streets were packed with people eating, photographing and kissing. One café where I remembered once being the only customer on a grey winter day now had a twenty-minute wait for a table. Near the river, a sign outside a 'Traditional Alsatian Restaurant' read FRESH SASHIMI HERE TODAY.

Like religion and doughnuts, Alsace has often been fought over. The split between what we now think of as 'France' and 'Germany' essentially dates to the ninth century, when the vast empire of Charlemagne was divided between his three lucky grandsons. In an effort to ensure each got their fair share, the empire was cleaved into three broad strips of territory, corresponding (very) roughly to the places we now know as France, the Low Countries, and Germany. The Rhine, for much of its length, formed a clear border between the middle and eastern sections. To the west of it, most people spoke French (a Romance language related to Spanish and Italian), while to the east, Germanic dialects (loosely related to English and Dutch) prevailed. Much later, at the end of the Seventy Years' War, the Peace of Westphalia gave Alsace to France, but many were never entirely happy. Even the origins of the name 'Alsace' were disputed – some said it came from the Germanic *Alis-lauti-sat* ('people over there') or *Ell-sass* ('people living on the river Ill'), while others insisted it came from the Celtic *Alis-atin* ('at the foot of the hills').

For the French, the idea of the Rhine as something to be proud of first took hold (or at least, was well defined) around the time of the Revolution. The revolutionary Georges Danton, for example, declared to a rapturous audience that the limits of France were 'indicated by nature'. 'We will,' he said, 'reach them at the four corners of the horizon: at the Rhine, the Oceans and the Alps.' The writer Armand Carrel, meanwhile, said France benefited from the 'incomparable situation' of being secure between 'two seas and its impregnable natural barriers', one of which was, of course, 'the barrier of the Rhine'. In 1792, when the mayor of Strasbourg called for a new marching song to inspire French troops, a lowly soldier called Claude-Joseph Rouget de Lisle responded by writing a ditty praising the 'roar of those savage soldiers' who soaked fields with the 'impure blood' of foreigners. The song was eventually adopted as the French national anthem, known as '*La Marseillaise*'. Few later remembered its original name: '*Chant de guerre de l'armée du Rhin*', or 'War Song of the Army of the Rhine'.

The Germans were, of course, not about to let such French triumphalism go unchallenged. Leaders such as Otto van Bismarck plotted obsessively to isolate and undermine France, while German historians and politicians argued French claims to the river were laughable. In France, meanwhile, nationalists were also encouraged by another unlikely source: maps. In 1874, a geography professor called Émile Levasseur published a *Petit Atlas de la France* which superimposed a hexagonal outline on the outline of the country. This neat trick was quickly adopted on countless French classroom maps and geography textbooks, suggesting France was – as the cartographer Catherine Dunlop wrote – 'preordained and almost God-given in its mathematical perfection'. In this context, the river had by the late nineteenth century become a dangerous potential flashpoint. One English correspondent warned that 'on the banks of the Rhine the tremendous force of the Germanic body is about to be put in motion, and the weakened [French] army . . . will probably be the first victim'.

After lunch, I walked half a mile or so to Place Kléber, a big grey-tiled square with bubbling fountains. There was a book market on, and I spent a happy half-hour browsing books from Bloy to Zola. An elderly bookseller sat amid his dusty tomes eating a feast of Alsatian ham and crusty bread, pausing only to sell a volume of Rousseau to a passing Deliveroo rider.

After a long time away, I found it wonderful to be back in France. The language helped. I spoke French almost as badly as I spoke German, but (like many Brits) fancied I had a certain reckless flair for it, honed over years of listening to Daft Punk and watching *Poirot*. When in doubt, I could always resort to the old trick of many an English linguist – adding a few extra vowels to an English word and doubling the volume: '*JE VOUDRAIS LA FISHA AND CHIPSA!*'

Strasbourg had long styled itself as '*le Carrefour de l'Europe*', 'the Crossroads of Europe', and with the border only a mile or two away, it bore the unmistakable traces of Germany. To my untrained eye, much of Strasbourg's architecture appeared an appealing but odd blend of influences, and I noticed that while most houses had French-style wooden shutters outside the windows, many had German-style hurricane-proof metal rollers. I heard dozens of people speaking German rather than French, and the book market sold only a handful of volumes in English but scores in German. Even the street names were a hotchpotch blend; *Rue des Veaux* and *Rue des Arquebusiers* sitting oddly alongside *Rue Wencker* and *Rue Ehrmann*.

The historical battles over the Alsatian Rhine are too numerous to list here, but one of the most significant came in 1870, with the conflict which became known as the Franco-Prussian War. This war was triggered when a vacancy opened up for a particularly plum job: King of Spain. The Prussian chancellor, Bismarck, decided to push the young Prussian Prince Leopold as his own candidate for the position. From Bismarck's perspective it was a savvy move, but the French were horrified at the idea of seeing Prussians on the throne behind the Pyrenees as well as across the Rhine. The French kicked up enough of a fuss that the Prussians were persuaded to withdraw Leopold's job application, and the crisis appeared to be over. However, Bismarck then stirred things up further by editing an official telegram so it sounded like Prussian and French leaders had deliberately insulted one another. Like a modern-day spin doctor teasing the tabloids, Bismarck leaked the dodgy correspondence to the press, which erupted in jingoistic fury. The two countries were soon arming for conflict, with Bismarck rather brilliantly declaring 'Germany wants peace and will make war until she gets it'.

These days, the details of the war of 1870 tend to get lost in a fog of a hundred other conflicts which clutter the pages of history books, but at the time, it was a brutal, passionate business. Bismarck's wife, for example, suggested all French people should be 'shot and stabbed to death, down to the little babies'. That didn't happen, but thousands of soldiers flooded into Alsace and Strasbourg, which one Prussian commander described as 'a standing menace to southern Germany'. Compared with the mighty steel guns of Krupp, French artillery was hopelessly obsolete. The Prussians marched across the Rhine and besieged the city, destroying houses with shellfire and leaving the grand cathedral pockmarked with bullet scars. Eventually, Strasbourg had no choice but to surrender. The Prussian general Helmuth von Moltke wrote gleefully that the city 'was now restored by German valour to the German fatherland'.

Further north, Prussian forces marched on Paris and besieged that city too. Conditions inside the walls were grim, but the Parisians were a determined lot. Hot-air balloons were used to ferry important passengers out, and pigeons carried letters to supporters elsewhere in France. Yet as food ran out, the Parisians were forced to abandon their usual fine dining. Even restaurants in the Latin Quarter were forced to lower their standards somewhat: one menu advertised delicacies including '*Brochettes de foie de chien*' (dog kebabs) and '*Emincé de rable de chat. Sauce mayonnaise*' (cat with mayonnaise). Castor and Pollux, the beloved elephants of the Paris zoo, were shot and sold in slabs to various restaurants, whose patrons allegedly ate them without knowing what meat it was.

Eventually, early in 1871, the French surrendered. Under the terms of the treaty which ended the war, France agreed to pay billions of francs in compensation, and the Prussians won control over Alsace and much of the neighbouring region of Lorraine. Worse still for the French, the Prussian Wilhelm was proclaimed the emperor of a newly united Germany.

The setting for the proclamation ceremony was a deliberate insult to French pride: Versailles, the historical seat of French royal power. The defeated Napoleon III went to live in a mock French chateau in Chislehurst, Kent, where he complained to visitors about the appalling English weather. The Rhine, which the French had always viewed as the rightful border between France and Germany, now lay almost completely under German control. The French had hoped to win sole custody of the river, but ended up without even visiting rights.

Leaving Place Kléber, I doubled back slightly to Strasbourg's star attraction, the cathedral, which towered over the old town like the spindle at the centre of a roulette wheel. Even for someone who'd spent weeks travelling from one cathedral city to another, it was an incredible sight: a colossal, rust-coloured building, squeezed in among the ancient townhouses with only a few feet to spare, with a front facade so delicately carved that it looked as if it were made of lace. I wasn't the first visitor to be impressed: Victor Hugo said the cathedral was a 'gigantic and delicate marvel', while Goethe 'experienced a revelation' when he saw the 'two towers rising to heaven'.

Just south of the cathedral, Strasbourg's weekly flea market was in process, and I browsed the picturesque junk for a while, wandering between rusty ice skates and musty fur coats, dented cellos and broken clocks. The river here was set a few metres below street level, and I walked along an attractive stone walkway which ran along the waterside like a balcony. The only slightly dispiriting thing was the number of soldiers on patrol. France's jihadi-induced state of emergency was still in place, and there were heavily armed soldiers everywhere. I took a photo of two camouflaged warriors in front of a faded news poster with the caption '*Comment La France a Changé*', 'How France has changed'.

A quick half-lap of the city took me past young couples picnicking over bottles of wine, poetic-looking young men reading thick novels and toddlers wobbling perilously close to the water's edge. Rounding a corner in the river, I came upon a floating grey houseboat emblazoned with the word *Boathome*. It looked rather ugly, but when I peered through in the windows, I realised it was a show home promoting houseboat life to prospective buyers, promising '*une nouvelle vision de la vie sur l'eau!*', 'a new vision of life on the water!' I didn't have the heart to tell them the Dutch had been living like that for centuries.

After their victory in the war of 1870–1, the Germans were naturally delighted with their new riverside territory, and determined to never give it up. On land, the new border between France and Germany was painstakingly marked out with over five thousand little stone pillars, all marked 'D' on one side and 'F' on the other. Some unfortunate villages found themselves divided: one church in the Vosges had to be split between two countries, with the congregation sharing out the silver plates and candlesticks.

As new owner-occupiers of the Alsace, the Germans were quick to undertake what might now be called nation-building; constructing railways and river ports. The stunning castle of Hoch-Königsburg, close to the Rhine in Alsace, was carefully restored on the orders of Wilhelm II; its hilltop fortifications serving as a renewed symbol of German power. German officials ran the region almost as if it were an undeveloped colony in some far-flung corner of the world. 'We Germans,' the nationalist Heinrich von Treitschke wrote in an 1871 pamphlet, 'know better what is good for Alsace than the unhappy people themselves . . . We will give them back their own identity against their will'. The use of the French language was restricted, and German schools and newspapers were established. A few years after the conflict ended, one British visitor reported that Strasbourg was already 'to all intents and purposes a German town', and 'the tongue spoken among the people sounds much more like German than French'.

For the French, however, the loss of the region seriously rankled. Over the following years, the French elite became obsessed with the idea of reclaiming the 'lost provinces'. In cities like Strasbourg, German efforts to promote their language proved particularly unpopular: one Alsatian student complained bitterly that his French lessons were given by teachers who'd been born in Königsberg and Cologne.

In short, while the maps of Europe declared that the Alsatians were German, in their bones most of them were still French. As one pro-French writer put it, in Strasbourg 'the Nibelungen . . . leave her cold, but the Marseillaise sets her tingling and vibrating with painful ecstasy'. 'France', the British *Spectator* magazine noted with envy, 'has secured a loyalty at once complete and obedient'. Unwilling to live under German rule, scores of French Alsatians packed up and left. At the dawn of the twentieth century, the two great countries of the Alsatian Rhine were ostensibly at peace but, like a bear living next door to a tiger, unlikely to stay friendly for long.

By the dawn of the First World War, Alsace had spent more than forty years under German control. However, most Alsatians never fully accepted the change of ownership, and many protested bitterly at being forced to speak German. One German newspaper put it bluntly: 'It must be frankly admitted that . . . Germanisation has failed utterly'. On French maps, Alsace was often depicted in violet, the colour of mourning. An English writer who visited wondered whether there should be a referendum to decide the fate of the region, before answering his own question: 'No one would think of demanding that a popular vote should be taken!'

When war erupted again in 1914, the fiercest battles were fought largely on the muddy plains of northern Europe, far from the banks of the Rhine. However, the Franco-German border zone was naturally in a tumultuous mood. French newspapers published cartoons depicting Germany as a hungry octopus, with tentacles reaching greedily across the river to grab Alsace. Thousands of Alsatian soldiers were conscripted and promptly went AWOL. 'Our hearts were beating for France,' said one young man forced to fight for the Germans in Cologne.

After the war, the final Treaty of Versailles awarded the French the whole of Alsace-Lorraine and much of the Rhine. At a stroke, more than 3 million German speakers lost their citizenship of Germany. Bridges across the river became French property, and Kehl, the German town opposite Strasbourg, was given to the French for seven years and managed by a Frenchman. The French naturally were delighted. Prime Minister Georges Clemenceau told an adviser: 'Fifteen years from now I shall be dead, but if you do me the honour to visit my grave, I am sure that you will tell me: We are on the Rhine, and we will remain there.' For the Germans, however, the humiliation was complete.

I was tired, and liked Strasbourg, and decided to stay for longer than I'd originally planned. I cancelled my hotel reservation and after five minutes browsing the internet, rented an apartment in the south of the city – a studenty little place crammed with dusty Tintin memorabilia. I spent several happy days drifting in circles through Strasbourg's old town and over the bridges, stopping every fifteen minutes or so to eat something. A particular favourite was the *keugelhof*, a strange sort of cake made with onions and lard, which tasted like a strange sort of cake made with onions and lard. Some days, I took long trips out of the city, jogging or taking the train to other towns and villages in Alsace, which continued to delight me with its culture. As with Germany, many foreigners had a tendency to think of France as somewhere with a single uniform culture, when in fact it was, of course, a rich tapestry of local sub-cultures and regional specialities. ('Nobody can bring together a country which has 265 types of cheese,' Charles de Gaulle was famously supposed to have declared.) In Alsace, the architecture, food and dialect were all significantly different to those just a few hours' drive away in Champagne or Burgundy, and I enjoyed poking around small towns like Obernai and Eguisheim, which were crammed with artisanal furniture, elaborate lace headdresses and blue-and-white pottery which looked as if it had been imported from Delft. High in the Vosges mountains, I hiked to the beautiful monastery of Saint Odile, built atop a ruined Roman fortress amid the trees. In Colmar, ten miles off the Rhine to the south of Strasbourg, I was amazed to come across a quarter-sized replica of a famous statue which a local man, Frédéric-Auguste Bartholdi, had built on the other side of the world: the Statue of Liberty.

On other days, when I stayed in Strasbourg, I quickly fell into a routine: get up and go for run around the Rhine docklands in the morning; visit a museum or wander around taking photos for a while; then spend the rest of the afternoon and evening eating cakes and reading novels. It all felt unspeakably decadent; an Englishman's fantasy of what life in France was like.

Eventually, though, I had to stop eating and do something. My belly bursting with *keugelhof*, I set out to explore a little further, cycling eastwards through Strasbourg towards the Rhine proper. Early in the morning, the streets were quiet. A thick riverine mist cloaked the city, and it was hard to see more than hundred metres or so. In the distance I could make out a few cranes and warehouses; the edges of the port of Strasbourg. Like many Rhine cities, Strasbourg hadn't let the fact that it lay hundreds of miles from the sea deter it from developing a sizeable port, handling more than 400,000 containers a year as well as over 700,000 tour boat passengers.

Historically, the river region in Alsace was also an important hub for mining; the source of significant lumps of iron ore and bauxite, as well as shiny pebbles of quartz-like rock crystal, which miners hacked by hand from the riverbanks. These glassy stones vaguely resembled diamonds but were very cheap, and became hugely popular as a component of jewellery and costumes for dancers. In the 1770s, though, a Frenchman called Georg Friedrich Strass, working not far from the Rhine at Strasbourg, figured out a way to make the gems even more sparkly, blending them with soft metals and adding reflective foil to the reverse side. In time, the technology improved to the point where the stones could be made completely artificially, and the riverside rock collection business died out. The fake crystals, meanwhile, were produced in massive quantities worldwide and beloved of low-key dressers like Elvis and Dolly Parton. The Rhine link was lost, but the original name of the shiny river stones stuck: rhinestones.

I continued east, heading through a wispy morning mist towards the border. Like many border zones, the last settlement on the French side of the river was slightly anticlimactic: an area of cheap hotels, petrol stations and cafés trying to entice passing truckers into having one last French meal. There were few reminders of the tensions which once had prevailed here, other than a plaque commemorating the fallen of the most recent war, and a restored French tank parked incongruously amid the Renaults and Citroëns.

The bridge over the river, however, was impressive: a long, white, bow-shaped footbridge suspended beneath two steel arches. I pedalled up to the centre and paused for a minute, enjoying being midstream between the French *Rhin* and German *Rhein*. A hundred metres or so to the east, the German town of Kehl was completely obscured by mist. An elderly woman marched past with a shopping bag, and I politely wished her '*Bonjour*'. She replied with a curt '*Guten Morgen*'.

It was somewhere around here, I remembered, that a teenaged Habsburg princess called Maria Antonia had in 1770 symbolically changed her clothes and marched across the river into France, ready to marry the grandson of the French King Louis XV as part of a great game of alliance-forming between Austrian and French royalties. Young Maria left her beloved pug, Mops, on the east side of the river, but acquired a place in the history books, along with a new name: Marie Antoinette.

More recently, in 2009, the modern bridge on which I now stood had briefly captured the world's attention when, as part of a NATO summit, Angela Merkel led world leaders including President Barack Obama, British Prime Minister Gordon Brown and Dutch

Prime Minister Jan Peter Balkenende on foot across it. Halfway across, the motley crew was met by President Nicolas Sarkozy for an awkward mid-river photo op before continuing their walk into France. Watching on TV from an election campaign headquarters in Westminster, I'd thought it a charming, iconic moment, marred only when Silvio Berlusconi left Angela Merkel waiting alone on the red-carpeted riverbank while he made a long phone call. Berlusconi was roundly criticised for his lack of manners, but it was an improvement on his previous performance in a similar setting, when he'd complimented Barack Obama on his suntan.

Descending into Germany, I cycled a short loop through Kehl. It was eerily quiet in the morning mist. The architecture looked boxier and more modern than on the French side, but there was otherwise little to suggest I'd crossed into another country. As at the Dutch–German border near Arnhem, there was nothing as unseemly as a customs booth or national flag; just a small sign explaining the German speed limits and another confirming this was *Deutschland*. I headed quickly back into France, before I was tempted to start eating sausages again.

The border zone around Strasbourg wasn't always so peaceful. After the First World War, the region (now back under French control) remained a flashpoint. In the late 1920s, right-wing nationalists in Germany were aghast when the French stationed black soldiers from their African colonies along the river, protesting bitterly at what they called 'the black horror on the Rhine'. In *Mein Kampf*, Hitler wrote of 'the contamination caused by the influx of negroid blood on the Rhine', absurdly claiming it was part of a plot to begin 'infecting the white race with the blood of an inferior stock'. In Britain, a fit of anti-German sentiment saw German Shepherd dogs renamed Alsatian wolf dogs.* The French, meanwhile, kept the region on a tight leash, expelling German immigrants, closing German-language newspapers and opening French schools.

In 1936, hungry for territory and eager to distract domestic attention from other crises, Hitler abruptly remilitarised the

---

* In 2010, the Kennel Club voted to scrap the name 'Alsatian', meaning the breed's only official name is once again 'German Shepherd'.

Rhineland, sending troops and arms into a region which was still supposed to be a neutral buffer zone. When the Second World War began in earnest, Alsace was invaded by the Nazis, and placed under the control of a German officer called Wagner. In the summer of 1940 Strasbourg was occupied, given the Germanised name of *Strassburg*, and subjected to all the usual degradations. Jews were rounded up and deported, and 46,000 people taken to a concentration camp in the Vosges. A squad of Hitler Youth burned down the Strasbourg synagogue, and others removed German Jewish names from old war memorials. Throughout the region, some locals bravely resisted, listening to illegal BBC radio broadcasts and plotting grenade attacks on Nazi patrols, but the occupiers were brutal and unyielding. As the historian John Sweets later wrote, the Nazis 'believed the French might misinterpret kindness for weakness', and as a result were 'savagely brutal and successful at instilling great fear in the population'. In 1941, the University of Strasbourg reopened, staffed by academics including Professor August Hirt, who conducted mustard gas experiments on prisoners and kept a collection of eighty-six human skeletons which he'd had produced to order in Auschwitz.

Fighting in Libya in 1941, the French general Philippe Leclerc promised that his men would not lay down their arms until the French *tricolore* was flying over Strasbourg cathedral, and so it eventually came to pass. Four years later, in November 1945, French tanks and jeeps directed by Leclerc spilled through the streets of Strasbourg, strafing Nazi soldiers and seizing control of the vital bridges over the Rhine. The French flag was raised over the cathedral. Ancient buildings were adorned with banners which read '*Il y a deux choses éternelles: la France et notre fidélité*', 'There are two eternal things: France and our fidelity'. Local children ran out into the streets to welcome arriving French and British soldiers, less thrilled by the prospect of peace than by the exciting foreign candies they were handed by the liberators. 'We'd never seen sweets like that,' one later said.

For the French, the liberation of Strasbourg was a proud, powerful moment after years of humiliation. However, the challenges of rebuilding Alsace were daunting. In a wearying echo of the events which had followed previous conflicts, the victorious powers once again tussled over how best to divide the spoils. Charles de Gaulle, the post-war leader of the French, was determined to avoid any outcome which might be seen as diminution of France, either in terms of physical size or in geopolitical prowess. He proposed splitting off the left bank of the Rhine from Germany, and giving the French (or their clients) control of not only Alsace but also parts of Hesse and the Saar. 'It is because we are no longer a great power that we must have a grand policy,' de Gaulle said, 'for if we have no grand policy . . . we will be nothing'.

De Gaulle didn't get everything he wanted, but ultimately the Alsace was returned again to French hands. Kehl, on the east bank of the river, remained under French administration for a few years, but for the most part, the boundaries of post-war Europe had been set in stone: Alsace was in France, and the Alsatian Rhine formed the border between France and Germany; a liquid frontier which both kept the two countries apart and bound them together forever.

Back in Strasbourg, I ditched my bike again and walked down to Petit France, the oldest part of the city. The twisting streets were about as crowded as the Eiffel Tower on Valentine's Day, but Petit France was undeniably spectacular; the kind of place so well preserved that it was impossible to take a bad photo. The highlight was an amazing wide basin; a sort of junction in the river where a massive stone barrage ran parallel to an ancient bridge topped with three mighty towers. I climbed to the top of the barrage, where a bride and groom were being bossed around by a wedding photographer. The view was one of the best I'd seen since leaving the coast: a wide pool of green water, stone bridges and towers, and behind it all, on the horizon, the reddish spire of the cathedral. I was still less than a hundred miles south of Ludwigshafen, but Strasbourg felt like not just another country, but another continent.

Looking south across the rooftops, I was surprised to see a big white bird flying past. It was a stork. Storks had long been a prized symbol of Alsace, and were everywhere in Strasbourg; on keyrings and T-shirts, signposts and restaurant menus. In 1888, *Scientific American* magazine reported seeing dozens of storks in and around Strasbourg, describing the bird as 'venerated by the Alsatians almost to the same degree as the ibis in ancient Egypt'. By the 1970s, though, the birds had become a rarity along the Rhine; poisoned by pesticides, killed by hunters and fried by power lines. At one point there were thought to be fewer than ten mating pairs in Alsace. However, a breeding programme and nest-building initiative had since been hugely successful. By 2015, there were thought to be around 600 mating pairs living in the region, and the stork was once again a common sight along the Rhine. Just as Alsace had returned to France, so the stork had returned to Alsace.

The storks were not the only ones whose status sometimes seemed uncertain. Despite the French authorities' *grand projet* to embed Alsace firmly in the French national culture, the sense of being a place apart never really died. While most Alsatians were adamant that they were indeed French, a minority thought of themselves as German. Others insisted they were something else entirely: proud, independent Alsatians, deserving of an *Elsass Frei*, or 'Free Alsace'.

For many years, separatism had been dulled by prosperity: Alsace was firmly within what the French called the *banane bleue* ('blue banana') of prosperous regions curving northwards along the Rhine to the North Sea. In the 1980s, however, an Alsatian economic downturn fuelled a resurgence in separatism. Surveys in the 1990s and early 2000s showed that when asked for their identity, about a quarter of Alsatians responded 'Alsace' rather than 'France'. Separatist parties became increasingly popular, including *Alsace d'Abord* (Alsace First), founded by right-wingers who broke away from Jean-Marie Le Pen's National Front.

Compared with the Basque or Northern Irish varieties, Alsatian nationalism was pretty mild – there were no car bombs or petrol bombs scarring the grassy banks of the rivers here. Alsace Firsters failed to win seats in the national assembly, and were unlikely to obtain independence any time soon. However, the authorities in Paris struggled to strike the right balance between supporting Alsatian development and culture, without fuelling separatist senti-ment. Like many on the populist fringes, the Firsters proved adept at winning headlines, and regularly made a decent showing in local and regional elections. They also benefited from regular controver-sies over elite attitudes towards the region, such as in 2011, when President Nicolas Sarkozy, giving a speech in Alsace, uttered the unforgivable phrase 'I'm in Germany'.

Other populists also found that railing against European integration and German domination often played well in the border region. During the 2017 presidential elections, Marine Le Pen was quick to jump on the bandwagon of Alsatian pride, declaring that the new administrative region of Grand Est was a 'mastodon' with 'no history, no soul, no meaning'. 'I will give you back Alsace!' she promised. In the first round of the elections, she comfortably topped the polls in the departments of Bas Rhin and Haut Rhin. Overall, though, Alsatian separatism was waning, even as the Scottish and Catalan variants thrived. As I travelled around, the people I spoke to were uniformly proud of their Alsatian identity, but also felt firmly French, and had little appetite for rocking the boat. 'I'm from Alsace, but I'm also from France,' explained one middle-aged cyclist I met near Colmar. 'And as for the Germans . . . well, we're all Europeans now. Apart from you Brits, that is!'

On my final day in Strasbourg, I headed out of town again, running along the river to the EU district. Like Brussels, Strasbourg was riddled with EU institutions and affiliated bodies. The tram stops had names like Rights of Man, and every other building housed an acronymic organisation pressing for better EU policies on dairy farming, dementia or digitisation. Around town, signs explained Strasbourg's ongoing role as a cultural crossroads in mystifyingly bad English: 'Regular couple, unusual stories: France and Germany', said one; 'Eyes everywhere, feet straddling the Rhine: an international enterprise'.

After half an hour or so of jogging I reached my destination, a big watery crossroads where the Ill split four ways. To my left was an enormous glass and metal structure the size and shape of a football stadium: the European Parliament. Glinting in the sunlight, it looked like a stack of silver plates waiting to be washed. I approached the main gate and peered through, but a female guard explained that despite the massive signs saying '*Wilkommen*' and '*Bienvenue*', I definitely was not welcome to visit at this time. In retrospect, I should perhaps have hidden my British accent.

The EU's location in Strasbourg was no accident. The European project was born, of course, amid the ashes of the Second World War, when it became clear that (as Winston Churchill put it) 'the first step in the recreation of the European family must be a partnership between France and Germany'. A happy marriage initially looked very unlikely. The French diplomat François Seydoux spoke for many when he famously described the new West Germany as an 'unknown country . . . of which we did not know whether it was the adversary of yesterday or already the friend of tomorrow'. When Robert Schuman, one of the architects of the EU, reviewed a guard of honour on a visit to Bonn, he allegedly noticed the German soldiers were wearing new boots with thick rubber soles. 'Good God!' he was said to have exclaimed, 'Next time we shan't hear them coming!'

However, centripetal forces were pushing the two countries together. In 1950, Charles de Gaulle, out of power but still revered in France, wondered aloud whether the Rhine might 'become a road on which the Europeans will join together, and no longer a ditch on whose banks they continue to fight'. Diplomatically, the key breakthrough came in the spring of 1950, with a memorandum written by Jean Monnet which proposed a grand scheme to phase out trade barriers and reduce tariffs. To modern ears, the scheme's official name – the European Coal and Steel Community – sounds like the theme of an exceptionally boring trade dinner. But at the time, the idea was revolutionary: two countries which had been at war five years previously would create a single, unified market in coal and steel – the very products which had helped fuel several disastrous conflicts. It marked the beginning of a long process of integration through which European politics would stop being a zero-sum game. Brussels would be one of the hubs for the new union, and it seemed only natural that another would be Strasbourg, a city as Franco-German as croissants with *kartoffelsalat*.

I jogged a little further, following a waymarked 'Europe Route' which criss-crossed the rivers between the institutions. On the way, I saw it all: the Parlement Européen, the Conseil de l'Europe, the Cour Européenne des droits de l'Homme, and the École Européenne. Near the parliament, cranes were busy pecking at an area of wasteland and the riverbank was piled with stone, sand and tile. Despite Brexit, European bureaucracy was clearly still a growth industry. Outside the court of human rights, I stopped to read signs pinned to the riverside fence by various protesters. Some were rather touching ('I really need help with my visa'), others, to put it politely, totally batshit crazy ('Tony Blair cut my throat and made it look like suicide').

Loonies with placards weren't the only ones who were annoyed by the way things worked in Strasbourg. In my native Britain, the very name of the city had become a by-word for bureaucratic excess and incompetence. 'If only we could be rid of Strasbourg,' lamented the *Daily Mail*. In particular, the city had become notorious in Eurosceptic circles for the so-called 'Strasbourg Shuffle'; the monthly process whereby hundreds of MEPs and their staff travelled by privately chartered train from Brussels to Strasbourg, where they worked for four days before returning north again. The Shuffle made an easy target for Eurosceptics, costing (depending on which newspaper one believed) £93 million, £130 million, £150 million, £300 million, £928 million, £1.3 billion or £2 billion per year. The *Daily Express* was outraged that 'British workers are forking out eye watering sums of money every day on the ridiculous vanity project, which was only ever set up to stroke France's bruised ego.' Other journalists, meanwhile, were outraged that the 'Eurocrat Express' provided 'eye masks and blankets' for travellers who dared to sleep on the train.

There was undoubtedly something farcical about the whole charade, but travelling around Strasbourg and Kehl, it was hard not be impressed by how old rivalries had been set aside. Thousands of people crossed the river daily to work and play, including French people looking for jobs in the healthier German economy, and Germans drawn west by better food and cheaper houses. A French–German TV station broadcast in two languages from Strasbourg, and trams shuttled back and forth over the river. Seventy years after heavy guns had last fired across the Rhine, war between France and Germany was like the idea of eating only one Pringle: theoretically possible, but almost certain never to happen.

Politically, the two former enemies were now deeply integrated, with a shared currency and central bank, and economies which moved in tandem like barges tethered together on the river. A Franco-German Brigade combined army units from the two countries, while the clumsily named 'Eurocorps' joint military force deployed French and German soldiers to hot zones including Bosnia and Afghanistan.

However, to any careful observer, it was clear Franco-German tensions hadn't entirely disappeared. The roots of the divergence were partly economic. Germany's population was only 20 per cent bigger than France, but its economy was roughly 45 per cent bigger. The economic bonds between the neighbours were intricate but unbalanced: in 2016, 16 per cent of French exports were sold to Germany, but the Germans sent only 8 per cent of their exports to France. In short, more French livelihoods depended on the Germans than German livelihoods depended on the French.

The French and German economies were also run in quite different ways. The whole issue was riven with cliché, but it was fair to say that while Germany's pro-business policies delighted the Davos crowd, French policymakers often behaved in ways likely to have Adam Smith rolling in his grave. At the end of the twentieth century, the level of state spending in France was roughly equal to that in Germany, but fifteen years later it was (as Jonathan Fenby put it) 'ten points higher on the west of the Rhine than on the east'. French presidents periodically pledged bold reform to pensions and working hours, but almost always balked in the face of union unrest and decided it really wasn't worth the heartache. To the Germans, it often seemed as if (the magazine *Spiegel* grumbled) 'Free trade, the market economy and liberalism are expletives in France.'

The French, meanwhile, were a little uneasy about how Germany had risen to dominate the Continent's political scene. The EU was essentially created on the basis of a grand bargain: the French would admit German economic supremacy in exchange for enjoying continued status as a political superpower. But as France faltered and Germany boomed, things didn't quite work out that way. A system designed to keep the Germans in their place had ended up putting them in the driving seat. The far left and right in France didn't agree on many things, but anti-German sentiment was one of them. In 2017, socialist presidential candidate Jean-Luc Mélenchon argued Germany was 'again a danger' because of its 'imperialism', while Marine Le Pen claimed the French president had been demoted to little more than the 'vice chancellor' of German Europe;

'administrator of the [German] province of France'. On trips to Paris and Strasbourg, it was common to hear bitter jokes about how the *franc fort* (strong franc) had been replaced by *Francfort* (Frankfurt, the German city where European monetary policy was made).

Tensions peaked a few years before my journey along the Rhine, during the euro crisis. The French were generally sympathetic to countries which found themselves in trouble, and sceptical of *rigueur* (austerity), which might undermine the welfare state. Many Germans disagreed. On the Syrian refugee crisis, Merkel may have seemed badly out of step with mainstream public opinion but before that, on the issue of Greek debt, she was perfectly in tune with the view from the street. For many Germans, inflation was anathema, and debt something to be avoided at any cost. The stock market was viewed as an unruly casino, and saving for the future was not only financially sensible, but a clear sign that someone possessed a good moral compass. Following the recent experience of East–West reunification, many also had a deep-rooted belief that countries had a moral duty to make economic sacrifices in exchange for political gains. Politicians won votes not by promising to spend more freely, but by pledging to chase the fabled '*schwarze null*', or 'black zero' – the point where budgeted spending exactly matches revenues. The strong German economy had long been a source of national pride, and austerity was generally seen as a natural state rather than an emergency measure. 'Not all Germans believe in God,' Jacques Delors once said, 'but they all believe in the Bundesbank.' In that context, many Germans, like the Dutch, saw bailouts for countries like Greece as a moral issue. The global recession was caused, Merkel said, 'because the world did not behave like we did in Germany'. Bailouts would only make things worse. 'We don't help an alcoholic by giving him another bottle of schnapps,' one of her allies said.

After a series of frantic European summits, stricken nations were eventually offered bailouts, but at a heavy price: they'd essentially have to remake themselves in the image of Germany, working harder, producing more and spending less. With dark-suited auditors from Berlin and Frankfurt dispatched to Athens and Dublin, for the second time in a century 'the Germans are coming' became a phrase which struck dread into the heart of many a European.

In Greece, protesters waved swastikas and Photoshopped pictures of Merkel in a Nazi uniform. The Germans, having worked tirelessly to lay old ghosts to rest, naturally were horrified to see old prejudices resurfacing. Many French, meanwhile, were dismayed by the attitudes on both sides. One young French minister reportedly was blocked by Merkel from participating in Greek bailout negotiations after he protested that the conditions the Germans wanted to impose were tantamount to another Treaty of Versailles. His name was Emmanuel Macron.

At the time of my stay in Strasbourg, Franco-German relations were at a high ebb, thanks to the same Emmanuel Macron. As president of France, Macron had quickly claimed Merkel as his strongest foreign ally and set out a bold, reformist agenda for liberalising the French economy and strengthening the EU. On a trip to Germany early in his presidency, he announced that one of his key aims was 'to restore the credibility of France in the eyes of the Germans'. For some, Macron's confidence and ambition hinted at an intriguing reversal – for the first time in years, the essential European might not be a German leader, but a French one. However, reform in France remained easier to promise than to deliver, and some of the old cross-border tensions remained. When the German newspaper *Die Zeit* reported Macron's victory, its headline consisted of a single question: 'Should we pay for France?' On visits to Berlin, it was common to hear German policymakers espousing the Atlanticist view that Macron's bold plans were destined to fail, and France was a nation in terminal decline. 'The French are failing,' a political adviser in the Bundestag once told me. 'They need to get their economy under control, but there's no one to make the tough reforms.' Another was blunter: 'It's quite appropriate that their national symbol's the cockerel. It makes a lot of noise but never lays any eggs.'

The French, naturally, were offended by such talk, feeling they'd been unfairly singled out for expressing even mild dissent from Bilderberg orthodoxy. One survey found that while only 5 per cent of Germans said they mistrusted the French, 14 per cent of French people said they distrusted the Germans. Going in the opposite direction, German attitudes towards France were a little less anguished and a little more patronising. Like the Brits, Germans were inclined to see the French as excellent hosts and cooks and dinner guests, but rather less excellent business partners. Nearly three-quarters of Germans said the French should be given no special favours because they were neighbours.

As a Brit, I found it hard not to see some truth in the idea that France was a more troubled place than its neighbour across the Rhine, and that the showboating and haplessness of successive French presidents contrasted starkly with German chancellors' steely efficiency. It was also hard not to see some of the oddities of French political culture – the prickly national pride, the obsession with the *Francophonie* in Africa – as a junior sibling's determination to prove that, no matter what anyone said, they were just as big and important as the Germans. Like the British, the French had lost an empire but still not quite found a new role.

Leaving the darkening parliament, I jogged back along the water to Strasbourg. At sunset, the old quarter was already spectacularly lit; the ancient townhouses reflected in the rivers like dolls' houses on a mirror. It was my last night in France, and I'd planned to go out for a delicious Alsatian dinner at one of the fancy restaurants in Petit France. On my way there, however, I passed a man of about seventy who was bedding down for the night in the chilly street, carefully unrolling his foam mat and plumping the wad of newspapers he used as a pillow. It was a desperately sad scene, and all the talk of European progress and unity and the prosperity brought by the Rhine suddenly seemed rather hollow. I handed over most of the money I'd planned to spend on gourmet *baeckoffe* and went for a pizza instead.

PART FOUR
Switzerland, Austria and Liechtenstein

II

Fortress Nation

Switzerland and the Edge of the Alps

A T SIX O'CLOCK in the morning, the river was bloody freezing. The Swiss city of Basle was famous for Rhine swimming, and I'd been looking forward to taking a dip, but it quickly began to seem like a terrible idea. Arriving from France the evening before, I'd seen several other people swimming in the river, drifting happily along in the current clutching special balloon-like waterproof bags filled with their clothes. However, when I went to buy a bag they turned out (like everything else in Switzerland) to be wildly overpriced. I'd therefore come up with my own low-budget alternative: three of the yellow plastic bags given to dog walkers to pick up their pets' poo. I crammed my T-shirt, shoes and socks in, knotted them tightly and strapped them to one arm with an old shoelace. Then, after a moment's hesitation shivering on the stone steps, I took the plunge.

My 'waterproof' doggy bags quickly filled with water, and the river's temperature was more Baltic than Mediterranean. Within moments, my fingers were too cold to move, and I was reduced to clawing weakly at the water like a dog digging a hole. Luckily, the scenery more than made up for the cold. The river curved right through the heart of Basle, like a canyon cleaving the city in two. To my right, a wide bank of stone steps led up to a wide promenade lined with trees, and on the left, ancient townhouses rose as steeply from the water as sea cliffs. Despite the urban setting, the water was turquoise-tinted and beautifully clear, and even without goggles I could see dozens of little fish when I dunked my head under the water. The city was silent and the current was fast – even pawing pathetically at the water with my numb arms, I could easily outpace a jogger making her way swiftly along the riverbank. I worried briefly that if I lost concentration, I might end up in Arnhem for breakfast.

In some of the Rhine towns I'd passed through, the river looked a little neglected. In Worms, for example, it might once have been an important commercial artery, but was now relegated to a minor distraction on the edge of town, like a pond lurking at the end of an overgrown garden. In Basle, though, the opposite was true. Here, the Rhine was the lifeblood of the city; a major channel which city residents relaxed alongside and crossed constantly, and which still brought much prosperity.

Basle* sat at the cap of the so-called Rhine Knee; the point where the river bent sharply from the north–south axis it had been following through France and Germany to head in an easterly direction, tracking the Swiss–German border for about a hundred miles to Lake Konstanz. Upstream from here, the Rhine quickly became narrower, choppier, fresher and colder; punctuated by waterfalls and swollen by snowmelt. As a result, Basle was the last really major city on the river's banks; the point at which most cargo ships turned around and headed back towards Rotterdam, and foolhardy swimmers like me had the water mostly to themselves. I paddled swiftly downstream, swerving to avoid some ducks, keeping a wary eye on the shore and trying not to think of the big signs I'd seen on display all along the river warning: '*Baden im Rhein ist Lebensgefärlich!*', 'Bathing in the Rhine is life-threatening!' A cheerful tramp raised a can of lager as I passed and hollered a salutation: '*Guten morgen!*'

Like France, Switzerland was a country where it was hard to argue that the culture had been shaped profoundly by the Rhine. Swiss lifestyles weren't affected by omnipresent flood hazards in the way Dutch ones were, and the Swiss didn't define their national identity in reference to Rhine myth and legend in the way the Germans did. Unlike the French, the Swiss had no history of fighting over the Rhine in recent times, and (as far as I could discover) had no particularly famous poems or songs inspired by the river.

However, it was also fair to say there were few nations more

---

* Even by the polyglot standards of the Rhine, the city's name can be confusing. Most people living there use the German 'Basel' (pronounced 'Ba-zul'), but others use the Italian/Romansh 'Basilea' or the French 'Bâle'. I have stuck with the anglicised 'Basle' (pronounced 'Baal').

defined by their geography than Switzerland; a place with dozens of peaks over 4,000 metres and a topographical profile which looked like a gambler's heart rate. Switzerland may have been more famous for its mountains than for its rivers, but looking at map, it was clear that for a landlocked country, a surprising number of the country's borders were liquid – including not only the Rhine, but also Lake Constance and Lake Geneva. Switzerland's role as the source of the Rhine also gave it a strong voice in debates about issues such as river pollution, while the port in Basle helped bind the country economically to France, Germany and the Netherlands. The river's presence along the northern border had also helped reinforce the image of Switzerland as an impregnable nation. As the nineteenth-century historian Heinrich Zschokke once wrote: 'the Rhine rolls its waves . . . [like] a moat at the base of a rampart, [and] thus has God begirt our fatherland, like an immense citadel'. The Swiss themselves were shaped quite profoundly by their landscape and the strange mix of isolation and internationalism it engendered; they were practical and no-nonsense, insular but worldly, hospitable but inclined to view the reckless antics of the rest of the world with one eyebrow permanently raised.

As I swam downstream, Basle quickly became less pretty. From water level the old city was heartbreakingly pretty, but after a mile or so I passed under a modern motorway bridge and things began to look very different. The ancient townhouses were replaced by modern office blocks, warehouses and dreary corporate campuses. Cranes and silos lined the water like soldiers on parade. The Switzerland of cliché was nowhere to be seen.

The drab scenery pointed to another crucial fact about the Rhine in Switzerland: that the river's main impact on the country was economic rather than cultural. Beyond Switzerland, the general assumption was that many Swiss spent their days counting gold bars, coddling dictators, and generally making money in ways of which a tax inspector would not approve. In truth, though, modern Switzerland is a deeply industrial society. In value-added terms, it presently manufactures more than 50 per cent more than either the Netherlands or Belgium, despite having a much smaller population, producing everything from rolled steel to medical equipment. Partly as a result, this tiny country, with a population split between four languages and few natural resources, has become astonishingly wealthy. In 2017, Swiss GDP per capita was roughly $60,000 per year – almost 50 per cent higher than in the UK or France. As one cultural guide put it, '[T]he laws of physics decree that the bumblebee cannot fly. Similarly, by the laws of economics, the Swiss should not be doing so sickeningly well.'

The Swiss economic miracle wasn't all due to the Rhine, of course. But as the grimy landscape around Basle showed, the river had been vitally important in helping the Swiss bumblebee take flight. Around the city, the Rhine provided massive amounts of water for manufacturing and factory cooling. Nationwide, roughly two-thirds of Switzerland's electricity came from so-called 'white coal', or hydro-power. The river was also, of course, a key highway along which things could be imported and exported, with a strong current heading northwards making it only about four days by boat from Basle to Hoek van Holland. At the time of my tour, more than 10 per cent of all Swiss imports arrived via the Rhine. 'The Rhine,' as the port authorities in Basle liked to say, was Switzerland's 'gateway to the world'.

Swimming along the river, I passed briskly by a big office building belonging to Novartis, a giant Swiss pharmaceutical firm which (like its rival Roche) might not be a household name abroad but was almost as important to Switzerland as Volkswagen and Audi were to Germany. Some production had been outsourced to cheaper locations overseas: according to the author and chemicals expert Martin Forter, a Sandoz-style spill turning the Rhine red couldn't happen in Basle today because 'dangerous production has been outsourced to India and China, and that's where today's [spills] take place'. However, even in a country not known for its poverty, the industry was a striking success story. Together, Swiss pharma and chemical firms exported goods worth around $90 billion per year – equivalent to more than a third of all Swiss exports – many of which were shipped in tankers along the Rhine to Rotterdam. Swiss scientists, often based in Basle, had led the way in developing HIV/AIDS and cancer-fighting drugs, cellophane, Velcro and aluminium foil – the last of which was produced using Rhine currents to power great metal rollers. The greatest discoveries were sometimes made by accident, such as in 1846, when a Swiss chemistry professor called Christian Schönbein spilled a mixture of nitric acid and sulphuric acid across the counter while experimenting in the kitchen at home. Grabbing his wife's apron, Schönbein used it to wipe up the mess before rinsing it clean and hanging it by the stove to dry. He was astonished when the apron then suddenly burst into flame, but later realised he'd accidentally discovered how to make nitrocellulose, which soon became one of the world's most popular explosives. (Sadly, a later attempt to use a form of nitrocellulose to make billiard balls had to be abandoned when the balls kept exploding during games.) A century later, in the late 1930s, it was at the Sandoz laboratory in Basle that a young scientist called Albert Hofmann made an even more exciting discovery. Hofmann was working on a project to synthesise compounds found in medicinal plants when he carelessly touched his hand to his face and accidentally swallowed a small amount of the chemical. 'I lay down,' he later wrote, 'and . . . perceived an uninterrupted stream of fantastic pictures, extraordinary shapes with intense, kaleidoscopic play of colours.' He had discovered LSD.

In the Rhine, the swimming was still beautiful, but my extremities were getting cold to the point where it seemed unlikely I'd ever be able to have children. I'd seen a few big signs warning swimmers to get out of the water, and as signs of industry increased, and my body temperature plummeted, I thought it might be time to obey. I hauled myself out onto some steps, tore open the heavy plastic bags and donned my soaking wet clothes.

Leaving a trail of wet footprints behind me, I followed a rusty old railway line further north along the river, heading back in the direction of France. Almost immediately, I came across Basle's inevitable hipster area, where the riverbank had been colonised by bars and cafés operating out of graffitied shipping containers. I pulled out my soggy notebook and began compiling a list of sassy English-language graffiti which adorned the walls along the waterfront: STOP THE WAR AGAINST MIGRANTS; THE PROBLEM IS BORDERS; BE REAL – GET MARRIED. The northern riverfront looked like the kind of place where Jeremy Corbyn's student son might spend his day off.

Early in the morning, the city was still quiet, but I passed a few dog walkers who laughed at my sodden appearance, and a young woman sitting on a bench reading Camus. A big chemical tanker slid by on the river, and I was surprised to see banners slung along its sides promoting a Dutch accountancy firm and a yacht charter business in Friesland. Nearby, on the riverbank, a truck with Dutch license plates had a map painted on the back showing truck routes between Holland and Schweiz, together with a Photoshopped image of a yellow clog floating in an alpine lake, and the dubious slogan *'Swiss precision is our success!'*

Crossing a small bridge, I heard a sudden cry and jumped back just in time to avoid being squashed by a freight train, with a driver in fluorescent overalls waving at me furiously out of a window. I stopped daydreaming and realised I'd arrived at the edge of Basle's port, a great wall of shipping containers and cranes lining a small harbour. On a wall by the water, multilingual graffiti was almost identical to that which I'd seen in the port in Duisburg; a multi-coloured testament to long-forgotten boats, sailors and home towns: *'Neus'*, *'Crespamo'*, *'Holko'* and *'Ahmemad'*. Basle's port was tiny compared with Rotterdam's – nearly 7 million tons of cargo per year, compared to nearly 500 million for Rotterdam – but still impressive given how far it was from the sea. Wonderfully, Basle was also the home base of the Swiss merchant navy, which sent Swiss-flagged ships all around the world from its landlocked headquarters.

Like so many Rhine cities, Basle had a long history as a trading centre. Despite being firmly landlocked, the city had for centuries benefited from an enviable physical position on the faultline between French- and German-speaking Europe, close to the northern end of important passes over the Alps, and directly on the river. In the thirteenth century, its Mittlere Brucke (Middle Bridge) became a key crossing point for trade on foot or horse, and canoe-like boats called *Lauertanne* were used to ferry goods downstream all the way to the Netherlands before being broken up and sold for timber. By the fifteenth century, Basle was already bigger than either Strasbourg or Frankfurt, and well on its way to becoming the wealthiest city in Switzerland.

At first, the importance of shipping to the city was limited by the simple dynamics of the Rhine current: in the days of sail and horsepower, it was only possible to travel easily downriver. In the nineteenth century, however, the advent of steam power made it possible for ships to chug swiftly upstream to Basle as well as downstream away from it. The city's docks were enlarged and business boomed. Like the Dutch, the Swiss were canny salesmen – in the 1860s, ice from Swiss glaciers was wrapped in cloth and shipped to big cities of the north, where fancy hotels charged a fortune for drinks cooled by the Alpine product. The city grew, and so did the bank accounts. By the 1870s, foreign observers had given Basle a nickname: 'Swiss Millionaire City'.

A few minutes' walk past the port, I arrived at the point I'd been aiming to reach: the *dreiländereck*, or three-country corner. It was here that the borders of three Rhine countries (Switzerland, France and Germany) met at a single point in the middle of the river, close to the tip of an artificial spur which stuck out into the water like the nose of a beached whale. I walked along to the end, passing a sign directing arriving cruise passengers to declare their imports. As someone born in an island nation, I found it remarkable to think that with a good arm, I could have pitched a ball into any of three different countries.

A friendly man with a small dog saw me taking photographs and stopped to chat for a while. Unfortunately, I found his singsong, Nordic-style accent impenetrable, and he couldn't follow my shouty Anglo-German.* We stood grinning and nodding at one another like fools until his English-speaking wife arrived and mercifully provided some translation. 'Is the Rhine clean enough to swim in here?' I asked, about an hour after I'd been swimming. 'Yes,' she replied, 'it's water from the Alps, so it's very clean. People say it's clean enough to drink, actually. But they also say there's bad chemicals in it, so I wouldn't drink it myself. Actually, I'm not sure I'd swim in it either.'

I walked back towards the centre, crossing a bridge into the old

---

* Switzerland is a famously multilingual place. About two-thirds of Swiss people are native German speakers, and about one-fifth French speakers, with the rest divided between Italian, Romansh and other languages.

town. It was still early but the city was coming alive, the riverside cafés filling with breakfast-seekers and the river filling with rowers racing downstream. A girl cartwheeled down the pavement and her mother told her off for getting her hands dirty. Nearby, a costumed clown was blowing bubbles for a group of delighted children. A big brown Labrador ran across the road and grabbed a bubble, yelping in surprise when he ended up with a mouthful of soap and air.

I'd already decided I liked Basle very much, even more than I'd liked Strasbourg. It was just small enough to be charming, but just big enough to be interesting. I decided to stay for longer than I'd planned, and through the sorcery of a smartphone, had within a few minutes rented a little apartment near the *Schwarzwaldbrücke*, and made firm plans to spend several days eating industrial quantities of fondue.*

The city authorities advertised Basle as a tourist destination on the basis of its 'Mediterranean flair' and the fact that it had 'up to 300 days of sunshine per year'. That 'up to' sounded a bit iffy to me, but the weather was indeed mild, and people seemed to make a habit of hanging around outside on the riverbanks in a way that they hadn't in, say, Mannheim. To my relief, the city was also less touristy than Cologne, Strasbourg or Amsterdam. The old town was remarkably well preserved, but there were few obvious signs of mass tourism, and no tour guides holding coloured plastic paddles in the air as if they were bidding at an auction. In four or five days of wandering around, I didn't see anyone taking a selfie.

As a lowland border city, Basle inevitably had a slightly more fluid identity compared with more isolated Swiss mountain towns. Some early visitors were disappointed to find the culture of Switzerland diluted by that of its neighbours – one nineteenth-century traveller grumbled, 'there [is] nothing Swiss about Basle'. Today, in a country not generally famed for its flamboyance, Basle was known as a relatively cosmopolitan place, with a boisterous carnival, a world-renowned art fair and dubious lumps of modern sculpture scattered around like dropped toys. Like Amsterdam,

---

* The name comes from the French verb *fondre*, meaning 'to melt' and not, sadly, because it's fun to do.

Basle had long served as a magnet drawing in writers, artists and scientists; it had served as a centre of humanism and of the Reformation. The city's university had hosted mathematicians including Daniel Bernoulli and Leonhard Euler, as well as the painter Hans Holbein the Younger, who lived in Basle for many years. Karl Jung also studied there, and when seeking to explain his theory of 'synchronicity' to explain apparently random coincidences, he wrote that the likelihood of chance events could be compared to the chance 'that the Rhine would flow backward just once'. The Nobel Prize-winning writer Hermann Hesse lived in Basle more than once, and set his novel *Steppenwolf* in a lightly fictionalised version of the city. Friedrich Nietzsche also taught at Basle in the 1870s, and in 1897 Theodor Herzl addressed the first Zionist Congress there, helping to lay the intellectual foundations for the state of Israel. Herzl later wrote in his diary: 'In Basel I founded the Jewish State.'

Years later, Basle wasn't exactly Burning Man, but was still a little punkier and funkier than the bland Swiss stereotypes would suggest. Walking along the river, I passed countless men and women with haircuts which looked as if the fire alarm had gone off halfway through their session in the salon. Provocative graffiti was everywhere. BURN THE PRISONS, one spray-painted slogan said.

Continuing towards the cathedral, I followed a pretty cobbled street uphill away from the river. The cathedral itself was relatively modest compared to the titanic glories of Mainz and Strasbourg, but still marvellous – a great pile of red stone, with a charming cloister garden and a glorious panorama of the river behind. The squares all around were filled with gorgeous horse chestnut trees; relics (a sign explained) of those brought to Europe by the Ottomans in the sixteenth century on their way northwards from Constantinople. Chestnuts themselves were still a delicacy in this part of Switzerland, sold on street corners to gullible punters who enjoyed eating horse food.

I was still wet and cold and reluctant to leave the sunshine, but was looking forward to visiting an old acquaintance from Rotterdam who lived inside the cathedral these days: Erasmus.

The great philosopher died in Basle, and with the help of a

friendly volunteer guide, I found his grave: a pinkish-brown marble plaque the size of a dining table, standing upright against a pillar. At the top was a strange little sculpture of a man (Erasmus, presumably) with long flowing hair, looking as if he were posing for a shampoo commercial.

Desiderius Erasmus was another quintessential man of the Rhine, born in Rotterdam in about 1466 as the illegitimate son of a priest and a doctor's daughter. He spent his early years in the Netherlands, including spells in Den Bosch and at a monastery near Gouda. After being ordained as a priest, he spent years criss-crossing between France, Belgium, England and Italy, where the Italians struggled to understand his thick Dutch accent and teased him for his enormous appetite. Before leaving the Netherlands, Erasmus had been known for his sharp critiques of the Dutch, but like many travellers, he found being away from his home country made him appreciate it more. Compared with the Dutch, he wrote, 'there is no race more open to *humanitas* and kindness, or less given to wildness'.

In 1515 Erasmus moved south to Basle, where he would (with regular intermissions) spend much of the rest of his life. Like many Dutch abroad, he quickly surrounded himself with a close-knit gang including several other Dutch people, and his years in the city were probably his happiest – towards the end of his life, he wrote: 'I can hardly say how much I like this Basle climate and the kind people who live there; nothing could be more friendly or more genuine.' His only complaint about Switzerland was: 'if only Brabant were closer'.

Erasmus arrived in Basle at a febrile time. For much of the Middle Ages, intellectual and social life in Switzerland and the Rhineland had been dominated by religious institutions; monks, monasteries and the Catholic Church. Now, though, things were changing fast. In Basle and elsewhere, the church was in crisis; beset by challenges from other denominations, and fighting desperately to reassert its authority. Many Catholic rituals and beliefs were still deeply embedded in Swiss culture, but church attendance was often low – one shepherd who was asked whether he knew about the Father, Son and Holy Ghost replied: 'The father and the son I know well for I tend their sheep, but I know not the third fellow, there is none of that name in our village.' In 1517, Martin Luther made his famous protest against religious corruption, sparking the Reformation, which spread quickly through the Rhineland thanks to Gutenberg's new printing press. Basle, where many people were disaffected with Catholicism, quickly fell under the influence of the Lutherans, and emerged (along with other Rhine cities) as one of the hotbeds of what later became known as the Northern Renaissance – an extraordinary period of discovery and exploration during which scholarship flourished, feudal systems crumbled, commerce boomed and daily life was transformed by inventions like movable type, the compass and gunpowder.

In the field of philosophy, the big shift was towards a new spirit of humanism. Humanism, like many philosophies, was somewhat difficult to define, but hit many of the same notes as Luther's Reformation, emphasising the dignity of man and a sense of confidence about the future. Humanist scholars could be sharply critical, but also emphasised many of the things which a modern reader might associate with the word *humanity* – empathy, dignity, mercy and compassion. The humanist movement began in Italy but soon spread northwards over the Alps towards Basle, where it found one of its greatest champions: Erasmus.

Erasmus had already been writing on similar themes to the humanists for many years, but as the cultural tides turned, he showed a new boldness in criticising contemproary society. Settling permanently in Basle from 1522, he wrote a series of polemics (published by the famous Basle scholar turned printer Johann Froben) in which he boldly called out the war-mongering and greed of the popes, preachers and princes who put their own needs above those of the people. 'If the Gospel were truly preached, the Christian people would be spared many wars,' he wrote. Erasmus's output was prolific, ranging from commentaries on the Bible to translations of Seneca, to collections of proverbs and management manuals for Habsburg princes.

Like many scholars at the time, Erasmus often found himself somewhat torn by competing loyalties. He believed fiercely in the unity of the church, but also agreed with many of Luther's complaints about its excesses, describing the dissident in a letter to the Pope as 'a mighty trumpet of Gospel truth'. For a while Erasmus maintained a delicate balancing act, declaring his support for the church while also issuing blunt critiques which were said to be suitable for honest 'Dutch ears'. However, this typically Dutch compromise couldn't last, and in 1529, as Protestants in Basle got increasingly annoyed with the Catholic population, he was forced to flee, travelling by boat down the Rhine to Freiburg. Erasmus eventually returned to Basle, where he died in 1536. The last words he spoke were in Dutch: '*Lieve God*', or 'Dear God'. In a divided Europe, he wasn't particularly widely mourned, but later he came to be seen as a titan of philosophy; the quintessential Renaissance man. Later, both the Dutch and Swiss would attempt to claim him as their own; naming a bridge and a university after him in Rotterdam, and an Alfa Romeo garage in Basle. Erasmus himself, though, had been determined to avoid such difficult choices. When offered the citizenship of Zurich he declined, saying 'I wish to be a citizen of the world.' Born near one end of the Rhine, it now seemed fitting that he rested here, near the other, within splashing distance of the river.

I descended a steep stone staircase to the riverbank and boarded a boat back across the water. My vessel wasn't an ordinary water taxi, but one of Basle's famous ferries – a gondola-style wooden boat which ran across the water attached to a fixed rope, like a dog pacing back and forth on a leash. The passage was powered purely by the current, and with no engine or winch, the journey was wonderfully peaceful. 'You look like you have a nice job!' I said to the young boatman who relaxed at the stern while the current carried us across. He didn't hear me; he was too engrossed in the novel he was reading. The only other passengers were a group of five young men all wearing white jeans. Whether this was a hilarious group prank or a hot new Swiss fashion, I couldn't rightly say.

After several days and nights in Basle, I reluctantly tore myself away and continued following the river east towards Austria. Leaving the city, the scenery quickly became greener, but still wasn't stereotypically Swiss. Here, in the far north of the country, there were no sawtooth mountains or steeply pitched meadows, just generic rolling European countryside. I wasn't in any particular hurry, and stopped often to have a coffee in the sunshine and eat my own body weight in either Emmental or chocolate.

Exploring a little further, I'd enjoyed teasing out some of the differences between Switzerland and the other countries I'd passed through. In keeping with cliché, Switzerland seemed much more orderly than France. The streets were spotlessly clean, the buildings were immaculately maintained, and uniformed safety officers shepherded pedestrians across the roads like traffic controllers at an airport. Despite all the talk of being overrun by immigrants, northern Switzerland still looked as white as a Republican Party convention.

Compared with the ebullient French, Dutch and Rhineland Germans, most Swiss people were also relatively reserved. 'We're Swiss, so we don't tend to get excited about things,' a guy I met in a bar explained. 'But you're very welcome here.' In keeping with the watchmaking cliché, the Swiss were also very punctual. 'Checkout is at 11 a.m.,' one hotel receptionist said to me. 'But I have an important appointment, could I please stay fifteen minutes longer?' I asked. 'I'll pay extra if necessary.' 'Checkout is at 11 a.m.,' she replied.

Like priests who'd won the pools, the Swiss clearly enjoyed their wealth, but in an unostentatious way. Parking spaces along the river were filled with Mercedes and BMWs, and when I lost my pen, it took me three-quarters of an hour to find a replacement which wasn't made by Mont Blanc and didn't cost more than my car. Travelling around Germany, I'd seen dozens of homeless people; in Switzerland I saw none. Riding a muddy bike and wearing a tatty old hoody and Jordanian *keffiyeh*, I felt like I might be deported for scruffiness at any moment.

The biggest surprise was how Dutch everything was. In terms of altitude, Switzerland couldn't have been more different from the Netherlands. However, the two countries were almost exactly the same size, and were (in very different ways) defined by their unique physical geographies. There were also certain historical parallels: both countries had become implausibly wealthy by becoming hubs for services and trade, and magnets for talent which felt unwanted elsewhere. Politically, both were famously stable and neutral in international affairs, with an instinctive love of consultation and compromise; but also shared a certain small-country conservatism, an unspoken fear that security wasn't guaranteed. Many Swiss I met seemed exceedingly Dutch in their pragmatism and conservatism. When a Basle man told me 'the problem with people in Geneva and Zurich is they're obsessed with money', I could practically hear the echoes of my Rotterdam friends' rants about flashy high-rollers in Amsterdam and The Hague. There were also many differences, of course. The Swiss seemed less direct and more diplomatic than the Dutch (although that perhaps wasn't much of an achievement). They were also slightly cooler than the Dutch – when I chatted with a woman on a ferry, for example, she was friendly but didn't ask about my medical history. The Dutch people I asked about Switzerland were riled at the idea they might have things in common. 'My God, no!' cried one Dutch colleague. 'We're not the same at all! Switzerland is just so boring! Their idea of a wild night out is to sit on a mountain and look at the view.' On balance, though, I thought there was more which united the countries than divided them. With their love of cheese, their enthusiasm for winter carnivals and their bizarre infatuation with TV dating shows where farmers searched for wives, the Swiss were the Dutch of the mountains.

Continuing eastwards away from Basle, the scenery still looked generically European rather than dramatically Swiss: low, wooded hills; flattish cornfields; and little grey church towers peeking through the treetops. The river was still surprisingly wide, and still the same blue-milk colour it had been when I went swimming. For the first time since leaving the coast, I went more than half an hour without seeing a single boat pass.

After about seven miles, the river passed a small town called Augst, clustered next to a small Rhine tributary called the Ergolz. Augst wasn't much of a place, but had once been important as the site of a Roman colony called Augusta Raurica, often said to be the oldest Roman colony on the Rhine.

The history of the Romans in Switzerland is not terribly well known, but (as elsewhere along the river) they had a profound influence on the country's culture. Moving northwards from their Italian heartlands over the Alps and down onto the Rhenish Swiss plateau, the Romans encountered a patchwork of Celtic tribes, including the Rauraci and the Helvetii (whose name now lives on in the 'Helvetica' label on Swiss stamps and coins). Just as they did in the present-day Netherlands and Germany, the Romans won control of Switzerland through a combination of conquest, coercion and cooperation, whereby some tribes decided it was better to join and trade with the Romans than to fight against them. Tribesmen from Switzerland signed up to join Roman armies and often served further afield – one Roman military grave later found in Cirencester, in England, contained the remains of 'Dannicus . . . of 16 years' service, a tribesman of the Rauraci'. Throughout Switzerland, major Roman settlements were built alongside rivers or lakes, including Basle, Geneva and Lausanne, and populated with the usual trappings of Roman rule: public baths, theatres, courthouses, arenas where gladitorial battles were staged. Passes over the Alps, including the famous Saint Bernard, were enlarged from narrow trails to proper paved roads. Along the Rhine, the Romans built sturdy stone bridges, which were connected by road to spectacular passes over the saddle of the Alps. The mountains, sloping down to the Rhine to the north, served as a formidable defensive shield between Rome and the restive tribal regions of present-day Germany, while the river itself was an important highway at a time when moving goods or soldiers might otherwise have involved weeks of hiking through snowy, mountainous terrain.

One of the most important settlements on the Rhine was at Augusta Raurica, which lay at the strategic point where the river (running from east to west) intersected with the north–south overland routes connecting the German Rhineland to Italy. Named after the emperor Augustus and the Rauraci tribe who had previously controlled the area, Augusta Raurica soon became a prosperous trading centre, home to thousands of people. The happy times ended, however, when the Alemanii and other tribes began to spill southwards over the Limes and the Swiss plateau around Augusta Raurica became a contested frontier zone. As the empire went into retreat, the Romans built a chain of stone watchtowers along the river from Basle to Lake Constance, each with walls 1.5 metres thick and a small landing stage for river boats. However, even this wasn't enough. Epidemics, climatic shifts and crop failures caused parts of Augusta Raurica to be abandoned, and by about AD 400 the Romans had all but withdrawn from Switzerland. The region fractured back into different tribal zones and cultural groupings, some of which remained Germanic in culture and some of which adopted the Latin language and culture – laying the foundations for linguistic and cultural differences which would keep shaping Switzerland for centuries to come.

Nearly two thousand years after the Romans packed their bags, Augusta Raurica seemed to me an interesting but rather odd place; a peaceful little hilltop village built around partially reconstructed Roman ruins, which were impressive in scale but sat oddly juxtaposed with the normal features of Swiss village life, as if a transparent map of a modern settlement had been carelessly laid atop a map of an ancient one. A great Roman temple overlooked people's back gardens and an amphitheatre stood across the road from the pizza place.

East of Augst, the Rhine looked much as it had in the prettier bits of Germany; tranquil and undramatic. However, as I tracked it further along a hilltop highway, I heard a growing rumble in the distance, like a fat dog snoring. Consulting my map, I realised what it must be: the Rhine Falls, a giant, tumbling set of waterfalls about 150 metres wide, described in my ancient Baedeker's guide as 'the grandest in Europe'.

The falls had been formed when alpine rockfalls forced the Rhine to change course slightly, passing over softer stone which gradually eroded into a 23-metre-high step. In terms of size, the falls were unlikely to worry the custodians of Niagara Falls or even their European rivals – several waterfalls in Norway were twenty or thirty times as high. However, after weeks travelling along bucolic river channels, the falls were an amazing sight: a roiling, boiling mass of foam spanning a wide, rock-strewn stretch of river. They looked rather like Niagara Falls, if Niagara Falls had been accidentally stepped on by a passing giant and squashed to about half their usual height. Unfortunately, the Swiss had done their best to kill off the natural glory of the place by building hotels, restaurants and tacky gift shops everywhere. I had to buy a costly entrance ticket before I could walk down to the falls' edge, past a row of shops selling cuckoo clocks and Toblerone. A sightseers' helicopter circled nosily overhead. 'This,' a German tourist told his young son, 'is the real Switzerland.'

The idea of making money from the falls was nothing new. As

Rhine trade increased in the nineteenth century, they were just about the only thing preventing a boat from drifting all the way from Lake Constance to the North Sea. There were regular proposals to dynamite the falls flat, or to bypass them with canals, but these never amounted to much – partly because locals were determined not to lose the profitable business they'd built up carrying cargo around the cataract. 'Engineers,' a preacher remarked of one dynamite proposal, 'are agents of the devil.' However, resourceful locals soon began to make money in other ways, building dams and waterwheels which powered riverside mills and ironworks, and even a factory making Swiss railway carriages.

The falls' main money-spinning role, though, was as a tourist attraction. As tourists flocked up and down the Rhine in the 1800s, the Rhine Falls emerged as one of Switzerland's star attractions; an essential stop on any Grand Tour. Turner visited, and made a grand oil painting imaginatively titled *Fall of the Rhine at Schaffhausen*. John Ruskin sat and stared at the torrent for an hour, while Goethe made extensive notes about the falls under the heading 'Excited Ideas'. Percy Bysshe Shelley did a boat tour and was typically cantankerous, complaining his fellow passengers were 'exceedingly disgusting' and punching someone who dared to take his seat.

By the late nineteenth century, this once tranquil part of the river was crowded with visitors, floodlit by night and equipped with a camera obscura which projected the image of the falls upside-down onto a nearby wall. In a way, the falls were representative of a broader trend, which saw Switzerland enter the public imagination as an idealised, pure, perfect piece of Europe; in much the same way that Germany's 'Romantic Rhine' appealed to those who thought the British countryside had been ruined by factory and furnace. Switzerland attracted and inspired an amazing number of writers and artists, including Rousseau, Conrad, Byron, Joyce, Fitzgerald, Hemingway, Twain, Dickens, Highsmith, Wells, Tchaikovsky, Zweig, Mann, Lawrence, Jung, Kandinsky, Louis Stevenson, Conan Doyle, T. S. Eliot, Paul Klee and Phil Collins. Wagner came and lived next to a lake at Tribschen. 'Nobody will get me out of here again,' he said.

Inns, guesthouses and hotels sprang up along the river and across the surrounding peaks. Tourists initially visited Switzerland mainly in the summer, riding boats on the rivers and going for gentle walks in the hills. Skiing was at first unpopular – Christoph Islin, one of the first to ski in Switzerland, had to practice in the dark to avoid people laughing at him. By the early 1900s, however, Alpine tourism had snowballed. Lazier travellers sometimes were carried up mountains on soft armchairs, but for some, even this was a bit rough. The critic Leslie Stephen wrote that guidebook-reading tourists displayed 'a total incapacity to live without *The Times*'.

As in other places along the Rhine, some visitors were disappointed by what they found. Travelling through Switzerland, Mark Twain grumbled that he met 'dozens of people, imaginative and unimaginative, cultivated and uncultivated, who had come from far countries and roamed through the Swiss Alps year after year – they could not explain why'. In 1883, an artist called William Brockedon was aghast to hear a Cockney accent in a Swiss restaurant, writing of his 'disbelief that such vulgarity could have . . . extended so far from the Thames'. However, there was also good news: in 1877, the Alpine Club in London sombrely informed its members that 'Goblins and Devils have long vanished from the Alps', and it had been so long since a dragon was seen that they too were 'assumed to have migrated'.

Well over a century after the initial tourist boom, the Rhine Falls were clearly still wildly popular. I had to queue for several minutes to pass the entry turnstile, and again to elbow my way down the steps to the river. Most of the other visitors were groups of Indians and Chinese, picnicking and taking group photographs on the viewing terraces. I wondered how many Swiss people were at that very moment visiting beauty spots in India and China, and thought again how odd modern tourism is; hordes of people switching hemispheres in a great sightseeing country swap. I stopped briefly for a can of cola, having already applied for a second mortgage to cover the cost.

Despite my impatience, however, the falls were extraordinarily beautiful; one of those places where a visitor can't help but be impressed, no matter how many people step on their toes. In the very centre of the river was a rock with a hole right through the middle, like a piece of Swiss cheese. High above the falls, the spray created a permanent rainbow; the perfect backdrop to a million grinning holiday photos. I took a grinning holiday photo and then sat for a while in the mist, listening to the river as it roared like a thousand badly tuned radios.

After leaving the falls, I stayed a night in Schaffhausen, a pleasantly twee little Swiss town with almost as many ice cream parlours as people. There wasn't much to do, but I shopped for maps of the mountains, and rolled around eating chocolate and fondue and rösti and generally behaving like an exceptionally lazy sightseer. I was going to be leaving Switzerland soon, so I also went shopping for cheese, visiting a little shop packed with great wheels and slabs of Gruyère and Emmentaler. I remembered reading that a typical three-foot-wide Emmentaler wheel was supposed to contain about one and a half tons of milk, as well as countless bubbles caused by microbes which burped out carbon dioxide, with modern cheese-makers sometimes using MRI scanners to check the bubbles were of the right size and in the right position. The amount of milk and work involved meant big cheeses had always been costly, and in the nineteenth century, farmers in some parts of Switzerland measured their wealth in terms of cheese, carefully stockpiling big wheels of the stuff. I thought that a good idea, and resolved to do the same. A lavish spending spree culminated with the purchase of seven slabs of different varieties to take home and savour, all wrapped like presents in crisp white paper. They didn't last long.

Schaffhausen's main claim to fame was the fact that in 1944 it was accidentally bombed by Americans looking for Ludwigshafen, in an outrageous breach of Swiss neutrality which killed dozens of people. Today, few signs of the destruction remained, but the Americans' mistake was perhaps understandable, given how confusing the borders were around here. When I went for a morning run along the river towards Gailingen, six or seven miles away, I found myself crossing the border no fewer than six times on my journey there and back – from Switzerland to Germany, to Switzerland, to Germany, to Switzerland, to Germany and back to Switzerland again.

For most of the distance between Basle and Lake Constance, the border between Switzerland and Germany was clearly demarked by the Rhine; the land to the north of the channel being German, and that to the south Swiss. Around Schaffhausen, however, things became fuzzier, with big pockets of Swiss land on the north side of the river, and even one lump of German territory – Büsingen am Hochrhein – which was completely surrounded by Swiss land, like a cherry in the middle of a crumbly pie.

I'd visited Büsingen once before, assuming its strange geopolitical status would make it a hedonistic free-for-all of nightclubs and casinos. Sadly, those high hopes were quickly dashed. However, the location meant other oddities abounded. The currency, for example, was naturally the euro, but given that Büsingen was surrounded by Swiss territory, Swiss francs were also widely accepted. Cars were issued special licence plates, and many addresses had two postcodes, one Swiss and one German. In the Schengen era, border controls were limited, and Swiss police reportedly were allowed to arrest people in Büsingen. However, no more than ten Swiss police officers were allowed in the town at any one time, in case they secretly planned an invasion. At one point I got lost and stopped a friendly looking man to ask which country I was in. He looked around for a second and answered, 'I'm not sure.'

For the Swiss, it all seemed perfectly natural, and they spent more time worrying about the rivalries between different Swiss cantons than between countries. ('The Swiss cantons bicker and quarrel among themselves as the American United States do,' one early traveller observed, 'but like the dogs in a snow-train, they get on together not the less rapidly for their barking and biting.') However, the strange shape and porousness of the border also sometimes generated international tensions, including around shopping.

Another of the true clichés about Switzerland was that it was (for tightwads like me, at least) breathtakingly expensive. This was partly a simple case of prices being higher: according to Switzerland's federal statistics office, in 2017 a basket of products which cost the equivalent of €153 in Switzerland would cost a mere €104 just over the border in Germany. For foreigners, the problem was also exacerbated by the strength of the Swiss currency. Despite being surrounded by Europhiles, the Swiss resolutely refused to join the euro and retained their own currency, the Swiss franc. This approach had its weaknesses – the Swiss were forced to adopt many European rules and regulations in order to gain access to the single market, and remained vulnerable to economic turmoil in the neighbouring countries which bought most of their exports. On the whole, though, staying out of the euro didn't seem to have done them much harm. During the years when the rest of Europe was roiled by economic crisis, Swiss unemployment was typically low, and output remarkably high. With Switzerland seen as a safe haven by investors, the value of the franc had risen by about a third relative to the euro, and Swiss interest rates had at times even been negative; meaning foreigners were willing to pay for the privilege of saving their money in Swiss accounts.

The downside of all this was that for visitors, the whole of Switzerland was about as expensive as a hotel mini-bar. My standard travelling lunch of a baguette and coffee cost the equivalent of about 11 euros in Basle, perhaps double what it would have cost in France or Germany. Worse still, a medium beer cost more than a whole bottle of wine had in France – one reason, perhaps, why the Swiss weren't exactly world-renowned as party animals.

For the Swiss themselves, high prices were less of a daily problem, but the strong currency meant shopping trips over the border were irresistible. Around Konstanz and Schaffhausen, thousands of shoppers headed from Switzerland to Germany every week to stock up on chocolate, food and petrol. Companies on the German side even rented out postboxes so Swiss shoppers could order cheap goods online and then collect them at the weekend. It probably wasn't a coincidence that in 2015, the listeners of one Swiss–German radio station voted as their Word of the Year the word *einkaufstourist*, 'shopping tourist'.

For Swiss shoppers it was all very convenient, but for the Germans it was sometimes annoying. On one visit to the German border town of Konstanz, I spoke to a local woman who was infuriated by the daily influx of Swiss big spenders. 'Konstanz used to be a lovely town,' she said, 'but now it's all foreign people buying things, and new supermarkets keep opening.' Watching great gangs of Swiss shoppers bustle back and forth, it was easy to understand her frustration. For a supposedly conservative people, the Swiss really liked expensive jewellery and perfume. I was reminded of something the famous Swiss writer Friedrich Dürrenmatt had once written about how the sceptre of European fascism been replaced in Switzerland by an 'omnipresent dictatorship of consumption, of production, of advertising, of commerce'. Switzerland, Dürrenmatt famously said, was like a girl who works in a brothel but wants to stay a virgin.

On the banks of the Swiss Rhine, I was still finding the tangled web of cultural influences difficult to untangle. Heading east from Schaffhausen, the French border was only a few dozen miles away, but the French influence seemed limited. When I got confused by Swiss German dialects and tried to speak French instead, most people looked at me as if I were speaking some strange alien language (although that may just have been my *Je voudrais la fisha and chipsa* accent). Culturally, too, the Swiss here were more German than French. Basle and Schaffhausen made even places like Düsseldorf look ill-disciplined and chaotic, and Strasbourg seem apocalyptically dysfunctional. 'The Swiss,' I remembered someone who worked in the European Parliament once telling me, 'are the only people who can out-German the Germans. If something doesn't work then they'll fix it, and if there isn't a rule forbidding something, then someone will make one.' Like the Netherlands, Switzerland was heavily dependent economically on its Teutonic neighbour: one-third of all Swiss imports came from Germany, more than those from Italy, the United States and China combined. In that context, and faced with global cultural juggernauts like the Oktoberfest and Wagner, it was perhaps inevitable that some Swiss felt their culture was overwhelmed by that of the 'big canton' to the north. 'You're writing a book about the Rhine?' a hotel receptionist in Basle said to me. 'Make sure you tell everyone it's a Swiss river!' One controversial survey conducted by the magazine *Spiegel* found nearly half of Germans believed 'a German' was 'someone who spoke German, even if they lived in Austria or Switzerland'. The response of the Swiss tabloid *Blick* to this claim was telling: 'Help! The Germans think we already belong to them!' Watching a German man and his son don Speedos and jump whooping into the river, I couldn't help thinking they might be right.

With dusk approaching, I packed my bags and headed quickly to Stein am Rhein, a small Swiss town close to the point where the river began to widen into Lake Constance. I wouldn't have dared say so to the locals, but Stein am Rhein again looked indistinguishable from the towns of the German Romantic Rhine – low green hills, ancient cobbled streets, half-timbered hostelries and slate church towers. It was lovely, though: peaceful and pretty and largely tourist-free.

I checked into a riverfront hotel and went for a short walk along the Rhine, which was peaceful and chalky blue-green. The weather was still warm, and I swam for a while from a sandy little beach, leaving my wallet and phone on the shore with no thought they might be stolen. The water was much warmer than in Basle but still deliciously clean; more like the spa in Wiesbaden than the Dutch canals I usually swam in. In the distance a church bell rang, and cowbells tinkled in the fields like wind chimes. I could practically smell the fondue waiting back at my hotel. The sun set and I clambered out, dried off and wrote in my notebook: 'Switzerland might just be the nicest country in the world.'

12

Into Thin Air

Lake Constance, Austria and Liechtenstein

T O M Y G R E AT surprise, the cow didn't much like being ridden.
She had all the right gear for it – saddle, reins, harness – and
so did I – black gloves, black helmet and a black leather crop
which made me look like a dominatrix on a field trip. Unfortunately,
all this didn't do much good. Almost as soon as I mounted her,
the cow charged straight off through a thorny patch of bushes. I
tapped her gently with the crop and asked her nicely to behave,
and she responded by turning around and marching back through
the bush again, leaving long scratches all down my legs. I bent
over in the saddle and whispered in her ear that I'd be having
steak for dinner.

There were four of us riding that day – me, and a trio of athletic-
looking young Swiss women who liked riding horses and had come
here as an amusing birthday treat. They were all mystified as to
why a lone Englishman was keen to join them. 'Why on earth do
you want to ride a cow?' one of them asked – a question to which
I struggled to give a coherent answer. 'Because . . . I've never done
it before?'

In truth, my reasons were slightly more complex than that. Cows
(particularly the sand-coloured Brown Swiss breed) are an enduring
symbol of Switzerland, and dairy products like chocolate and cheese
are as closely identified with the Swiss as tulips are with the Dutch
or sausages with the Germans. Like the Dutch, the Swiss also have
a deeply held belief that dairy products are unusually healthy, and
consume them on an epic scale: according to some statistics, the
average Swiss person eats more than ten kilos of chocolate and well
over 20 kilos of cheese each year; slightly more than the Dutch do,
and more than double the British. Swiss cheeses (Gruyère, Emmental,
Raclette) and chocolates (Lindt, Cailler, Toblerone) are world

famous, and the tinkling cowbell provides the quintessential soundtrack to any mountain meadow scene.

Against that backdrop, it didn't seem right to spend so long in Switzerland without getting up close and personal with a cow. Just as importantly, the cow riding offered a way to see the river from another angle. Here in the tranquil north-east of Switzerland, the Rhine was far more sedate and sleepy than it had been in France or Germany. The waterfalls to the west blocked any river traffic, and the channel itself was no longer big enough to have supported major urban development. After leaving Basle, I'd spent a pleasant couple of days moseying along the Rhine in the direction of Austria. The river was pretty and the towns it passed through were pleasant, but I found it all a little unexciting, in a vanilla kind of way. On the stretch between Lake Constance and Schaffhausen there were no cities, and few of the tour boats and ferries which had so crowded the waterways around Koblenz and Bonn. And so, in search of a new perspective on the river, I'd ended up here, near the Swiss village of Hemishofen, where narrow bridleways tracked the channel through green fields, riding a cow.

The day began with a 'Meet the Cows' session which felt a lot like speed-dating, but was even more likely to end with at least some of the participants nursing a sore crotch. There were four cows, obviously – three which looked calm, gentle and hornless, and one which had big horns and was clearly in a bad mood, bashing the other cows with its head and tugging furiously at its harness. I subtly sidled over to one of the gentle-looking ones and draped a possessive arm around its neck, just in time to hear the instructor shout 'Ben, this one is yours!' while untying the stroppy, horny one. I began to wish I was still in Basle.

Thankfully, riding the cow initially turned out to be quite pleasant – a slow ramble through flattish fields of red cabbage and lettuce, with the river burbling in the distance. The slow pace made it clear why cows had never caught on as a means of transport, but compared to a horse, the cow turned out be surprisingly comfortable, with a back which was as wide and as flat as a sofa. However, the big problem was that the cow was also sofa-like in its ability to follow instructions. I'd ridden horses a lot as a child, and was used to the idea that I could adjust my speed or direction with a subtle twitch of the heels or tug on the reins. The cow, though, apparently was unaware of these protocols, and kept moving resolutely wherever she damned well pleased, regardless of anything I said or did. When she decided to head off into a field for a snack, it took three people – me, the cow instructor and a sympathetic passer-by – five minutes of shouting and shoving before she even considered turning around. Riding a cow was like being a passenger on top of a tank: you might enjoy the ride, but you also didn't have much say in where you went.

We trundled slowly across the fields for a couple of miles, me doing my best to enjoy the view as the cow zigzagged from one patch of grass to another. 'For cows, eating fresh grass is like eating cashew nuts!' the instructor explained cheerfully. 'If they have one little bit then they just can't stop eating.' Eventually, with blistered hands and a sore backside, we arrived at the banks of the wide, fast-flowing and milky-green Rhine. I assumed we'd just look at the view for a while before turning back, but the cow plunged right in, wading until exactly the point where my shoes dangled in the water, and then stopping for a long drink. I hauled on the reins and shouted at her to reverse, and she thought for a moment before walking even deeper, soaking my legs to the knee. I sat there for ten minutes, unable to get her to move. A kayaker passed by and did a cartoonish double-take when he saw us, sad Englishman and happy cow, half submerged in the water. 'I've seen a lot of things on this river,' he said in German as he passed, 'but I've never seen that!'

Three days after riding the cow, I could still barely walk. My legs felt as if I'd been riding a bull at a rodeo, and my hands were badly blistered. Luckily, I had something new to distract me: Lake Constance. Moving east from Hemishofen, the river had widened gradually, and then suddenly become very wide indeed, splaying into the vast expanse of Lake Constance – a 200-square-mile behemoth which formed a giant bulge in the Rhine, like a big blue bead on a string.

From Konstanz, on the western tip of the lake, I caught a boat all the way across to Bregenz at the opposite end, in Austria. Old travel guides warned of 'the horrors of sea-sickness' when crossing the lake, but the surface was smooth and the weather mild. The ferry was much like those on the middle Rhine: a stately white cruiser packed with chatty holidaymakers enjoying the picture-postcard scenery, and wondering what that loner was scribbling in his notebook. The scenery, though, was perhaps even better than it had been along the Romantic Rhine; a vast panorama of glassy water reflecting a Hockney-blue sky. Leaving Konstanz, the lake quickly widened to the point where it was hard to believe we weren't heading out to sea. Including a few stops, the journey from Konstanz to Bregenz would take four hours; more than twice as long as it took to sail from England to France. Nevertheless, the weather was bright and breezy, and after weeks following a narrow channel hemmed in by hills, it was a thrill to be somewhere so open again. The wide, watery vistas and massive skies would have reminded me of the Netherlands, had not the weather been so nice.

Lake Constance was another one of those strange places which was hugely important to people who happened to live near it or holiday there, but practically unknown further afield, despite the fact that it was not only enormous but extremely attractive. Hermann Hesse lived nearby at Gaienhofen, and described it as a place of 'tranquillity, clean air and water, beautiful cattle, fabulous fruit, decent people'. The artist Otto Dix, who lived on its shores, was even more poetic: the lake was 'so beautiful that you have to vomit', he said.

The limited global interest in Lake Constance was perhaps because it had a lot of local competition, with scenic monsters including Lake Geneva, Lake Lucerne, Lake Como and Lake Garda all within half a day's drive. It was also perhaps because (like the Rhine as a whole) Lake Constance suffered from an identity crisis. Even the name wasn't fixed: while English-speakers referred to it after the Roman emperor Constantius, who built Roman defences along the shores of the lake, German speakers called it the Bodensee, after the Carolingian imperial palatinate of Bodman. One of the nineteenth-century travel guides in my backpack cheekily called it 'the most beautiful lake which Germany possesses', but in practice, ownership of the icy waters had long been a source of dispute. On land, the lake's shoreline was divided clearly between three countries,

with Germany holding about a hundred miles of waterfront property to the north, Switzerland about forty-five miles to the south
and west, and Austria around sixteen to the east. Out on the water,
though, things were considerably less clear. Maps showed the dotted
lines demarcating international borders ending like hedgerows at
the water's edge. Cruising across the water, it wasn't clear if I was
in three countries at once, or none. As one writer put it, the whole
lake was effectively 'a borderless black hole in the middle of Europe'.

The history of how the black hole came to be was convoluted,
but essentially came down to the fact that, like a group of five-
year-olds given a cake, the neighbouring powers had never been
able to decide how to share it. The Austrians claimed all three
countries owned the whole lake equally, under a kind of joint
custody agreement which diplomats called a 'condominium'. The
Swiss, meanwhile, argued the international boundary sliced neatly
through its centre, dividing it evenly like a pie chart. The Germans
had an affection for the lake almost as deep as its waters, but were
wary of being accused of land-grabbing and so had no official legal
opinion on the matter. As a result, by the twenty-first century, the
three countries essentially had agreed to disagree, making the lake's
ownership a diplomatic grey (or blue) area. Whenever disputes arose
– for example, over how to divide up fishing rights – they were
settled by individual treaties, with the bigger picture left untouched.
To legal scholars, the whole situation was deeply odd, but it struck
me as another example of modern Europe at its best: a sign of how
old rivalries had faded, and how many Europeans were happy to
think of borders between their countries as fairly unimportant. Or
perhaps one early traveller was right when he wrote Lake Constance
simply was 'a gem too costly for the possession of a single kingdom'.

Heading east from Basle, the small size of the Rhine meant development was limited, and I'd seen few towns big enough to merit
bold type on a map. Lake Constance, however, was ringed with
sizeable ports and resorts. In particular, Friedrichshafen, on the northern
shore, was the closest thing southern Germany had to a sea port, and
had long thrived as a centre for both tourism and trade, once hosting
special steamer services which carried trains across to Switzerland.

Like a performance of Shakespeare in a city park, Lake Constance
also inevitably attracted romantics. In Romantic literature, lakes

played a very different role to rivers like the Rhine: they were less dynamic and more passive, and the mirror-like surfaces were thought to offer special opportunities for reflection and revelation. In that context, as the rest of Europe industrialised, Lake Constance was seen as a magical, mysterious place where stressed-out city dwellers could hark back to a greener, cleaner age. The Germans discovered the Alps in their own backyard in about 1770, and as German travellers were drawn southwards, German writers increasingly drew inspiration from the unspoiled places on their doorstep. (Goethe, for example, wrote in *The Sorrows of Young Werther* of the contrast between the bureacratised drudgery of city life and the 'paradise' of wilder zones and the 'glowing, sacred life of nature'.) Lake Constance, only a hundred miles from the city of Stuttgart, made a natural gateway for wholesome pursuits like swimming, hiking and mountain climbing, as well as being a tourist attraction in its own right. 'Lakes', wrote one German traveller as he cruised across Constance, 'are the secret working-places of nature'.

In the nineteenth century, well-off Germans flooded south from cities like Frankfurt, ferried by train to the nearest thing they had to a seashore. Lake Constance lay high above sea level, but the way the water stored and reflected heat meant the climate was unusually warm for the altitude. Grapes and fruit grew along the lake shore, and visitors revelled in the opportunity to enjoy alpine fresh air and snow-capped scenery without needing thick socks. The lake offered fine (if rather cold) swimming, and ferries headed regularly to the towns across the water and to pretty little fortified islands. The island of Lindau, connected to the mainland by bridges, was a particular draw: Baedeker's guidebook recommended visiting it for the bronze statues, lighthouse, 'monument in memory of the war of 1870–71' and 'admirable view' of the Alps. Crossing the lake, many travellers were amazed to discover that southern Europe wasn't completely uncivilised. In 1859, for example, a reporter from London joined some locals for dinner in Bregenz and was astonished to find a local 'forest dame' was capable of conversation 'carried on with such grace . . . that I might have fancied myself in the first society, had it not been for the garb, and her own statement that she [managed] the Crown Inn'. Hotels and sanatoriums sprang up along the lake shore, and early visitors swooned at what they saw. 'What wealth of colour gratifies our eyes!' wrote one visitor. 'The water glistens like an emerald.'

By the time of my visit, budget airlines had rather stolen the ancient steamships' thunder, and Germans were more likely to holiday in Greece or Turkey than in Friedrichshafen. However, the lake was still a popular retreat, with places like Lindau marketed as the 'Bavarian Riviera' or 'German Mediterranean'. When I visited, those sales pitches seemed rather optimistic, but the scenery was indeed lovely and the climate surprisingly mild. Wandering past palm trees and sparkling blue waters, I could almost – *almost* – have been somewhere in the Greek islands rather than a couple of hundred miles from Mannheim.

By the time I arrived in Bregenz, on the Austrian shore of the lake, the weather was sadly not quite so Mediterranean. The sun had resumed its usual position behind the bulky clouds, and a stiff breeze swept across the surface of the lake like a broom. Here, the atmosphere seemed in keeping with the altitude: at roughly 400 metres above sea level, the light was sharp, and the air as hard and clear as glass. Leaving my clothes on a step, I swam a short distance out from the shore, shivering fiercely but enjoying the view of the steeples of Bregenz and the forested peaks behind. The water was amazingly smooth, like a tinfoil chocolate wrapper rubbed so smooth by a finger that only a cobweb of fine ridges remained. The day I'd spent held hostage by the whims of a grumpy cow began to seem like a bad dream.

Looking up as I swam, I was startled to see an enormous grey airship passing low over the lake; a giant floating cigar whirring its way steadily northwards. Turning around, I was even more surprised to see another, passing high over Lindau, and what looked like a third heading towards Konstanz. I belatedly remembered reading that airships were another quintessential Rhine invention.★ The world's first airship was designed by Ferdinand, Count Zeppelin, who was born in Konstanz in 1838 and spent much of his life tinkering with flying technology on, next to and over the waters

★ Technically, an airship is any lighter-than-air craft that is powered and steerable, as opposed to floating free like a balloon. A dirigible is the same as an airship; a Zeppelin is one made by the Zeppelin airship company, and a blimp is similar but usually has no solid skeleton inside.

of the lake. In the summer of 1900, Zeppelin's masterpiece, the hydrogen-filled LZ1, made its maiden voyage, taking off from a vast floating hangar on Lake Constance near Friedrichshafen. In an age when aircraft were still vanishingly rare, crowds were thrilled to see something the size of a building floating serenely along the lake shore, and people soon were rushing to book tickets for voyages.

The technology wasn't without flaws, including the minor detail that hydrogen was highly flammable. Manufacture was also complicated by the fact that the intestines of 250,000 cows were needed to make a single airship. Nevertheless, Zeppelin voyages across Europe and even the Atlantic became wildly popular; a by-word for travel glamour. By the First World War several airships had also entered German military service. In 1915, one even managed to cross the Channel to London, where it drifted serenely over Regent's Park before dropping a number of bombs on High Holborn. The British, who'd long thought themselves secure behind the great moat of the Channel, were faced with the horrifying realisation that war could come from the air. The head of the Metropolitan Police was forced to issue a leaflet warning the panicking public what to do 'When the Zeppelins Come' – essentially, close the windows, stockpile water and sand, and hope for the best.

In time, though, airships proved too unwieldy, unsafe and expensive to compete with newer high-speed aeroplanes. Zeppelin's own commercial prospects were effectively destroyed along with the airship *Hindenburg*, which crashed in flames in 1937 in New Jersey. For many decades thereafter, airships were rarely seen. In recent years, however, they'd undergone something of a renaissance, with several airship companies – including Zeppelin's own – focused on making vessels for moving heavy cargo like wind turbines, as well as for the military, backed by deep-pocketed investors including Bruce Dickinson, better known as the lead singer in Iron Maiden. Around Friedrichshafen, Zeppelin's inventions were a common sight over the lake again, ferrying sightseers up and down the bulges of the Rhine for eye-watering prices.

Even the most excitable travel writer would be hard-pressed to describe Bregenz as thrilling. The lake itself was lovely, but the town itself perhaps wasn't quite as classy as it wanted to be, with too many pedal-boats and Bavarians wearing Speedos to draw the real Gatsbys and Clooneys. It was, however, all very pleasant; sedate and breezy, with an almost nautical atmosphere, and green hills wrapping around the back of the town like a shawl. Autumn wasn't far off now, and the leaves on the trees were just starting to turn rusty, littering the lake like confetti. The white sails of yachts filled the horizon; folded white napkins on a blue tablecloth.

Sketching out my route plan in Amsterdam, I hadn't planned to spend much time in Austria, largely because its exposure to the Rhine was limited. In a country shaped roughly like a tadpole facing Russia, the Rhine ran along the edge of a tiny section of the tail, passing undisputed through Austrian territory for a grand total of about three miles, and then forming the border with Switzerland for about fifteen more. The small size of the river here meant there was little in the way of Austrian Rhine industry, and most traffic moved by road or rail rather than by river. On previous visits to other parts of Austria, I'd detected few signs of people having much deep affection for the Rhine. The national anthem called Austria the 'land on the river', but this referred to the Danube.

However, the Rhine had played a significant role in Austrian history in a couple of odd ways. Firstly, foreign minister and chancellor of the Austrian Empire, Klemens von Metternich, was born in the river city of Koblenz, lived in Strasbourg and Mainz, and spent many of his younger days tramping around the Rhine–Moselle region, before going on to play a decisive role in establishing Austria as a major power on the world stage. Secondly, and more importantly, the river and its tributaries had been the setting for the creation of the dynasty which ruled Austria for generations.

In Switzerland, travelling eastwards from Basle, I'd briefly crossed over the River Aare, a tributary of the Rhine which flowed into it from the mountains. About fifteen miles south of the junction, on a pretty green hilltop, lay Schloss Habsburg, a grand pile with a turreted square tower, built by Count Radbot in about 1020 and named (probably) for the hawks, or *habicht,* which often circled overhead.* Radbot's descendants later took the name of the castle

* An alternative theory says the name means (rather less romantically) 'Castle of the ford'.

– Habsburg – as their own family title, and enjoyed a significant income from the toll booths which were stationed on the surrounding rivers and roads. Using the castle as a power base, the Habsburgs assumed control over a patchwork of territories around the upper Rhine, stretching across the Black Forest, Alsace and present-day Switzerland. However, even this wasn't enough to satisfy the dynasty's ambitions, and they gradually projected their power further eastwards along the Rhine, controlling an even bigger patchwork of duchies and principalities which stretched across the Tyrol, Carinthia and beyond.

For the original Habsburg castle, the burgeoning empire's pivot to the east was bad news: with their attention now focused elsewhere, the Habsburgs eventually opted to surrender to Swiss confederate rebels (led, according to legend, by William Tell). The empire itself, though, continued to grow and grow, aided by the Habsburgs' habit of marrying into other noble families or simply marrying among themselves. This shallowing of the gene pool meant Radbot's descendants eventually became horribly inbred: the Habsburg Charles II of Spain, for example, had two-thirds of the normal number of great-great- and great-grandparents, and was afflicted with nasty skull deformities as a result. But in empire-building terms, it was a masterstroke: the Habsburgs were, at one time or another, the rulers of much of present-day Austria, Germany, the Netherlands, Belgium, Spain, Portugal and the Balkans. And they didn't stop there. As the kings of Spain, they also ruled the Philippines, much of Latin America and the east coast of the United States. In Vienna, the Holy Roman Emperor Frederick III famously had a wall of the cathedral decorated with angels bearing the letters AEIOU, shorthand, scholars believe, for *Austria Est Imperator Orbis Universae*, 'Austria is emperor of the whole world'. As Martin Rady wrote, 'no dynasty was as tenacious and fortunate in its acquisitions', and the Habsburgs became 'Europe's premier dynasty for almost half a millennium'. Eventually, just as the Roman Empire had crumbled before it, so the mighty Habsburg Empire collapsed, smashed under the rubble of the First World War. The Habsburg Castle still stands, though, glowering down across the vineyards towards the Rhine.

★

Bregenz, like many towns located near international borders, was a slightly odd place – extremely pleasant, but also a little mixed up in its outlook and identity. Further east, in Vienna and Graz, Austrians exhibited a proud cultural identity which often seemed to have more in common with those of Hungary, Slovakia or the Balkans than it did with Germany or Switzerland. Around Bregenz, though, the river and Lake Constance helped tether west Austrians to their Swiss and German neighbours, with the result that the culture seemed more west than central European. Bregenz lay only about four miles from Germany and six miles from Switzerland, compared with roughly four hundred from Vienna, and the cultural shifts when crossing between western, Rhenish Austria and neighbouring countries were subtle rather than dramatic. The Austrians still spoke German, were still boringly wealthy and sensible, and still led lives of which the average Mediterranean playboy would not approve. There were some differences, though. Politically, the Austrians and Germans were usually close allies, but Merkel's liberal immigration policies had generated significant unease – about half of new asylum seekers arriving in Germany came from Balkan countries such as Serbia, Bosnia, Macedonia and Kosovo, and many of the major trafficking and migration routes passed through Austria.

Culturally, the Austrians seemed to me a little more relaxed and broad-minded than the Germans; naturally conservative, but convivial. 'Germans are always worried about doing the wrong thing,' one Austrian woman told me. 'We also don't like to make fuss, but we're a bit bolder; we've still got some of that old imperial grandeur.' Like the Germans, the Austrians were also proud of their regional identities, with strong regional accents and cultures, and often saw themselves as Tyrolean or Carinthian first and Austrian second. However, around Bregenz, many things looked generically Rhenish rather than specifically Austrian; yet another reminder that in modern Europe, identities often faded gradually in and out across international borders, rather than stopping abruptly at them. In Bregenz, the souvenirs were Swiss, the books were German and the food was Italian. When I asked a fellow boat passenger (an Austrian returning from a work trip to Friedrichshafen) about the dialect of German spoken in the Rhine region of Austria, she replied: 'An Austrian from around here has more in common with a Swiss or a southern German person, in terms of language, than they do with people in lots of our own country. The dialect's a bit different, but if I go over to Bavaria it's almost like I haven't left home. But Vienna, that's really different!' I remembered an old quote I'd read somewhere: 'Hypochondriacs worry about their illnesses, and Austrians worry about their identity.'

On my second morning in the town, I set off on a long walk around the lake shore, heading east from a little marina. Early in the day, the footpath was quiet, but I did pass a big group of American birdwatchers, dressed for heavy combat in multi-pocketed green jackets and trousers. Lake Constance, I remembered reading, was one of the major stopping-off points for migrating birds on their way from Africa to northern Europe, and as a result had become a major stopping-off point for bird-lovers too. 'I've hardy seen anything today,' one birdwatcher said, trudging morosely along the waterline with his binoculars.

In the past, lake towns like Bregenz were even more strongly linked with their neighbours across the water, particularly during cold winters. Lake Constance was recorded as having frozen more than thirty times since records began, and the Austrians and their neighbours had established a charming tradition of exchanging gifts across the lake whenever the weather was cold enough. During the last major freeze, in 1963, some adventurous Germans even drove over the lake in their Beetles, only to be welcomed by Swiss police who told them it was illegal to drive on the lake, confiscated their cars and forced them to take the train home. Sadly, with a warming planet, it was unlikely such high jinks would happen again any time soon.

Today, Bregenz had a lot of Bavarians and Viennese soaking up the sun. Walking around the lake, I'd seen dozens of election campaign posters, often heavily graffitied with swastikas and anti-racist slogans, and containing quite provocative language. '*Die Islamisierung gehört gestoppt*', said one, 'Islamisation will be stopped'. Like most non-Austrians, I'd rarely given Austrian politics much thought, but voters were due to go to the polls a few weeks after my visit and, in keeping with the spirit of the times, the election campaign was proving unusually sparky. In the decades since the war, Austria had often been run jointly by the leftish Social

Democratic Party (SPÖ) and centre-right People's Party (ÖVP), working together in grand coalitions which made Dutch or German governments look Congolese in their flamboyance and volatility. However, in recent years the country's politics had become increasingly fractured and bad-tempered, with debate dominated by the refugee crisis and the faltering economy. Smaller political parties had risen to challenge the old duopoly, and the far-right Freedom Party (FPÖ) had become a significant force, fiercely protesting the *Islamisierung* of Austria. In late 2016, the FPÖ's Norbert Hofer missed out on being elected president of Austria by just 31,000 votes, despite appearing on the campaign trail carrying a pistol and wearing a blue cornflower, an old Nazi-era symbol of nationalism.*

At the time of my visit, all eyes were on Sebastian Kurz, a thirty-one-year-old right-winger who looked (depending on one's point of view) like a strong, dynamic leader or an exceptionally sleazy estate agent. The '*wunderwuzzi*', some Austrians called him: the 'whizz-kid'. Under Kurz's leadership, the once stately ÖVP had swerved sharply to the right, taking a hard line against 'Islamisation' and pledging to close down migrant routes which passed through Austria from the Balkans. During my stay in Bregenz, in late 2017, the incumbent centre-left chancellor Christian Kern was facing a tough fight to hold on to his job. The result was hard to predict, but it was clear the old era of corporatist, consensual, courtly politics was over. 'What is happening in this country?' the Austrian news magazine *Profil* asked in anguish. 'Austria is unrecognisable.' Others were pleased, though. Near the lake, I paused to take a photo of a poster and was hailed by a passing Austrian man of about sixty. 'Sebastian Kurz, very good!' he said, giving me a big smile and a brusque thumbs up.

Tiring of Bregenz's balmy charms, I left and headed south, following the lake shore a few miles to the point where Constance met the Rhine again. I'd read that early English travellers avoided this area for fear of catching malaria, but today it was blandly suburban; the river a narrow grey channel which looked like an inner-city canal.

---

* This first presidential election was declared invalid for technical reasons, and in a rerun Hofer was comfortably defeated.

For the first time since leaving the coast, I felt that the umbilical link provided by the Rhine might finally have been broken: there were no ferries carrying tourists from the north, no ships flying Dutch flags, and no containers on their way downstream to Düsseldorf, Mannheim or Rotterdam.

I began to fear the last stage of my journey might be something of an anticlimax. I needn't have worried, though, as Mother Nature soon came to the rescue. A few miles south of Lake Constance, mountains reared up dramatically from either side of the river, like great green teeth biting upwards into wispy white clouds of candy-floss. By Swiss or Austrian standards, the peaks were unremarkable – roughly 1,000 metres high – but to an honorary lowlander like me, they looked extraordinary; on a completely different scale to any other hills I'd seen since leaving the coast. 'The immensity [of the Alps] staggers the imagination,' Percy Bysshe Shelley wrote when he travelled not so far from here, 'and so far surpasses all conception that it requires an effort of imagination to believe that they do indeed form a part of the earth.'

South of the lake, the Rhine followed a straight line southwards through Austrian territory for a few miles to St Margrethen, from where it formed the Swiss–Austrian border for about twenty miles more. I dawdled happily along it, crossing a small bridge back into Switzerland as easily as if I were crossing an Amsterdam canal. The scenery was gorgeous, and I was just thinking how nice it was to be back in Switzerland when suddenly I wasn't. Another small bridge over the river was marked with a single flag and a single small sign, and before I'd realised what they were, I was in Liechtenstein.

Like a long-forgotten deputy prime minister or a champion hot-dog eater, Liechtenstein often seemed to exist mainly for the purpose of generating content for pub quizzes. To the extent that the outside world was interested in the country at all, it was only because of its tiny size: the whole of Liechtenstein was only slightly larger than the island of Jersey, and one-sixteenth the size of mighty Luxembourg. Liechtenstein's capital 'city', Vaduz, was barely bigger than the English country village where I'd grown up, and the national population of 38,000 people would fit comfortably into a place like Purbeck or Middelburg, with enough room left over to invite some Swiss friends round.

Within fifteen minutes or so, I'd crossed a sizeable part of the country. Vaduz sat right alongside the river, at the foot of a steep bank of mountains, with the Rhine forming the eastern border of the country as well as the city. At this time of year, the water level was low, and the channel was interrupted by great shoals of gravel and rock. For the first time since leaving the coast, it looked as if it would be feasible for someone to wade through the Rhine without getting their hair wet. Some kind of football match was in progress in a stadium on the riverside, and I walked into Vaduz to the sound of cheering echoing up the steep mountainsides, as if the whole city was delighted I'd finally arrived. In terms of character, Liechtenstein immediately felt like Switzerland on steroids: more clean, more rich, more boring.

Like Austria, Liechtenstein was another country which perhaps didn't automatically spring to mind when one said the word *Rhine*, but its history had been profoundly shaped by the river. The Rhine here was narrow, but in a country so small and potentially vulnerable to assault, it assumed an outsized significance. Running from south to north, the river formed a neat, continuous border with Switzerland; a major water feature in one of only two countries in the world to be 'doubly landlocked' – that is, landlocked and surrounded by countries which were also completely landlocked (the other is Uzbekistan). The steep terrain dominating the rest of the country meant most of Liechtenstein's population was squeezed onto a narrow wedge of land next to the river, along with factories producing an odd assortment of goods including dog food and false teeth. As the crow flies, nowhere in the entire country was much more than ten miles from the Rhine.

The Rhine was also somewhat important to Liechtenstein's national identity, given that many people questioned why the country even existed at all. For Liechtensteiners themselves, such existential questions were surprisingly hard to answer, but the most common refrain was simply that Liechtenstein deserved to be a country because it was different from Switzerland or Austria. In that context, the Rhine served as an important national identifier; a major landmark and natural boundary which helped make Liechtenstein more than just a strange typo on a map. As the scholar Robert Ostergren once wrote: 'Tucked between three larger

German-speaking states, locked into a close but unequal relationship
with its Swiss neighbours . . . [Liechtenstein] must work hard to
maintain its own distinctive persona. Its borders matter, not so much
in their role as static, fixed barriers, but in the way that [they] make
Liechtenstein what it is.' The national football team played in the
riverside Rheinpark Stadion (where it was possible for an errant
kick to send the ball into another country) and the national anthem
was '*Oben am jungen Rhein*', or 'High Above the Young Rhine';
this was sung in German to the exact tune of the British 'God Save
the Queen'.

I'd been to Liechtenstein twice before, as a scruffy road-tripping
student about a dozen years previously, doing what scruffy road-
tripping students do best: passing briefly through the place merely
so I could boast about having been there. In that, I was fairly
typical: Vaduz was filled with bus tourists who'd crossed briefly
over the border and often were more interested in saying they'd
'done' Liechtenstein than in actually doing it. The modern guidebook in my backpack was typical, recommending visitors come for
just a day or so, for 'sheer novelty value'. Given how astonishingly
beautiful the scenery was, it seemed a little unfair.

Outside the annals of stamp collecting, Liechtenstein rarely
attracted much outside attention. 'Liechtenstein? Is that a city in
Austria?' a knowledgeable friend in London had asked. When the
country did appear in international news, it was usually because of
some quirky story which helped confirm it was a Lilliputian joke.
Perhaps the ultimate example came in 2007, when the Swiss army
accidentally invaded Liechtenstein. A group of 170 Swiss soldiers
were on a training exercise when they accidentally marched over
the border, armed with assault rifles. The Liechtensteiners (who
didn't actually have an army) apparently didn't notice the incursion,
and the imperialist Swiss were deeply apologetic. 'It was all so dark
out there,' one of the lost soldiers complained. In Switzerland, the
incident was barely thought worth reporting, but it utterly delighted
the international press, who gleefully covered what they called the
'Swiss Miss' at some length. 'Switzerland is hard to tell apart from
its neighbours,' the *New York Times* explained. Brilliantly, the acci-
dental invasion was actually the second most ridiculous thing ever
to happen to Liechtenstein in military terms. The most ridiculous

happened during the Austro-Prussian War of 1866, when the eighty-strong Liechtenstein army was called into service to defend a mountain pass between the Tyrol and Italy. Not only did the Liechtensteiners lose not a single soldier in action, but they actually came back with one more soldier than they'd left Vaduz with, having made a friend on the way.

Liechtenstein's tiny size essentially was a throwback to the days when much of Europe was a patchwork of tiny principalities and fiefdoms. The Principality of Liechtenstein was established within the Holy Roman Empire in 1719, after a powerful local dynasty called the Liechtensteins managed – in a move which would put the Kardashians to shame – to buy two parcels of land, unite them together in a single principality and rename it after their own family. (Curiously, the purchase of Vaduz seems to have been negotiated in Dutch guilders.) Later, the country's history was unsurprisingly dominated by trial-and-error attempts to form alliances with its more powerful neighbours, sometimes voluntarily and sometimes not; like a schoolyard weakling forced to make friends with bigger, tougher boys. Today, Liechtenstein remained outside the EU but was closely allied with Switzerland, using the Swiss franc as its national currency. The food was mostly Swiss or Italian, and Germany also cast a long shadow linguistically, culturally and economically. Liechtensteiners were predominantly Catholic and overwhelmingly German-speaking. In a mildly interesting twist, the country's current ruler, Prince Hans Adam, was a great-nephew of Archduke Franz Ferdinand, the Austrian whose assassination sparked the First World War. He looked like a retired accountant.

Chatting with Liechtensteiners in Vaduz, I found them firmly and proudly independent, and rightly annoyed at any suggestion that theirs was anything less than a proper nation. 'We're a real country – no different from the United States or Germany,' one hotelier told me. The national football team entered every World Cup, and Liechtenstein was also a regular participant in the Games of the Small States of Europe, a sort of micro-Olympics in which Liechtensteiners competed for medals against the mighty Andorrans, Maltese and Montenegrins. 'Liechtenstein might not be the biggest country in the world, but it's definitely the best,' a young guy told me as he filled his BMW. Such views were typical. Despite their country's small size, the Liechtensteiners I met were all cheerfully, unabashedly patriotic, with an us-against-the-world mentality which was both odd and inevitable for a country which many outsiders had never even heard of. To be fair, they had plenty to be proud of. Liechtenstein was not only extraordinarily attractive, but had no military and no poverty, and (according to the CIA) the government's external debt was $0. Crime rates were low, and life expectancies high. For a while in the 1980s, unemployment in Liechtenstein stood at exactly three – not per cent, but people.

Yet despite these achievements, the country still suffered from a sense that – like an independent republic of Cornwall or a free state of Rotterdam – it was a bit too small to justify. 'Switzerland,' one man in Basle said, 'is the country Liechtenstein could have been. I really don't know why they don't just join Switzerland and become one of our cantons.' The answer to that question, I soon realised, was simple: the Liechtensteiners had become so extravagantly wealthy that they could do whatever they damn well pleased. Like the Swiss, they largely sidestepped the Second World War, and afterwards made up for their geopolitical reticence by becoming an unlikely economic powerhouse; a hub for German-speaking banking and financial services. Regulation was light and taxes were kept remarkably low – it was sometimes said that if the personal rate ever hit 10 per cent, there would be a revolution.

Above all, Liechtensteiners made it their business to attract business. Walking through Vaduz, I saw few sights other than the surrounding mountains, but scores of bland office buildings with brass signs and postboxes listing tenant companies I'd never heard of. Taxes paid by companies based in Liechtenstein were as slender as a supermodel on her wedding day, and the country was often said to have far more private corporations than it did people. Significantly, Liechtenstein law also made it relatively easy to create foundations which could control a business without revealing the true identity of its owners, or exposing them to excessive tax or transparency demands. The furniture giant IKEA, for example, did well off its reputation for Scandinavian purity, but was controlled partly through a *stichting* (foundation) based in the Netherlands, and partly through a foundation based in Liechtenstein. IKEA's billionaire founder Ingvar Kamprad claimed the structure was the only way to ensure 'eternal life' for the company, even as its cheap beds and bookshelves fell apart.

In recent years, Liechtenstein's willingness to cash cheques for any passing dictator or robber baron had often caused tension with its European neighbours. The Liechtensteiner authorities naturally claimed the problems were all down to a few bad apples, and German attempts to force reform seriously rankled. One local newspaper reported: 'We're not a very patriotic people, but under pressure from Germany, everyone is banding together.' At one point, Prince Hans Adam jokingly said that if the situation didn't improve, he'd be forced to sell Liechtenstein to Bill Gates. Thankfully, that hadn't yet proved necessary. However, Liechtenstein had been badly dented by the 2008 financial crisis, and in 2012 was officially designated by the US State Department a 'major money laundering country . . . whose financial institutions engage in currency transactions involving significant amounts of proceeds from international narcotics trafficking'. Under pressure from abroad, Liechtenstein reluctantly scrapped many of its banking secrecy laws, and won the great honour of being removed from the OECD's official 'grey list' of countries who adopted shady financial practices. 'We're not a tax haven, we're a safe haven,' the country's chief financial regulator told reporters. However, even after all the reforms, it remained a popular place for billionaires to park their riches, and was still clearly doing well from it. In 2016, Liechtenstein's GDP was an astonishing $90,000 per capita – 50 per cent higher than Switzerland's, and more than double that of the UK or France. In terms of the wealth on display, it made Amsterdam look like a refugee camp.

Vaduz was one of those places which could have been lifted from the pages of a children's colouring book: a pocket-sized package of medieval turrets, steep winding streets and snow-capped mountains. Outside of ski season, there is little to do apart from go for walks and buy Swiss watches. 'Vaduz,' I overheard an American visitor say, 'is the kind of place which makes Zurich look like Rio.' However, the city more than made up for any dullness with the stunning beauty of its location. The surrounding peaks could've been lifted from the label on a can of air freshener.

On my first morning in Liechtenstein, I did what almost all

visitors did, and walked up to the castle. The royal seat sat high above the city, dominated by a big round tower like a coffee-coloured top hat. I hiked there up a steep gravel path which zigzagged through a patchy forest, following a group of Japanese tourists. The views back over my shoulder were predictably tremendous; the little city nestled between the steep valley walls, with the milky-blue river beyond. I still found it amazing to think that with enough patience, and a powerful outboard motor, I could (barring a big drop over the Rhine Falls) have chugged all the way from Vaduz to Amsterdam, London or even New York by boat.

Wheezing and cursing from the effort, I eventually arrived at the castle, which looked like the kind of place where Shrek might live happily ever after. The ruling prince still lived there, reportedly surrounded by a priceless art collection, but there were no security cameras and no guards, just a low gate and a sign saying '*Eintrott Verboten / Entrée Interdite*'. I noticed a doorbell next to the gate and thought about ringing it to see if the prince answered, but decided not to disturb him. He was probably busy counting his money.

Lichtenstein's political system was another mild oddity, thanks largely to the role played by Prince Hans Adam. Technically, the prince was (like many European monarchs) a kind of non-executive chairman who left the day-to-day running of the country up to elected leaders. In practice, though, he was (in royal terms) something of a badass; willing to wade into public controversies in a way which would make Windsors or Oranje-Nassaus blush. In 2011, for example, it looked likely that a referendum would lead to reform of Liechtenstein's abortion laws, which remained among the strictest in Europe. However, at the last moment the prince (a devout Catholic) suddenly announced he'd veto any attempt to change the law, and the pro-choice side narrowly lost the referendum. On another occasion, he proposed a new constitution which gave him the power to hire and fire governments more or less as he pleased. Two-thirds of voters eventually backed the change – but only after the prince threatened to quit and move to Austria if he didn't get his way. 'If the Prince came out tomorrow and said the sky is pink, I believe 15 to 20 per cent of the population would agree with him,' a democracy campaigner once sighed.

★

The end (or beginning) of the Rhine was barely a hundred miles away by now, but I liked Liechtenstein, and didn't want to leave. Departing from Vaduz, I ascended further above the river, up a narrow ribbon of tarmac which zigzagged its way relentlessly uphill between 2,000-metre peaks. With the end of my journey almost literally in sight, I decided to slow down for a while, and holed up in the mountains near Malbun for a few days. The wooden ski chalet where I stayed had heartbreaking views, log fires and a jovial Liechtensteiner proprietor who made it her business to feed me up and teach me about her country. I planned to stay one night but stayed four, eating fondue, going for long walks, spending long evenings reading in the starlight, and not really thinking about the Rhine at all.

Sadly, my mountaintop exile couldn't continue indefinitely. F. Scott Fitzgerald once wrote 'Switzerland is a country where very few things begin, but many things end', and with that in mind, I tore myself away from Liechtenstein and crossed the border one last time, heading south back into Switzerland. Beyond Vaduz and Malbun, the river quickly became even smaller, steeper and rockier, more of a tumbling mountain stream than a continent-spanning colossus. Footpaths and cycle lanes alongside the Rhine became rare and I took to the road, heading up a gently sloping highway which tracked the narrowing channel. Mountains rose like walls on either side, but looking back down the valley behind me there were flatter plains, widening like an inverted funnel towards Lake Constance. I had the clear sensation of being on a topographical threshold; a place where lowland Europe ended and the highlands began. Fiddling briefly with my phone, I found that technically, this hunch was largely correct – about forty or so miles to the south, in a place called Pianazzo, the bottom of a rocky valley marked the exact spot where the African and Eurasian tectonic plates met. The Italian border was now only about forty miles away, and I started to see more signs in Italian as well as German. 'Scola da snowboard', said one.

Ascending the road towards Chur, the scenery became literally jaw-dropping. The valley continued to narrow and steepen, and the landscape was increasingly Alpine: cows with bells, wood-walled chalets and barns, steep green meadows and craggy cliffs. In the winter this would be a prime skiing area, teeming with visitors bragging of their exploits both on piste and off. Now, though, late in the summer, the weather was balmy and mild, and the pistes as green as hockey pitches. The plain at the bottom of the valley, which had been several miles wide in Vaduz, narrowed until the river sat in a deep V-shaped cleft barely wider than a residential street. Looking around at the snow-capped peaks, I thought of something the Everest climber George Mallory once wrote: 'On the whole, the Himalayas are disappointing and infinitely less beautiful than the Alps.'

By another miracle of logistical planning, I'd managed to get my dog dropped off in Chur by someone who was driving south for the summer, and she joined me for my last day following the river; literally bouncing with excitement at the prospect of another big day out. Footpaths alongside the river were now completely non-existent, so we hiked up a steep, switchbacking road which could've been designed for filming car commercials. Down to the left, in the bottom of the valley, I could still clearly see the river; it was as narrow as a double bed now, and rockier than a soap star's marriage. Across the hillsides, the colours were spectacular – grey rocks, sandy-brown grass, purple heather, green scrub. Signs warned of rock falls and of cows on the road. It looked like the moors of Scotland, reimagined by a set designer from *Lord of the Rings*.

After a few miles of ridiculously steep ascent, we arrived at the top: the Oberalp Pass – one of the highest and most famous paved passes in Europe, at over two kilometres above sea level. Walking away from the road, I was surprised to see a nautical red lighthouse standing atop the pass, hundreds of miles from the sea. It was (a sign explained) an exact replica of the lighthouse which previously had stood on the end of the concrete pier at Hoek van Holland, from where I'd stared at the sea a few months previously. The clouds were closing in but the view back down the valley was still breathtaking: a sweeping vista of crags, peaks, rocks and grass, veined with several rocky little streams winding their way down towards Liechtenstein – including, of course, the tiny Rhine. Not for the first time, I wondered why on earth I'd chosen to build a life for myself in the pancake-flat Netherlands, when there were places like this in the world.

A small yellow sign pointed away from the lighthouse to my final destination: Lake Toma, or the Tomasee. The dog and I set off along an undulating, rocky trail barely wider than my shoulders, cutting across the hillside from the lighthouse towards the river. The path was steep, and I quickly found myself wishing I'd followed the river in the opposite direction, from source to mouth instead. I stopped to drink from a deliciously cool stream and was interrupted by a passing pair of elderly Austrian hikers, with ruddy cheeks and walking poles, who asked in German: 'Is this the way to the source of the Rhine?' 'I hope so!' I wheezed in reply.

The weather forecast had predicted some unseasonal light snow, and I was keen to make it to my destination before the weather turned, so moved quickly, running over the rocky terrain. The dog was utterly delighted. Feeling flush after a lucrative corporate report writing job, I'd splashed out on an absurd canine mountaineering jacket for her, complete with fleece lining, karabiner clips and pockets to carry her own snacks. She now wore it with pride, charging up near vertical rockfaces and howling impatiently whenever I failed to scramble uphill quickly enough. At one point, she stopped suddenly at a corner and began barking furiously. I rushed to catch up, thinking she might have hurt herself or found something dangerous, but she was just protecting us from a metre-wide patch of snow. It was the first she'd ever seen.

The path got steeper and slippier, and I gasped for breath. I began to wonder how much further it was to the lake, and whether it was worth the effort. And then, suddenly, there it was: a V-shaped cleft in the hillside opening up ahead of me, and inside it a pretty lake, bottle-green, roughly circular and about as big as a couple of football pitches. A small sign confirmed it: this was Lake Toma, the source of the river Rhine.

I'd expected the end (or beginning) of the river to be something of an anticlimax, but it wasn't. It was astonishingly beautiful. The dog drank thirstily from the water, and we walked around the edge of the lake to the point where the river flowed out of it; a thin, foamy thread tumbling out of sight over a cliff face, like the spill-over from an overfilled bath. Here at its birthplace, the river was almost narrow enough to step over, but someone had built a sweet little bridge out of a few slabs of stone. I sat on it for a while, looking at the steep, rocky peaks surrounding the lake and watching the reflections of clouds scudding over the glassy water. Having travelled so far, it was strange to think this was it; the end of my journey. I picked a sprig of heather and threw it in the river, and thought of all the places it might end up drifting past: the castles in Vaduz and Koblenz; the cathedrals in Strasbourg and Cologne; the hipster bars in Basle and Rotterdam; the Roman ruins in Utrecht and the rocks of Lorelei; the naked bathers in Wiesbaden and the trekking cows in Hemishofen; the beach at Hoek van Holland and the rower's river in Amsterdam. I splashed some cold water on my face, then turned around and started walking back downhill, towards Holland, and home.

Epilogue: LSD Dreams
The New Politics of the Rhine

OUTSIDE THE SUBWAY station, a fashionably dressed young man sat on the pavement amid a crowd of people drinking and dancing, clutching a raggedy piece of cardboard scrawled with the plea: NEED € FOR BEER. I felt moved by his plight, and gave him a few coins. A few feet further along, a rival had upped the ante, and was hunched behind a plastic cupful of coins with a neatly printed sign saying: MONEY FOR MARIJUANA. Finally, a third beggar had really pulled out the big guns: I NEED MONEY FOR LSD. I stopped to copy the slogan in my notebook, and thought: only in Berlin.

It was a few weeks after my hike to Lake Toma, and I'd come to the German capital to do some follow-up on the recent elections. Voters had gone to the polls around the time I was holed up in the mountains in Liechtenstein, and awarded Angela Merkel another term as chancellor. It was in many ways a stunning achievement: the new Iron Chancellor, written off by many after her immigration policies proved unpopular, now looked as if she'd stay in office continually from 2005 until 2022. Merkel was already on her third US president, fourth British prime minister and fourth French president, and had outlived almost a football team's worth of Italian prime ministers. Like Japanese knotweed or the Rolling Stones, her career seemed impossible to kill off.

Berlin was an even more dubious place to end my exploration of the Rhine than Amsterdam was to begin it. Standing in the centre of the free state of Friedrichschain, I was almost as far as I could get from the river without leaving Germany; further from Cologne and Düsseldorf than I was from Prague or Wrocław. Berlin also wasn't exactly a peaceful writers' retreat: at 2 a.m., the street outside my hotel was busier than it was at lunchtime. However, the pizza was cheap and the beer plentiful, and Berlin made a good place to hole up for a few days, and gather my thoughts about what I'd seen and done over the previous busy months travelling along the river.

Before setting out from Amsterdam, I'd known that the Rhine was important to Europe in the historical sense, but wasn't entirely sure what role it played in an age of twenty-euro flights and rail freight links to China. I'd been relieved to confirm, therefore, that it did still seem very important indeed: as a border; as a means of cultural exchange; and above all, as an artery for trade. The world's media might not care very much about the likes of BASF, ThyssenKrupp and LyondellBasell, but they arguably had done more to shape the past and future of Europe than Tesla or Snapchat ever would.

Like a true Brit abroad, I'd also enjoyed poking fun at the attitudes of people, and at the differences in cultures and attitudes on either side of the frontiers which intersected the river. In modern Europe, borders between countries often were practically invisible on the ground, but were clearly still very real things in the minds of many. The frontier between the Netherlands and Germany, for example, had been almost unnoticeable in physical terms, but it would be a brave travel writer indeed who told someone from Arnhem that they were the same as a German. For almost everyone I met, being a citizen of an integrated, borderless EU and having a strong national or regional identity were not mutually exclusive.

Yet despite these differences, I'd also been interested to see that people up and down the river shared certain key traits, attitudes and opinions – a Rhine culture, if you will. There were of course many big differences between different places, and to bundle millions of people together in a single stereotype was a gross generalisation. But as I wandered around louche, bohemian Berlin, it seemed clear to me that there were certain values which didn't prevail in this city, but which were shared by most people of the Rhine, whether they happened to live in Vlaardingen or Düsseldorf, Basle or Bregenz, Everdingen or Mannheim.

All along the river, the people I spoke to were hard-working and deeply attached to the mental security blanket of having a decent house, clean car and steady job. They were relatively wealthy, but at the same time quite ambivalent about wealth, and disdainful of anything which smacked of excessive consumption. Family was important, but having expensive jewellery or a fancy haircut usually were not. People considered it essential to be productive and efficient, but would also think it an outrage if expected to reply to a work email on the weekend. From Rotterdam to Ludwigshafen, they counted pennies and returned empty bottles, avoided running up debts, and were careful to save for rainy days. Food was enjoyed but unimportant, and a 'salad' was anything covered with mayonnaise, preferably fried first.

Socially, the people of the Rhine were welcoming and hospitable; used to a constant parade of foreign workers and tourists coming and going. They loved few things more than an evening sharing a raucous meal with family, or drinking and laughing in a *kroeg* or a *brauhaus*. Even small towns displayed a surprising degree of worldliness and internationalism, Polish boatmen and American businesspeople rubbing shoulders with Norwegian chemical engineers, Dutch diplomats and Australian tourists.

Yet despite all this, the people of the Rhine were also instinctively conservative, with a reflexive aversion to risk. I'd often thought in the past that the constant threat of flooding and the relatively recent history of conflict had inspired a certain tidy conservatism in the Dutch, making them forever keen to keep everything in its place and on schedule. Now I wondered if the same might apply to places upriver too, where turbulent, destructive histories had fostered a deep desire for stability and continuity.

People living along the Rhine also had deeply held beliefs and traditions, and tempers which could flare quickly if they felt their hard-won lifestyles were being challenged or threatened by outsiders. They could be undiplomatic to the point of rudeness, loudly declaring their opinions with the confidence of a talent show judge, and were inclined to assume everyone in the world shared (or at least should share) their values. Woe betide the careless English visitor who mixed up their *du* and *sie* or *u* and *je*, and accidentally addressed a Bacharach innkeeper or a Dordrecht doctor with the informal form of address. For the Germans and the Dutch in particular, being sensitive was for soaps and shampoos.

Politically, the people of the Rhine were generally pro-business and pro-welfare; pro-free trade and pro-hard work; and (until recently, at least) relatively pro-American. They were perhaps more socially responsible and environmentally aware than the Brits or Americans; more conservative and cautious than the Mediterraneans; and more liberal and internationalist than those from the east of Germany and eastern Europe. While it was easy to overdo the stereotyping, I thought the Rhinelanders (in the broadest sense of the word) represented Europe at its best – pragmatic, internationalist, industrious, gregarious and interconnected, blending cultures and influences as seamlessly as the river did the waters of the Neckar and the Aare. They got rich through trade and diplomacy rather than by putting up walls, and they ate a lot of cheese in the process.

Thinking things over in a Berlin bar, I quickly found easy ways to demolish all these theories. The most obvious bar-room criticism of my Unified Theory of Rhine Culture was that these days everyone was pretty much the same, and my newly cherished Rhine values were actually just generic western European ones. Or alternatively, perhaps it was simply a case of religion. Many of the regions I'd travelled through – in the southern Netherlands, western Germany, Alsace, northern Switzerland, western Austria and Liechtenstein – had sizeable Catholic populations. Wasn't it possible the values I was describing – hospitality, family, hard work, fiscal responsibility – were just Catholic values, rather than Rhine ones? Perhaps. But I could also think of many other places which were west European and Catholic yet didn't quite seem to share the same blend of conservatism and cosmopolitanism. Lisbon and Barcelona were both predominantly Catholic, and both in the EU, yet if transplanted to the Rhine, those cities would stick out like a scuba diver at a disco.

Overall, it didn't seem too far-fetched to think that the river might have encouraged the spread of certain social values, generating an influx of foreign visitors and migrants, food and literature which made quiet towns more cosmopolitan than they might otherwise have been, and engendering a reliance on trade which made people more business-minded and open to the world. Regardless of what the maps might say, Basle and Vaduz were closer to the North Sea than they were to the Mediterranean.

Berlin, needless to say, was the antithesis of Rhine values: scruffy, youthful, rebellious and punkish; a dodgy student art project writ large. I may well have been the only person in town who didn't have a tattoo – although it was still only 10 p.m., so anything was possible.

I hadn't visited Berlin for a while, but it appeared to be thriving, and I noticed there were even more bars, restaurants, shops and nightclubs than there had been a couple of years previously. As in Rotterdam, formerly drab industrial ruins were being converted almost by the day, and property prices were skyrocketing. From the bridge outside my hotel, looking in one direction only, I could see a total of fourteen big construction cranes within a few hundred metres. A big sign nearby explained what many of them were building: a new shopping centre, the East Side Mall, being flung up almost literally in the shadow of the communist side of the Berlin Wall. To a certain extent, though, the signs of development were a mirage. For all Berlin's shabby glamour, it remained something of an albatross in economic terms. After the reunification of Germany, big companies based in places like Düsseldorf had little incentive to relocate to Berlin, but artists, freelancers and bohemians flocked to the city, attracted by low rents and the empty industrial spaces which made ideal studios or party venues. This influx helped rejuvenate the new capital in quite a remarkable way, and attracted millions of tourists keen to combine a visit to Cold War horrors with a fun night out on the town. For many foreigners, Berlin *was* Germany in the twenty-first century: scruffy but hip; party-friendly; filled with well-dressed young people inventing apps, riding fixed-wheel bikes and writing screenplays. Yet in many ways, it was all a fantasy. The east of Germany was still far poorer than the Rhineland, and Berlin was (in GDP per capita terms) far poorer than Düsseldorf. Almost uniquely for a capital city, it acted as a drag on the national economy, and Germany without Berlin would be richer than Germany with it. The city's freewheeling creative spirit gave it a wonderful energy, but also a distinctly un-German dysfunctionality – epitomised, a cynic might say, by the flagship project to open a new Berlin aiport, which missed at least seven different opening dates and ran ten years and billions of euros over schedule. Berlin was, in the words of one former mayor, 'poor but sexy' – the exact opposite of places such as Bonn, Koblenz and Wiesbaden. In economic terms, Germany's centre of gravity was still nowhere near the border with Poland.

Leaving Amsterdam, I'd also been keen to explore how the Rhine region was changing over time. The answer to that question, sadly, wasn't entirely positive. Like generations of travellers, I'd probably developed a tendency to over-romanticise the Rhine region; seeing it as somewhere which effortlessly combined both the best of yesterday and the best of tomorrow. Yet it was also clear the region faced serious challenges. Economically, the river was still a crucial artery for trade, but new long-distance rail lines were encroaching, and robots were plotting a *Terminator*-style takeover of ports in Rotterdam and Duisburg. Only a fool would bet against the Dutch and the Germans, but it was unclear exactly how places like the Ruhrgebeit could keep thriving as the messy work of making things was outsourced to other corners of the world. Environmentally, there'd been huge progress since the dark days of the 1980s, but it was still exceedingly difficult to keep the river clean while it operated simultaneously as one of western Europe's busiest highways, biggest sewers, most important wildlife habitats and main sources of drinking water.

Politically, too, the outlook was mixed. Angela Merkel's victory had come near the end of a remarkable year for Rhine politics. In March, the Netherlands voted. No fewer than thirteen parties made it into parliament, but after seven months of tortuous negotiations, the centre-right prime minister, Mark Rutte, eventually cobbled together a coalition which enabled him to stay in power and keep doing what most Dutch prime ministers had always done: running the country reasonably well, without doing anything very interesting or upsetting too many people. A few months later, in France, the youthful technocrat Emmanuel Macron managed the neat trick of persuading everyone that a millionaire banker-turned-minister was a rebellious political outsider, and decimated a startlingly weak field of opponents to become president. And then finally, it was Austria's turn. In October 2017, the Austrians elected as chancellor the conservative Sebastian Kurz – a man who, at thirty-one years old, had become head of government a mere six years after leaving university, and was viewed by some as Austria's own version of Emmanuel Macron. Across Europe, the worst populists had been kept out of office, and pro-trade centrists reigned supreme again. Pundits could sleep easy in the knowledge that the virus of populism had been defeated.

Unfortunately, the reality wasn't quite so simple. The new politics of the Rhine were almost as murky as the river itself. In the Netherlands, Mark Rutte's centre-right party had won the most seats in parliament, but the far-right Geert Wilders had come a strong second, and only been kept out of power because he'd done such a good job of offending everyone that no one was willing to form a coalition with him. In France, Emmanuel Macron, a son of post-industrial Amiens, seemed both bold and thoughtful, and had won a spectacular victory, but second place again went to someone for whom globalism was a dirty word – the Alsace-loving Marine Le Pen. It remained to be seen whether Macron's blend of reformist zeal and old-school Gallic pomp could actually translate into meaningful change for people living in places like Strasbourg and Colmar. In Austria, the far-right, anti-Europe, anti-immigrant FPÖ had scored more than a quarter of the vote, and Sebastian Kurz had secured the chancellorship only after aping much of their anti-immigrant rhetoric. When he later invited them to join him in a governing coalition, the reaction from the rest of Europe was muted. In Switzerland, the electoral cycle was at a quiet point, but the right-wing Swiss People's Party (SVP) had spent several years tapping a rich vein of anti-immigrant sentiment. In 2015, they became the largest party in the Swiss legislature, winning almost 30 per cent of the vote in national elections, and a referendum to deport foreign criminals had passed easily, aided by an SVP poster campaign which featured white sheep kicking black sheep off a Swiss flag with the caption: '*At last make things safer!*' Finally, in Germany, Merkel had returned to power, but only after seeing her party's vote share fall sharply. It took her months to negotiate a new 'GroKo', or grand coalition; a loveless marriage between her CDU/CSU bloc and the leftish SPD, which somehow managed to put both sides in power but leave both diminished. Having long praised German governments for their stability, some began to mutter that political turnover was unhealthily low, noting that between 1949 and 2018, Germany had only eight chancellors, while Britain had fourteen prime ministers. Merkel herself remained a clever strategist, but was nearing retirement age, and many Germans were already imagining a future without her. The far-right Alternative for

Germany (AfD), whose lead candidate Alexander Gauland said Germans 'have a right to be proud of the achievements of German soldiers in two world wars', had poached more than a million voters from Merkel's alliance, entering the Bundestag and officially becoming a major force in German national politics. 'We will take our country back!' Gauland said.

The details of all this were probably a subject for a longer and more boring book, but the centrists' victories struck me as welcome but hollow. Up and down the river, the old behemoths of the centre-left – including the Dutch PvdA, German SPD and French Socialists – had been decimated, and the centre-right in places like Britain was looking more right than centre. The political middle ground was shrinking, and what I'd come to think of as Rhine values – internationalism, free trade, Atlanticism, social liberalism – were under threat. For parties which thought all Muslims were terrorists to come second in a national election was now seen as not just normal, but a triumph for peace-loving democracy. Most worryingly, there were few signs that the mainstream parties had much idea of how to fix the problem. For all their strengths, the leaders of more centrist parties like the CDU, SPD and VVD still had a worrying tendency to dismiss voters who'd backed Wilders or Gauland as gullible, ignorant or racist, without ever really trying to understand why they might be unimpressed by the globalist status quo. In many places, people seemed a little too busy laughing at authoritarian strongmen elsewhere to notice the authoritarian strongmen in their own front yards.

Reviewing all the election results in Berlin, I was wary of reading too much into the data, but it was curious to note that some of the populists' strongest support had come in places which the river passed through. Geert Wilders hoovered up votes in the working-class river suburbs of Rotterdam, while Marine Le Pen might've been president had voting been restricted to residents of Alsace. In Germany, support for the far-right was far higher in the east of the country than in the globalised Rhenish borderlands, and big anti-immigrant rallies more often took place in eastern cities like Dresden and Leipzig. But in Duisburg, which once had been an unassailable stronghold of the leftish Social Democrats, the far-right AfD won more than 13 per cent of the vote. 'People here are tired,' one

Duisburg resident told a journalist from *DW*. 'They're tired of promises from politicians.'

The correlations between river proximity and alt-right support probably wouldn't stand up to rigorous mathematical analysis, but I found it odd – and a little sad – that some of the very places which had done best out of free trade and openness to the world now were fertile hunting grounds for the nationalist, isolationist right. One could only hope that now, having returned to power, triumphant technocrats like Rutte, Merkel and Macron wouldn't just be content to see riverside warehouses converted into craft beer outlets, and see real workers replaced by robots, but would instead ensure the Rhine remained a free-flowing conduit for goods, people and ideas.

Finally, my own experiences of the region had also, inevitably, been coloured by the impending Brexit, looming on the horizon like an iceberg. There were certainly legitimate reasons to dislike the EU, which often spoke softly and carried a small stick, and I wasn't so dogmatic as to think Britain was doomed to an apocalyptic future. But having spent so much time thinking about borders, trade and identity, it was disappointing to see British leaders failing to make the case for openness and integration, and instead portraying geopolitics as a zero-sum game where foreigners were weird and trade always meant one person winning and another losing. Brexit might yield benefits in the future, but for now, the impending loss of my own right to live, work and travel freely up and down the river felt like a very tangible loss. My Malawi-born dog had an EU passport, but I soon would not.

In Berlin, I resolved to stop thinking myself into a geopolitical pit of despair, and continued my pub crawl. Hours after bedtime in Bacharach and Oosterbeek, Friedrichshain was alive with activity: buskers beatboxing, skateboarders grinding, couples dancing in the street. The streets were still packed, and almost everyone who walked past had a beer bottle in hand. I found a cheap Italian restaurant and sat at a table in the corner. Nearby, two couples on neighbouring tables began to talk; formally and politely at first, purely because they happened to be sitting close to one another. 'Are you on a date?' one woman asked the other. 'Yes we are,' came the reply. 'Are you?' 'Sort of. We've been seeing each other for a while. He's married, but we're together.' The conversation got louder and more animated. Chairs were turned so they were all half facing each other, and after half an hour they were sharing bottles of wine and life stories. After another half an hour, they shook hands and exchanged names. One of the couples, who'd been planning to leave, took off their coats and settled in for the long haul. The two tables were pushed together as one. It was getting late by now; I was the only other customer in the restaurant and they invited me over. I surreptitiously pulled out my notebook and wrote in it: 'Germans are friendlier than everyone thinks'. We drank a final, noisy toast – 'To new friends!' – and all went off to a nightclub together. The whisky sours there were only three euros each, and I really paid for them in the morning.

The next day, it was time to go home. I went for a final quick walk before catching the high-speed train to Amsterdam, wandering down to a remnant of the Berlin Wall which was graffitied with the phrase How's God? She's Black. I loved Berlin, but if anything, being there for a few days had made me like the Rhine cities even more. Travelling between them, I'd found plenty of reasons to grouch and grumble and worry about the future, but also plenty to admire. Between them, the places the river flowed through had it all: bustling cities; glorious churches; lively bars; ruined castles; mountains to climb; lakes to swim in; places where restaurants could serve a mountain of cheese and ham and call it a nutritious meal.

After a rough few years, the economies of the Rhine were in relatively rude health, and solid growth was forecast in every country through which the river passed. In France, unemployment had fallen below nine per cent for the first time in years. In Germany, the arrival of more than a million asylum seekers had tested voters' patience, but crime subsequently had fallen to its lowest level since 1992. The Franco-German alliance had been rejuvenated, and the Dutch were keen to fill the political gap left by the British in Europe. The river's cathedrals and museums still amounted to the world's greatest repository of history and art, while its factories, ports and warehouses remained a terrific source of wealth and innovation. Journalists and think-tankers may have been focused on the rise of Silicon Valley, Dubai and Shanghai, but there were still few better places for an inventor, investor or entrepreneur than this chaotic, boggy little corner of Europe. For all its problems, the Rhine region was prettier than most of northern Europe, and more prosperous than most of southern Europe. It was happy, rich and safe. Above all, the people remained as welcoming and as fun as a puppy on a boat tour. As Thackeray wrote in *Vanity Fair*: 'To lay down the pen and even to think of that beautiful Rhineland makes one happy.'

I walked along the river Spree towards Treptower, tracking the side of the wall. A group of French schoolchildren galloped past, racing back and forth across a frontier they once would have been shot for touching. A busker tuned an electric guitar, and a Frenchman extravagantly kissed his girlfriend. An American man with a camera walked by, overflowing with the enthusiasm of someone on the first day of a much needed holiday: 'Isn't Europe amazing!' he cried to his wife. 'What a fantastic place! And what a great time to be here!' I mentally agreed, and looked down towards the coffee-coloured river, flowing slowly westwards. I thought: I wonder where that goes?

Acknowledgements

THE IDEA OF visiting places which you don't come from so that you can explain them to others is inherently a rather presumptive or even arrogant thing to do. However, I'm grateful to the countless people – both friends and strangers – who were willing to overlook this, and shared the ideas and stories recorded in these pages, and so helped me understand some of what makes the Rhineland (in the broadest sense of the word) tick. I hope they'll forgive my occasional criticisms of their homelands and habits and will welcome me back again in the future. Despite what the papers say, there are still Brits who love the world beyond the Channel, and the people who inhabit it. *Dank jullie wel*, *danke* and *merci* to you all.

I wrote most of the book while travelling along the river, but also researched and drafted some big sections of it while further afield. The Zomba gang were there at the inception, and the Kampala-ites kept the coffee and *waragi* flowing while I submerged myself in the history of Roman Switzerland, Dutch flooding and the German car industry. The staff at the wonderful Casa Rossa, Kardamom & Koffee and Tin Roof Café provided oases of peace in which to think, read and write. Most importantly, in Kenya, a motley crew of friends and experts helped put my wife and me back together after an unusually nasty car accident. Eternal thanks to Julie Sandys-Lumsdaine, Carlette Langat, Frans Makken and his team at the Dutch embassy, and – last but by no means least – Margriet van Unen in Karen, and Amer Karim and Mujahid Feroze Din at Aga Khan. It's no exaggeration to say that without them, this book would not exist, and my wife and I might not either. *Asante sana*.

In London, I owe a huge debt to the team at Nicholas Brealey

/John Murray Press/Hachette who helped take the book from ice-skater's fantasy to published tome. Nick Davies saw the potential of the idea early, gave good advice on how to structure things and was then brave enough to let me get on with it. Kate Craigie did excellent work bashing the text into shape and advising on the content, including gently telling me to cheer up at times when I despaired at Dutch weather, German food or French timekeeping. Caroline Westmore ably steered the book through the editing and production process, and Hilary Hammond did a fine job of editing the text. Louise Richardson and Ben Slight skilfully handled publicity and promotion.

Finally, thanks to my friends and family, in the Netherlands, Britain and elsewhere, for everything. Thanks to my parents for their unlimited kindness and to my sister for the celebrity gossip. And thanks to Kim, of course, for somehow staying sane and supportive through it all; fixing houses and walking dogs and paying bills while I busied myself drinking beer and riding cows. She's still the best.

Apologies to those I have forgotten to thank. Any other errors are entirely my own.

Select Bibliography

NB. English-language titles only

Backouche, Isabelle, and Blackbourn, David, *Rivers in History: Perspectives on Waterways in Europe and North America*, University of Pittsburgh Press, 2008

Beattie, Andrew, *The Alps: A Cultural History*, Signal, 2006

Bentley-Taylor, David, *My Dear Erasmus: The Forgotten Reformer*, Christian Focus, 2002

Black, Jeremy, *The British and the Grand Tour*, Croom Helm, 1985

Blackbourn, David, *The Conquest of Nature: Water, Landscape, and the Making of Modern Germany*, Jonathan Cape, 2006

Bradley, Ian C., *Water Music: Music Making in the Spas of Europe and North America*, Oxford University Press, 2010

Braudel, Fernand, *The Identity of France: History and Environment*, HarperCollins, 1988

Brüggemeier, Franz-Josef (ed.), *How Green Were the Nazis? Nature, Environment, and Nation in the Third Reich*, Ohio University Press, 2005

Callow, Simon, *Being Wagner: The Triumph of the Will*, William Collins, 2017

Carré, John le, *A Small Town in Germany*, Penguin, 2011

Childress, Diana, *Johannes Gutenberg and the Printing Press*, Lerner, 2009

Cioc, Mark, *The Rhine: An Eco-Biography 1815–2000*, University of Washington Press, 2006

Clark, Lloyd, *Arnhem: Jumping the Rhine 1944 and 1945*, Headline, 2000

Cole, Robert, *A Traveller's History of Germany*, Interlink, 2004

Craig, Gordon A., *The Germans*, Penguin, 1991

Davis, John R., *The Victorians and Germany*, Verlag Peter Lang, 2007

Delsen, Lei (ed.), *The German and Dutch Economies: Who Follows Whom?*, Springer, 1998

Dornbusch, Horst, *Prost! The Story of German Beer*, Brewers Publications, 1997

Dunlop, Catherine Tatiana, *Cartophilia: Maps and the Search for Identity in the French–German Borderland*, University of Chicago Press, 2015

Fenby, Jonathan, *On the Brink: The Trouble with France*, Abacus, 2002

——, *The General: Charles De Gaulle and the France He Saved*, Simon & Schuster, 2011

——, *The History of Modern France: From the Revolution to the War with Terror*, Simon & Schuster, 2015

Fischer, Christopher J., *Alsace to the Alsatians? Visions and Divisions of Alsatian Regionalism 1870–1939*, Berghan, 2014

Friend, Julius, *The Linchpin: French–German Relations 1950–1990*, Praeger, 1991

Frijhoff, Willem (ed.), *Dutch Culture in a European Perspective*, Palgrave Macmillan, 2004

Goldsworthy, Adrian, *Pax Romana: War, Peace and Conquest in the Roman World*, Weidenfeld & Nicolson, 2016

Gordon, Charlotte, *Romantic Outlaws: The Extraordinary Lives of Mary Wollstonecraft and Mary Shelley*, Random House, 2015

Green, Stephen, *Reluctant Meister: Germany and the New Europe*, University of Chicago Press, 2017

Hay, Daisy, *Young Romantics: The Shelleys, Byron and Other Tangled Lives*, Bloomsbury, 2010

Hazen, Charles D., *Alsace-Lorraine under German Rule*, Forgotten Books, 2018

Heinzelmann, Ursula, *Beyond Bratwurst: A History of Food in Germany*, Reaktion, 2014

Hofmann, Paul, *The Viennese: Splendor, Twilight, and Exile*, Anchor, 1988

Huizinga, Johan, *Erasmus and the Age of Reformation*, Princeton University Press, 2012

James, Harold, *Krupp: A History of the Legendary German Firm*, Princeton University Press, 2012

Judson, Pieter M., *The Habsburg Empire: A New History*, Harvard University Press, 2016

Kershaw, Robert, *A Street in Arnhem: The Agony of Occupation and Liberation*, Ian Allen, 2015

Kornelius, Stefan, *Angela Merkel: The Authorized Biography*, Alma, 2013

Kossoff, Philip, *Valiant Heart: A Biography of Heinrich Heine*, Cornwall, 1983

Krebs, Christopher, *A Most Dangerous Book: Tacitus's Germania from the Roman Empire to the Third Reich*, W. W. Norton, 2011

La Baume, Peter, *The Romans on the Rhine*, Argonaut, 1967

Lambert, Audrey M., *The Making of the Dutch Landscape: Historical Geography of the Netherlands*, Academic Press, 1971

Lendering, Jona, and Bosman, Arjen, *Edge of Empire: Rome's Frontier on the Lower Rhine*, Karwansary, 2013

Lendvai, Paul, *Inside Austria: New Challenges, Old Demons*, C. Hurst, 2010

Lever, Paul, *Berlin Rules: Europe and the German Way*, I. B. Tauris, 2017

MacCarthy, Fiona, *Byron: Life and Legend*, John Murray, 2002

MacMillan, Margaret, *Peacemakers: Six Months That Changed the World*, John Murray, 2001

Man, John, *The Gutenberg Revolution: The Story of a Genius and an Invention that Changed the World*, Headline, 2002

Manchester, William, *The Arms of Krupp*, Michael Joseph, 1969

Middlebrook, Martin, *Arnhem 1944: The Airborne Battle*, Pen & Sword, 2009

Mierzejewski, Alfred C., *Ludwig Erhard: A Biography*, University of North Carolina Press, 2004

Morris, Edmund, *Beethoven: The Universal Composer*, HarperPress, 2007

Murray, Donald S., *Herring Tales: How the Silver Darlings Shaped Human Taste and History*, Bloomsbury, 2015

O'Shea, Stephen, *The Alps: A Human History from Hannibal to Heidi and Beyond*, W. W. Norton, 2017

Ozment, Steven E., *A Mighty Fortress: A New History of the German People*, HarperCollins, 2004

Plowright, Adam, *The French Exception: Emmanuel Macron – The Extraordinary Rise and Risk*, Icon, 2017

Poulsen, Bo, *Dutch Herring: An Environmental History 1600–1860*, Aksant, 2008

Pye, Michael, *The Edge of the World: How the North Sea Made Us Who We Are*, Viking, 2014

Qvortrup, Matthew, *Angela Merkel: Europe's Most Influential Leader*, Duckworth, 2016

Ramsden, John, *Don't Mention the War: The British and the Germans Since 1890*, Little, Brown, 2006

Rees, Goronwy, *The Rhine*, Weidenfeld & Nicolson, 1967

Reid, James H., *Heinrich Böll: A German for His Time*, Bloomsbury, 1987

Richards, John F., *The Unending Frontier: An Environmental History of the Early Modern World*, University of California Press, 2003

Ridley, Glynis, *Clara's Grand Tour: Travels with a Rhinoceros in Eighteenth-Century Europe*, Atlantic, 2005

Robb, Graham, *The Discovery of France*, Picador, 2008

Roding, Juliette (ed.), *The North Sea and Culture 1550–1800*, Verloren, 1996

Rooney, Padraig, *The Gilded Chalet: Off-Piste in Literary Switzerland*, Nicholas Brealey, 2015

Sammons, Jeffrey L., *Heinrich Heine: A Modern Biography*, Princeton University Press, 2014

Schulze, Hagen, *The Course of German Nationalism: From Frederick the Great to Bismarck 1763–1867*, Cambridge University Press, 2008

Smyser, W. R., *Yalta to Berlin: The Cold War Struggle over Germany*, Palgrave Macmillan, 2000

Steinberg, Jonathan, *Why Switzerland?*, Cambridge University Press, 2015

Swafford, Jan, *Beethoven: Anguish and Triumph*, Faber, 2015

Sweets, John, *Choices in Vichy France: The French Under Nazi Occupation*, Oxford University Press, 1986

Tanner, Michael, *Wagner*, Princeton University Press, 1996

van Ginkel, Rob, *Braving Troubled Waters: Sea Change in a Dutch Fishing Community*, Amsterdam University Press, 2014

van Heezik, Alex, *Battle over the Rivers: Two Hundred Years of River Policy in the Netherlands*, van Heezik Beleidsresearch, 2008

van Zanden, Jan L., *The Economic History of The Netherlands 1914–1995*, Routledge, 2015

Viviès, Jean, *English Travel Narratives in the Eighteenth Century*, Routledge, 2016

von Elbe, Joachim, *Roman Germany: A Guide to Sites and Museums*, P. von Zabern, 1977

von Moltke, Helmuth, *The Franco German War of 1870–1871*, Greenhill, 1992

Whitaker, Denis and Shelagh, *Rhineland: The Battle to End the War*, Mandarin, 1999

Williams, Charles, *Adenauer*, Little, Brown, 2000

Wintle, Michael, *An Economic and Social History of the Netherlands 1800–1920*, Cambridge University Press, 2000

Wise, Michael Z., *Capital Dilemma: Germany's Search for a New Architecture of Democracy*, Princeton Architectural Press, 1999

Wokeck, Marianne, *Trade in Strangers: The Beginnings of Mass Migration to North America*, Pennsylvania State University Press, 1999

Wood, Gillen D'Arcy, *Tambora: The Eruption That Changed the World*, Princeton University Press, 2014

Wood, Karl E., *Health and Hazard: Spa Culture and the Social History of Medicine in the Nineteenth Century*, Cambridge Scholars Publishing, 2012

Zschokke, Heinrich, *The History of Switzerland*, Forgotten Books, 2018